Love, the Word, and Mercury

Love, the Word, and Mercury

A reading of John Gower's *Confessio Amantis*

Patrick J. Gallacher

UNIVERSITY OF NEW MEXICO PRESS

Albuquerque

Publication of this book was assisted by the American Council of Learned
Societies under a grant from the Andrew W. Mellon Foundation.

For Patricia

non potè suo valor sì fare impresso
in tutto l' universo, che 'l suo verbo
non rimanesse in infinito eccesso.
Paradiso XIX. 43–45

CONTENTS

PREFACE

Advocates of continuity in the history of ideas can find no better example than the notion of the Logos or Word, which appears at different times in a variety of cultures. Ernst Cassirer in the first volume of *The Philosophy of Symbolic Forms* asserts that the first sense of order in the universe derives from a sense of order in language. Since primitive peoples place a magically causal relationship between word and thing, power in speech gives command over the external world. Common to Babylonian, Egyptian, and Indian cosmogonies is the belief that the divine word is the agent of creation; and in the Rig-Veda, the commander of the word governs all things with power, because the celestial Vac—the eternal, imperishable word—underlies all human words. The Logos is important in Greek philosophy, and the beginning of St. John's Gospel guarantees its influence in medieval culture. Coleridge found the scheme useful in his theoretical criticism; Kenneth Burke in *The Rhetoric of Religion* has elaborated in what he calls logology his most explicit statement of language as symbolic action, a principle which has motivated his practical criticism for decades. T. S. Eliot makes use of the dialectic of words and Word in *Four Quartets,* as does Charles Williams in his "theological thriller," *All Hallows' Eve,* to which Eliot has written an introduction. In the *Siddhartha* of Herman Hesse, there is the climactic and unifying function of *Om,* a term which not long ago gained a faddist currency in popular culture. And finally, to cut the list short, the distinguished psychologist, Erik H. Erikson, writes in *Young Man Luther* of the dramatic outcry in the choir of Erfurt:

> . . . was it not a "dumb" spirit which beset the patient before Jesus? and was it not muteness, also, which the monk had to deny by thus roaring "like an ox"? The theme of the Voice and of the Word, then, is intertwined with the theme of Luther's identity and with his influence on the ideology of his time.[1]

My decision to apply this tradition to John Gower's *Confessio Amantis* resulted from noticing that Mercury, who as god of speech was necessarily assimilated to the Verbum tradition, occurs in four significantly placed stories. Particularly, I discovered that Anubis, a popular, syncretistic avatar of Mercury, appeared in the first story of the poem in a context of clear allusion to the Annunciation, in which, of course, the Word plays a central role. Having noted further that the poem is based on the institution of sacramental conversation—that is, a confession of a penitent to a priest—and that it ends with the penitent being given beads to pray on "por reposer," it seemed to me feasible to investigate other conversations in the poem. I concluded by making the following architectonic model: a story that inevitably involves a vice or virtue of speech, and contains an amorous conversation resolved or completed in some form by the word of God. A brief list of the Mercury stories will help clarify my intention: in chapter 2, Anubis, the Egyptian Mercury, in an Annunciation story; in chapter 3, the slaying of Argus by Mercury as a resolution of the analogy between prayer and amorous persuasion; in chapter 5, the beheading of Medusa with the sword of Mercury, and, later in the same chapter, the use of Mercury rather than Apollo in a well-known story about the origin of law. Mercury as the Word completes a process which shows that a realization of the inadequacy of words results in a desire for the Word by conceptual necessity.

My first chapter defines the literary principles that are deducible from the Verbum tradition and relevant to a critical reading of the *Confessio Amantis*. The rationale for my other chapters is as follows: In chapter 2, the love situation which alludes to the Annunciation is the most perfect illustration of my normative model, and, just as important, the three Annunciation stories have a key position in the poem itself. The first two are the first and last stories of Book I of the poem and deal respectively with Pride and Humility, the chief vice and the chief virtue. The third and last Annunciation story is the justification for the extensively encyclopedic Book VII and becomes thereby the principle of a summary of knowledge. In chapter 3, I discuss the progress from words to Word in relation to the contrast between amorous persuasion and prayer, which is cited explicitly as a remedy for sins of speech exemplified in Pride, Wrath, Sloth, Avarice, and Gluttony. In chapter 4, the Word appears in the words spoken by the ladies in the exempla and the lover's own lady as a necessary complement to the lover's rhetoric. Chapter 5 concerns the similarity between the act of repentance and the recognition scene of narrative plot (a likeness which became historical reality in Tudor drama) and deals with the Word as the object of such recognition. Chapter 6 shows first that the command of Venus to pray is a recapitulation of the fact that the words of love brought Amans to the Word of prayer; and, second, how Gower applied the dialectic of imperfect and perfect speech to himself by writing his poem in the tradition of the confession-autobiography.

My discussions of the mythography of Mercury are necessarily scattered, since Mercury appears in various forms in different parts of the poem and practical criticism requires that each such appearance be explained in context. Specifically, the most extensive treatment of Mercury is in chapter 5, which treats the beginning and end of the confessional process. My sources for Mercury indicate the vitality of the figure in the mythographical tradition, from Servius the Grammarian in the fourth century, through Rémi of Auxerre in the ninth, Arnulph of Orleans in the eleventh, Alexander Neckam in the twelfth, John of Garland in the thirteenth, and, in the fourteenth century, Giovanni Boccaccio, Giovanni del Virgilio, Thomas Waleys, and Robert Holcot.

Gower criticism as such has borne less directly on my subject, although Maria Wickert brings up the use of Verbum as the name for Christ in her discussion of the *Vox Clamantis* and medieval preaching;[2] and Donald G. Schueler points out the importance of the dialogue structure.[3] James J. Murphy, in a study of Gower and rhetoric, has noted in passing the similarity between a fourteenth-century English homily on the prologue to the Gospel of John and the discussion of the nature of words in the *Confessio Amantis*.[4] J. A. W. Bennett discusses the relation of the poem to the medieval love tradition;[5] and Derek Pearsall has contributed to the rescue of Chaucer's much-abused contemporary from critical neglect.[6] The insights of C. S. Lewis are still illuminating, in my opinion, as will be apparent in my second chapter.[7] Russell A. Peck has made the *Confessio Amantis* more accessible in his Rinehart edition;[8] and J. A. Burrow's classification of Gower as a Ricardian poet will do much to highlight his importance, especially in regard to the literary use of confessional psychology, to an understanding of which I hope my book makes a contribution.[9]

Finally, I happily acknowledge my gratitude to those who read the manuscript at various stages, first of all to Professor Robert E. Kaske of Cornell University, at whose suggestion I began to read Gower and mythography for a doctoral dissertation, and whose wholehearted and candid encouragement was never lacking; Professor O. B. Hardison, Jr., director of the Folger Shakespeare Library, who very practically helped me retain the conviction that literature is not the handmaid of history or source study; Professor Jerome Taylor of the University of Wisconsin, whose commitment to the practical criticism of medieval literature was most supportive at a crucial time; Professor Winthrop Wetherbee of Cornell University, whose critical comments were most helpful; Professor Judson Allen of Marquette University, whose friendship so often occasioned the sort of conversation about the nature of verbal art which is, in large measure, the goal of this book. To the many other colleagues and friends who directly and indirectly aided my efforts, especially Professor Joseph Zavadil, chairman of the English Department at the University of New Mexico, and Mrs. Elizabeth Heist, my editor, whose good sense and meticulousness were invaluable, I express my most hearty thanks.

1

The Rhetoric of the Word

Speech manifests and affects character in a variety of interesting ways in medieval literature; and each of the Seven Deadly Sins has a verbal manifestation. Pride makes a man boastful; Envy nettles him into backbiting; Wrath provokes quarrelsomeness. Sloth holds him in a stupified silence. Avarice makes him stingy even in what he says. Gluttony inordinately whets his appetite for his lady's voice, and Lust makes his conversation lascivious. Quite simply and fittingly, the sovereign remedy for all these vices of speech is the Speech of God, or the Word, who also resolves the tension and fulfills the yearning caused by an experience of the verbally inexpressible.

It would seem inevitable that a poem patterned largely on medieval confessional and ascetical manuals—in both of which the threefold analysis of thought, word, and deed is basic—should show a recurring emphasis on the various aspects of human speech. Both these kinds of manual are intended to elicit a verbal response: in the one case, an audible declaration of sins; in the other, prayer, discussions of which usually begin with its relationship to speech in general.

The confessional manual followed two main lines of development. The first, initiated by Raymond of Pennafort in his *Summa de Casibus* (ca.1235), was intended to provide priests with the information necessary to evaluate the state of the penitent's soul and is cast in a catechetical dialogue form. The second type of confessional manual, intended for laymen, provided classifications of sins to be used in an examination of conscience and reached its classical expression in the *Summa de Vitiis et Virtutibus* of Guilielmus Peraldus.[1] The ascetical manual, according to Father J. B. Dwyer, had a principally devotional function, and its contents were chosen and arranged as a preparation for and a supplement to prayer. For those who could not read, sermons and conferences, or the spoken word, took the place of the manuals.[2]

The other main emphasis on conversation comes from the fact that, in terms of the blend of the devotional and amorous in the *Confessio Amantis*, words are as important to the winning of a lady as to confession and prayer.

1

Since the art of verbal persuasion played a major role in the medieval love tradition, listening and speaking receive the concentrated attention of poets and theorists of the art of love.

The function of speech in the *Confessio Amantis* can be viewed in two principal ways. According to the purpose for which Amans or the characters in the individual tales speak, there are friendly conversation, amorous persuasion, counsel, preaching, confession, and prayer. On the other hand, speech can be looked at from the point of view of its origin, qualities, and effects. According to an enduring tradition, speech originates in man's soul, which is made in the image of the Divine Word. The components of speech are the external, significant sounds; the most important quality of speech is the correspondence between the significant sounds and the mind of the speaker. That is, man's speech must be truthful. This obligation, theologically considered, stems from the truth of correspondence between man's soul and the Divine Word, and the mysterious correspondence of identity between the Word and the Father. The most important effect of speech is the union of speaker and listener, which is real and stable in proportion to the truth of the speech. The word *trouthe*, which occurs frequently in the *Confessio Amantis*, thus has an intimate connection to the theme of the spoken word.

This chapter is a background study in which I examine the convention of the lover's apprehensiveness and fear to speak, and review the solutions offered to the lover in this situation by the viewpoint represented in the *De Arte Honeste Amandi* of Andreas Capellanus. In this review I have introduced conversational criteria from the medieval Aristotelian virtues of truth and friendship because of their analytical usefulness[3] and because of the explicit presence of the issues of truth and friendship in the medieval love tradition. I pursue the criteria of truth and friendship in my examination of both the sacrament of confession and the tradition of prayer. Finally, I explore briefly the tradition of the Verbum, where the quality of truth receives its ontological fulfillment and love takes the specific "conversational" form of union with the Verbum.

From the many theological, epistemological, and moral aspects of the Verbum tradition, three important, closely related literary principles emerge. First, there is a natural progress toward perfection in the use of words motivated by an awareness of the inexpressible. Second, this goal of perfection inhabits in some sense each stage toward that goal. Third, the Word, which is the perfection of words, remains One while being present in an infinity of verbal instances.[4]

First, all things are to some extent inexpressible; the human achievement of truth is always incomplete. That words are an inadequate means of describing either the things of the world or one's subjective experiences is an epistemological commonplace which occurs in Plato and Aristotle, and extends throughout the Middle Ages into contemporary semantics. In Plato, since words describe only a partial reality to begin with, words are but shadows of shadows. Even Aristotle, who believes that words are objectively adequate signs of things, admits that men use these signs imperfectly. Nevertheless, this realization sets up a motion in the use of words toward an increasingly accurate expression of one's thoughts, a motion toward verbal perfection conceived finally as an attribute of a divine being but accessible in some way also to man. Objectively, from man's point of view, if words are incomplete signs of ordinary realities like trees and stones, or even beauty, how much more inadequate they are to the expression or discussion of the ultimate reality, God Himself. Augustine's awareness of this commonplace comes to its most influential fruition in his meditations on the inadequacy of words to describe God, or His Ineffability,[5] the response to which is negative theology. Nothing positive can be said of God: He is immutable, infinite, timeless. Conveniently for my purposes, a modern critic, Kenneth Burke, applies this concept to all uses of language and asserts that the inadequacy of an ordinary word to a concept or thing is a reduced model of this theological principle.[6] A medieval counterpart of this could be found by applying to words a notion from Boethius's *Consolation of Philosophy*. Since we cannot judge things to be imperfect unless a norm of perfection exists,[7] an awareness of imperfect speech proves the existence of perfect speech, or the Word. The inexpressible becomes the Ineffable and the Ineffable in turn shapes the inexpressible. Both inexpressibility and perfect expression find their logical resolution in the Word.

Burke further asserts that, goaded by the spirit of hierarchy, words are used most thoroughly when they are applied to the most inclusive and transcendent concept, God, and that even the trivial use of words retains some vestige of this thorough use. "Grace" is a lucid instance of this. Borrowed from the realm of social experience and referring originally to something done for nothing, without pay, through sheer kindness, it was applied to the free act by which God redeems man. It was then borrowed back, aestheticized, and used to designate "grace" in a literary style or in a hostess.[8] The most important corollary of this is the reversibility of the process. The mere structure of belief in the creative, omnipotent Word, the Second Person of the Trinity, lends a dynamic orientation to words in their most trivial use. With this theory of language, medieval theologians from Augustine to Aquinas would enthusiastically agree, but they would insist that such a structure describes the way things are. In one sense, reversibility is simply a way of saying that the Word became flesh and is an application to words of the *fides quaerens intellectum*. If the goal of man's speech is redemption in the Verbum, then this goal is present in some fashion at each stage leading to that goal and even in various ways at the same stage. The Word is the final cause of all the verbal causes.

The Word is present then in man's attempt to overcome both subjective and objective inexpressibility and in the redemption of man's faculty of speech. And yet the presence of the Word in both man's movement to God and God's movement to man is temporal and eternal; in time and outside of time. Augustine, in his *Confessions,* finds an analogy of this belief in the sentence, where there is a temporal succession of words whose sounds come into existence and pass away, while the meaning of the sentence is in each part and remains after the sounds are gone.[9] A more expansive example of this is the tradition of the Verbum Abbreviatum which describes the belief that all the words of the Old and New Testaments are summed up in the One Word who is Christ.[10] A more particular application occurs in the Annunciation commentaries where the words spoken by the Angel Gabriel are compressed to the Word Whose Incarnation is being heralded. Literarily rather than theologically, this usage resembles the figure of synecdoche, which Quintilian defines as "letting us understand the plural from the singular, the whole from a part, a genus from the species, something following from something preceding; and *vice versa.*"[11] Paralleling Augustine's observations on the sentence and the tradition of the Verbum Unum is an ordinary idiomatic usage of *word,* found in the *Confessio Amantis,* to designate many words, a sentence, or a whole discourse.

A slightly different synecdochic idiom extends the use of *word* to an event or action, which can of course be a series of smaller incidents. Christ's actions are "words" articulated in time but made one and eternal by the Word which He is.

These examples serve to illustrate how the Verbum, or Mercury, can enter narrative not only as character, but even as plot or theme, since the Word is the pattern of both action and meaning in Scripture.

In tracing a progress from the words of amorous conversation through confession and prayer, I wish to show how an awareness of the inexpressible leads inevitably to the Word and that this process is reversible and synecdochic. That is, the redemptive power of the Word traverses the way down, descending easily into such cognate spiritual actions as confession and prayer, but assuming flesh even in the amorous conversation itself.

I

The virtually insurmountable difficulty that the true lover experiences in trying to speak his devotion to the lady is one of the central conventions of medieval love poetry. In the *Romance of the Rose,* after the lover has been wounded by the arrows in the garden of Mirth and becomes the thrall of the god of love, speechlessness is enumerated among the pains he will experience. When he meets the lady, he will not have the hardihood to speak and she will leave before he says anything. His color will change and words will fail him. Even if he does speak, he will forget much that he planned to say.[12] In *La Vita Nuova,* there are no conversations between Dante and Beatrice, and he is content, ecstatic rather, with simply the lady's greeting.[13] Even in the laconic

Njalssaga, Gunnar of Hlidarend, before his disastrous marriage to the sinister Hallgerd, falls in love with Bergljot, but fails to ask for her hand:

> At the Yule festival the earl gave him a gold bracelet. Gunnar fell in love with Bergljot, one of the earl's kinswomen, and it was obvious that the earl would have married her to Gunnar, if Gunnar had sought it at all.[14]

His marriage to Hallgerd, which takes place almost immediately after this, and, as it were, in default of his not speaking to Bergljot, results eventually in his death. In Chaucer's *Troilus and Criseyde,* Pandarus is able to exercise his dubious function primarily through the inability of Troilus to speak directly with Criseyde.[15] The convention extends indefinitely on either side of the medieval period, to be sure, and the fact that Don Quixote never speaks to the fair Dulcinea is one of the final variations of the convention in the medieval romance tradition. In the *Cligés* of Chrétien de Troyes, famous for its analysis of the psychology of love, there are two pairs of lovers who do not know what to say: their emotions are inexpressible. If they do speak, they are tortured by the possibilities of untruth or multiple meaning. Alexander seeks the presence of the queen in order to be close to Soredamors, but he dares not speak to her, and she in turn would gladly inform him of the truth of her affection.[16] He calls himself a demented, wounded man who dares not seek aid and healing. Soredamors, in turn, asks herself why Alexander should care about her in his ignorance unless she informs him of her desire. If someone wants a thing, she should request it. She cannot, though, because she is a woman.[17] After repeating her reflection on the necessity of communication of some sort, she consoles herself by the realization that she has not yet begun to suffer unbearably, and decides to wait until his attention is aroused. She assumes that Alexander has heard of love, but contrasts the inadequacy of such hearsay knowledge, which in her experience has been mere flattery, to the authentic feeling.[18] As a solution to the dilemma, she decides upon allusive circumlocution. As the story develops, however, the two lovers are brought together only by the perceptive courtesy of Guinevere.

Cligés, the son of Alexander and Soredamors, and Fenice, his beloved, encounter a similar inexpressibility in the second part of the poem. Their eyes discourse in the exchange of glances, but their tongues are cowardly; they dare not speak of the love that possesses them.[19] At one point, Fenice's anxiety about verbal communication begins a striking analysis of the hope and fear latent in the words "toz suens" which Cligés has addressed to her. The uncertainty of meaning present in her reflections on the phrase demonstrates the inadequacy of words, and her attempt at a complete understanding shows the need to remove the imperfections from language:

> With what intention would Cliges say "I am altogether yours" unless it was love that prompted him? What power can I have over him

that he should esteem me so highly as to make me the mistress of his heart? Is he not more fair than I, and of higher rank than I? I see in it naught but love, which could vouchsafe me such a boon. I, who cannot escape its power, will prove by my own case that unless he loved me *he would never say that he was mine* unless love holds him in its toils. Cliges could never say that he was mine any more than I could say that I was *altogether his* unless love had put me in his hands. . . . But now I am sore dismayed because it is so trite a word, and I may simply be deceived, for many there be who in flattering terms will say even to a total stranger, "I and all that I have are yours," and they are more idle chatterers than the jays. (My italics.)[20]

Analysis increases the meanings of the phrase and it becomes a symbol of a wider semantic area, analogously to the way in which *word* can refer to a whole sentence. The passage then gives us an illustration of the awareness of what words should—but do not—do; and "toz suens" becomes a synecdochic emblem. When the two lovers finally speak to each other more fully, their conversation is a maze of indirections with the convention of the absent heart used to delay the final disclosure of love.

One of the most remarkable examples of this realization that words are imperfect occurs in the Provencal romance *Flamenca*, where William the clerk, proffering Flamenca the gospel book to be kissed during mass, says simply "alas."[21] Flamenca, reflecting on this word later, first assumes that he was mocking her marital unhappiness. Counseled by her maid, she decides to speak to him the words "why grieve?"[22] at the same point in the mass on the following Sunday. During the week William suffers a similar onset of alternating joy and despair about the possible meanings of the phrase. This process of exchange of phrase and analysis goes on for many weeks and over a thousand lines, motivated by the semantic incompleteness of the words; and constitutes a progress to a final understanding by consolidating synecdochic stages.

One could go through Chaucer, mentioning, for example, the fact that when Theseus finds Palamon and Arcite in the forest ankle-deep in each other's blood, they have not yet made their love known to Emelye;[23] and on into the Renaissance, citing Orlando's trembling reticence before Rosalind in Shakespeare's *As You Like It* and the consequent dramatic necessity for her disguise. To cite further examples of the connection between love and the inexpressible would only belabor the obvious, however, for the convention is truly archetypal.

What is the lover to do, then? The very existence of a technique of amorous persuasion, advocated in Ovid's *Ars Amatoria* and codified in the *De Arte Honeste Amandi* of Andreas Capellanus, puts him in a dilemma, which, though often amusing, has serious moral implications. If he masters such a technique, does that not radically endanger the authenticity of his love? The dialogues of

Andreas, like all rhetorical manuals, attempt to provide the lover with a means of coping with the inexpressibility of his subjective experience, but they also illustrate an important stage in the progress from words to Word. The central truth about the lover of the *Confessio Amantis* is that he is to be rejected as a human lover in order to find his vocation as a Christian in prayer. His experience of words is the means by which he will come to this truth, but the several stages along the way consist of a progressive realization that some modes of speech provide access to a more perfect kind of truth and hence relate his sense of the inexpressible to the divine affability. Before examining the degrees and kinds of truth in the *De Arte Honeste Amandi*, we will do well to establish coordinates.

The rhetorical tradition contains the principle that human truth can be achieved only through praise and blame; that it is through an assessment of the positive and negative elements that the whole can be achieved. The Aristotelian virtue of truth, widely discussed in the Middle Ages, consists of saying neither too much nor too little about oneself; neither boasting nor deprecating; avoiding excessive praise or blame of oneself. Discussed in the *Nicomachean Ethics*, explained in a commentary of Thomas Aquinas and repeated in his *Summa Theologiae*, truth in this tradition is a virtue that governs the way a man speaks about himself and is a mean between two extremes. On the excessive side of the mean, we have the boaster:

> He says therefore that the boaster, who sins through superabundance, makes certain pretensions to glory. And this in two ways. In one way, they pretend to have certain grand qualities which they do not have. In another way they say that their qualities are greater than they are.[24]

The opposite extreme is represented by the man who indulges in false modesty, or *ironia*. The mean is achieved by a kind of perfect self-revelation:

> But he who possesses the mean is called *autocastos*, that is, admirable in himself, since he does not seek to be greater in admiration than is suitable to him according to himself. Or he is called *autophastos*, that is, manifested through himself, because he manifests himself such as he is.[25]

Though few may attain the grand simplicity of this ideal, it describes a goal and framework valid for conversations of every sort—an important stage in the progress from imperfect words to perfect Word. The requirements for the speech of confession and prayer, for example, fit neatly and predictably into the framework, and the theological tradition of the Word fulfills the implied model of perfect verbal expression.

Correlative to the importance of "trouthe" in medieval love literature is the frequent occurrence of the "friend." Looking at *The Romance of the Rose* once more, we find that the lover is advised to seek a friend to counsel him, and this he does.[26] The role of the counseling friend in love literature is of frequent occurrence, like the difficulty of speaking. La Vielle performs this function for the woman in *The Romance of the Rose;* in Chaucer's *Troilus and Criseyde,* Pandarus does the office.[27] The role of the friend in both of these poems is, I believe, ironic. La Vielle and Pandarus are used to define friendship by showing what it clearly is not and to suggest genuine friendship as the criterion for sexual love as well.[28] Genius in the *Confessio Amantis,* although he is the priest of Venus, draws this role of the friend into the context of a Christian sacrament and brings the convention to a theological fulfillment, a process to which we shall return later in this study.

Just as the Aristotelian virtue of truth matches the "trouthe" of the love poetry, a corresponding virtue of friendship parallels the role of the friend. Defined also as a virtue that regulates speech, it is a mean between saying more and less than is true about someone.[29] Although the elements of these two virtues, friendship and truth, together with their four extremes to be avoided—flattery, contentiousness, boasting, and false modesty—are touched upon in the *Confessio Amantis* only within the specific structure of the Seven Deadly Sins, they underlie conceptually all the other kinds of speech in the poem.

Measured against these conversational norms, the dialogues in the *De Arte Honeste Amandi* are both deficient and encouraging.[30] They are, in large part, remarkable instances of amorous flyting. Their purpose is clearly rhetorical, and the comments of Andreas abound in proleptic admonitions. The tone throughout the dialogues is that of a comically perverse debate, with both parties sedulously avoiding what is true and friendly; indeed, the object seems to be to distract, embarrass, distort, and, further, to employ any kind of sophistry that will give one speaker an intellectual or emotional edge over the other. Addressing the famous Walter, Andreas, who naturally takes the masculine point of view, fills the treatise with unabashed exhortations to flattery founded upon the pervasive assumption that the purpose is to deceive the lady. At the beginning of the dialogues, he lists the five principal causes of love, giving precedence to beauty, character *(morum probitas),* and eloquence:

> The teaching of some people is said to be that there are five means by which it [love] may be acquired: a beautiful figure, excellence of character, extreme readiness of speech, great wealth, and the readiness with which one grants that which is sought. But we hold that love may be acquired only by the first three.[31]

In the same chapter, Andreas asserts that only excellence of character is worthy of love. Instead of advising the honesty of straightforward self-revelation—the requirement of the virtues of truth and friendship—Andreas recommends flattery, subtle boasting, and a canny avoidance of contentiousness. Since eloquence makes the listener assume a good character, he dedicates over half of his treatise to illustrative patterns of speech instructing Walter in the technique of courtly persuasion:

> Character alone, then, is worthy of the crown of love. Many times fluency of speech will incline to love the hearts of those who do not love, for an elaborate line of talk on the part of the lover usually sets love's arrows a-flying and creates a presumption in favor of the excellent character of the speaker. How this may be I shall try to show you as briefly as I can.[32]

With the suggestion that "presumption" *(praesumi)* implies that only the impression of a good character need be given, we receive our first inkling that Andreas's concern for the quality of truth in speech is only perfunctory. The obvious antithesis between excellence of character and the techniques recommended by Andreas becomes more apparent in a remark about the feminine appetite for praise prefatory to the first dialogue:

> But if the woman waits too long before beginning the conversation, you may begin it yourself skillfully. First you should say things that have nothing to do with your subject—make her laugh at something, or else praise her home, or her family, or herself. For women, particularly middle-class women from the country, commonly delight in being commended and readily believe every word that looks like praise. Then after these remarks that have nothing to do with your subject, you may go on in this fashion.[33]

The lady, in this view, is anything but inexpressible.

The matter-of-fact way in which he calls attention to this defect in women, his unequivocal affirmation of their vain credulity, as it were, suggests the wry atmosphere of the whole treatise. The lady is to be flattered prudently according to her social rank and intelligence. This initial advice, however, is complicated by what actually takes place in the dialogues. To the man's opening assertion that "when the Divine Being made you there was nothing that He left undone," our middle-class woman responds simply that he's telling fibs.[34] This kind of exchange constitutes the pattern of the dialogues. The women are always aware of the flattery and verbal manipulation employed by the men, and they respond by a vigorous and deflating vilification on physical, social, and intellectual levels. On one occasion, the lady calls attention to the man's fat calves and huge, flat feet. The man has to reply to the charge of physical ugliness and demonstrate its irrelevance.[35] On another occasion, the man's mercantile occupation is the object of unmitigated scorn.[36] Again, he is accused of seeking the love of a woman of a lower class because of failure on his own social level.[37] Since the man is always the initiator of the dialogues, he must insist on his complete conviction of the lady's excellence, and naturally he employs flattery. The lady doesn't make it easy, though, and her attitude is consistently satirical. Moreover, the men in the dialogues are just sufficiently harsh themselves when it becomes necessary to respond to a particularly devastating remark from a lady.

An almost truculent criterion of truth would seem to be the guiding principle here, but such is not the case. The men from various ranks of society are interested, after all, only in the seduction of the lady. The excellence of character, or *morum probitas,* everywhere invoked as the only basis for accepting a lover clearly does not involve authentic "trouthe." On the other hand, paradoxically, the impetus toward candor, or the virtues of truth and friendship, is an intrinsic part of the dialogues' structure. Although they patently and perhaps deliberately fall short of giving a lover a model of "trouthe," they nevertheless raise the issue in a thorough and lively fashion. The rhetorical completeness of the dialogues, the explicit awareness on the part of the speakers of flattery, their skillful use of insult, the man's denunciation of false modesty, the lady's savage thrusts at any appearance of pretentiousness—all serve to build a pattern that superficially resembles the virtues of truth and friendship. This adherence to the letter of virtue without its spirit perhaps makes the dialogues more insidious than the obviously deceitful and rather repulsive advice given by the "friend" and La Vielle in *The Romance of the Rose.* But the blatant directness of the dialogues, whatever their immoral purposes, has virtue in it. The lover is put through a confrontation with his defects and pretensions which is an excellent preparation for confession, and when Amans in the *Confessio Amantis* refers to his conversations with his lady, his experiences have clearly been painfully similar to those of the beleaguered male speakers of Andreas's dialogues. And, most important, Amans's experience of blame is crucial to his growth in self-knowledge in several parts of the poem and particularly in his final conversation with Venus.

The progress from words to Word is advanced even, or perhaps especially, by excessive praise and blame of this kind. The hyperbole does after all describe an ideal that can have only a divine fulfillment; and the waspishness of the satirical jibes uncovers human limitations. Amans will finally choose God as the only object that an absolute or hyperbolic use of words can fit.

Repeatedly throughout the dialogues the speakers call attention in various ways to the disparity between truth and verbal skill, until, in the eighth dialogue, the lady proposes that, because of the inadequacy of words, the man abandon speech completely. A patient silence would enable her to be more faithful to the nature of love, which is a free gift and should not be sought with importunate pleading. She gives this line of reasoning an additional gaminess by mentioning a rival:

> There is another man, equal to you in character and family and no different in his desire to serve me, who asks for love by his services alone and is reluctant to mention the matter with his tongue, and it is

most fitting that in love he should be preferred to you. For I think that the man who puts all his hope and trust in the purity of my faith and does not trouble me with constant importunities, since he feels confident that his hope will be fulfilled just because of my liberality, deserves to get from me what he wants more than the one who has laid before me in so many words the secrets of his heart and puts all his trust in his fluency of speech, having more trust apparently in the force of his own remarks and the duplicity of his words than in the honesty of my judgment.[38]

The rival has the good sense to know that such feelings are inexpressible and that to talk about them is vulgar.

What the lady has almost advised is a return to the situation with which we began—that of the sincere, inarticulate lover. If the lover says nothing, presumably he cannot lie, or reduce the inexpressible to the banal. This will not do, however. In response, the man asserts the right to speak on the basis of a natural analogy and a biblical command:

It seems to me that your opinion in this case is open to a good deal of argument, for what wise man ever said that a mute who tries with unintelligible gestures to indicate what he wants deserves to have it more than a man who can ask with words of deepest wisdom and all the ornaments of language for what his soul desires. Among the popular sayings men quote is "Never have a mute for a sailor on any ship." Besides there seems to be every argument in favor of my being permitted to ask for what I want and urgently desire; even the Author of truth Himself said, "Ask, and it shall be given you: knock and it shall be opened to you." For the custom has grown up in the world that far from getting what we want or obtaining the result we hope for, by keeping silent, we can hardly get it by the most insistent demands.[39]

The last two quotations from Andreas present my critical pattern in miniature. They show how talking to the lady leads to talking to God, and how talking to God affects talking to the lady. The lady says that the lover should not talk to her because words are inadequate. If the Author of truth, however, urges the use of words, then words can achieve a truth proportionate to the Person or person addressed. But words must be adequately proportioned to their object; and words that pertain only to God should not be addressed to the lady, unless they are understood analogically. If a man has a divine imperative to make requests of Divinity Itself, he need have no reticence before the lady. Although the tone here is hardly serious, the very notion provides a means by which the timid lover can overcome his initial low self-esteem and speak successfully to the lady. Prayer and the mute, however, give occasion for another argument against articulate speech:

> But the labor of a mute should not go without its proper reward, even though he cannot express in words what he wants, and the example you cite from the Gospel cannot make any difference here. He whose own merits speak for him and who is aided by the purity of his faith is considered, so far as the judgment of the Eternal King goes, to be asking urgently and knocking incessantly at the door. If you wish to restrict the meaning of the word and take only what it actually says, you will be forced to say emphatically that all mutes are absolutely denied entrance into Paradise, since because of a natural defect in their tongues they can never ask in articulate words for what they desire in their hearts.[40]

Reflecting upon the relationship of prayer and amorous conversation can also bring into focus the greater ease and power of prayer as a mode of communication and, of course, the option of abandoning amorous conversation altogether. My purpose in looking at the dialogues of Andreas has been to point out that in terms of their explicit purpose they offer no solution to the plight of the speechless but authentic lover. In their concern for the rhetorical appearance of truth, however, and by the implications of the speciously introduced allusions to prayer, they point the way to the kind of hierarchical ascent from human to divine speech which Gower presents in the *Confessio Amantis.*

II

Gower's use of the sacrament of confession demonstrates its value at this point. The intention of the dialogues of Andreas is seduction, and no amount of surface striving for honesty can change this. But the insistent, implicit criterion of truth effects an important transition in the process by which man discovers God in the faculty of speech. The lover first realizes his fear or inability to speak to his beloved and entertains the possibility of learning a technique of amorous persuasion, which fails him without his realizing it. Finally he comes to confession, where he finds a kind of dialogue of complete self-disclosure which was foreshadowed in his desire to speak to the lady in the first place and which rejects the rhetoric of amorous persuasion while it fulfills the deepest implications of its structure. By entering the context of religious thoughtfulness, the experience of inexpressibility, encountered in conversations with the lady, modulates into a more adequate use of words in the self-disclosure of confession, and at the same time takes on a new dimension.

The sacrament of confession can be looked upon as an attempt to penetrate inwardly to the principle of a man's being by clearing away the dishonesties and hypocrisies standing in the way of self-knowledge and of achieving the virtue of truth.[41] A great aid to this, in contrast to the dialogues of Andreas, is the initial presumption of inadequacy: the penitent is supposed to be unimpressive and is under no rhetorical pressure to represent himself otherwise. A sense of exhaustion and qualified defeat should provoke in the penitent a deep reassessment of his self-awareness. The situation, viewed as a dramatic rather than ecclesiastical structure, is like the moment of inanition in tragedy when the hero is forced through suffering to see what he is and has done, in all its painful and humiliating implications. The articulated vision won from this encounter with human guilt in its most universal context is what we value in tragedy and, less apparently, what is received in some form in confession, but with an explicit sacramental intention.[42]

In the sacrament of confession, however, the penitent reaches understanding not through events but through conversation about events. He is urged in innumerable confessional manuals to tell neither more nor less than is true about himself. The confessor, in turn, must practice the virtue of friendship, certainly without flattering the penitent, and without reproaching him carelessly. The extremes to be avoided in the sacrament of confession are the same as those Aquinas warns against in his discussion of the virtue of truth. The penitent should not be led by a misguided sense of humility to confess to sins he has not committed. On the other hand, he should not omit any sins, which would be a fault of defect, or saying too little. In the *Sentences*, Peter Lombard contrasts the two extremes of concealment and misguided self-revelation: "Just as the penitent should not hide a sin, because that is pride; so he should not, for the sake of humility, confess himself guilty of what he knows he did not commit, for such humility is careless and makes him a sinner." Similar advice is found in Robert de Sorbon and Alan of Lille.[43]

The kind of indirection that shocks and delights us in the amorous dialogues of Andreas is strictly out of place. According to Pierre de Poitiers in his *Liber Poenitentialis*, confession must be simple, without excuses, without Adam's archetypal tendency to blame someone else.[44] A similar openness of shrift is enjoined by Robert Mannyng of Brunne in *Handlyng Synne*. Although openness is usually listed as the tenth requirement of a good confession, Mannyng puts it in third place:

> The thryd poynt of thy shryfte,
> 'Opunly thyn herte vp lyfte:'
> So Byt God tome and the,
> That opunly shal thy shryfte be.   (11401–4)

He continues the discussion of this point in its proper place (11757–60) and states further that one should not minimize his sins by fair words (11761–68).[45]

Through these qualities of speech, the penitent cleanses himself, as it were, or prepares himself for the reception of an ordered view of the universe, which is ultimately the Verbum Himself. By declaring that his own actions were disordered, he asserts by implication the validity of an ordered universe. The role of the confessor, in addition to helping the penitent make his disclosure and giving absolution, is to provide the knowledge necessary to such a view. It is precisely this function that is the artistic justification of the *Confessio Amantis,* for the confessor's innumerable stories serve to define the proper attitude toward all human action, as far as possible.

Just as the penitent, as we shall see, ought to imitate the Word in the truth and completeness of his self-revelation, the confessor—whose speech is edifying, if ambiguously so at times—is an instrument of the Word by virtue of his sacerdotal teaching function. The importance given to this teaching, referred to as counsel in the traditional discussions of the sacrament of confession, demonstrates the special artistic relevance of a number of stories about individuals who seek advice, the best advice being related to the word of God. In relation to this theme of counsel, the fact that Venus herself gives the final judgment and advice to Amans unites the confessional and amatory themes in a coda and points the way to divine love. It is the fact that counsel is an integral part of the sacrament of confession that makes the *Confessio Amantis* important as the handbook of a king.

We are fortunate in being able to turn to Gower himself for a description of the relationship between confession and the recognition through knowledge of the proper world order. He explains the three parts of the sacrament of confession—contrition, confession, and satisfaction—at some length in the *Mirour de l'omme* under Science, which is the fifth daughter of Prouesce (14593–15096). Early in his treatment of this virtue, Gower outlines a progression from *science,* or knowledge, through the interior word to its outward manifestation in speech and action:

> Science poise la parole,
> Ainçois que de la bouche vole,
> S'il soit a laisser ou a dire;
> Car ja ne parle du frivole.
> Molt est apris de bonne escole
> Cil q'a sa discipline tire;
> Bien dist, bien pense et bien desire,
> Bien sciet, bien fait, bien se remire,
> Du fine resoun se rigole,
> Fole ignorance fait despire,
> Bien sciet la meene voie eslire
> Parentre dure chose et mole.   (14605–16)

> (Knowledge weighs the word
> before it flies from the mouth,
> whether it should be spoken or not;

for it never speaks frivolously.
He is well taught of a good school
who draws from its discipline.
He speaks well, thinks well, desires well,
knows well, does well, regards himself well,
he channels himself with careful thought,
he despises foolish ignorance,
he knows well how to choose the middle way
between the hard and the soft thing.)

The knowledge, or *science*, from which the word of human action is begotten is itself conveyed by words.[46] Sin weakens this knowledge and the flesh would lie open to grave dangers

Si voie n'eust a revenir
Du vray Science, que la guye
Par confess et par repentir:
Pour ce confession oïr
Primerement fuist establie.   (14828–32)

(If there were not a way to come back
through true knowledge, which guides it
by the confessor and repentance:
for this reason, to hear a confession
was first established.)

Since man is so susceptible to deceit and the forgetting of this "vray Science," he must have frequent recourse to the counsel (14797–832) that is most efficaciously available in the sacrament of confession:

Mais ly sage homme en governance,
Ainz q'il deschiece en ignorance
Qant a ce point, molt sagement
Consail demande et sa vuillance
Reconte et met en l'ordinance
Du prestre par confessement.   (14803–8)

(But the wise man in governance
lest he fall into ignorance
in this regard, very wisely
asks for counsel, and recounts
his will and submits it to the ordering
of the priest through confession.)

Sacramentally, the truth achieved by the penitent is at least a preparation for the reception of Truth in the Augustinian sense, and because the process of purgation is verbal, the reception of the Word is a fitting, perhaps an inevitable, goal of the process. Be that as it may, in another part of the *Mirour de l'omme,* separate from the discussion of the sacrament of confession, Gower very definitely relates counsel, the source of knowledge or *science,* especially to the word of God:

> Sovent par bon consail d'amy
> Homme ad vencu son anemy;
> Pour ce bon est consail avoir
> Du saint sermon, comme je vous di. . . .   (18181–84)

> (Often by the good counsel of a friend
> a man has overcome his enemy;
> for this reason it is good to have counsel
> of the holy word, as I tell you.)

But among the effects of hearing the word of God, one of the most appropriate to the theme of the *Confessio Amantis* is the defense against lust. Aspre vie, the fifth daughter of Chastity and a personification of the ascetic life, has two armors, hearing the word of God and transforming this into action:

> Qui valont contre la pointure
> Du Foldelit et de Luxure:
> Dont le primer adoubbement
> C'est d'umble cuer oïr sovent
> De dieu sermon le prechement,
> Q'om dist de la seinte escripture;
> Et ce que par l'oreille entent
> Parface bien et duement. . . .   (18088–95)

> (Which are strong against the sting
> of foolish pleasure and lust
> against which the first armament
> is to hear often with a humble heart
> the preaching of the word of God
> which they speak from the holy scripture;
> and what he hears with his ear,
> let him perform well and properly.)

This quotation introduces an analysis and commendation of the word of God that continues for some hundred lines. The counsel of the word of God can build a knowledge in the penitent, a *science* commensurate with its scope, which is climaxed in the following lines:

La dieu parole ad grant vigour,
Et grant vertu deinz soy contient:
Car par parole soul du nient
Dieus ciel et terre ove leur atour
Tout les crea comme creatour;
Auci nous veons chascun jour
La dieu parole, q'en nous tient,
A no creance sanz errour
Le corps du nostre salveour
Fait que du pain en char devient.   (18159–68)

(The word of God has great vigor
and contains great virtue within itself:
for by the word alone from nothing
God created heaven and earth
with their adornment, as a creator;
also we see every day
the word of God, which dwells within us,
according to our belief, without error,
make bread become the body of our Savior
in the flesh.)

The word of God has created the universe from nothing and every day transforms bread into the body of our savior.

What is established, then, by this analysis is the particular relevance of the word of God, whatever its manifestation—Second Person of the Trinity, scripture, the voice of the preacher—to the sacramental conversation of penance. The constitutively verbal nature of this sacrament permits the Word to invade the speech of both penitent and confessor and thereby to fulfill the desire of the inarticulate lover for self-expression. Using words more accurately in the context of the penitent's relation to order in the universe moves the experience of inexpressibility closer to its theological fulfillment in the Word; and the word of God, in all its manifestations, as the best counsel for Amans is a concrete manifestation of the Word as final cause of all the verbal causes.

If the communicative anxieties of the lover are diminished in the dialogue of confession, the speech of prayer removes them completely. Worry about the right kind of verbal approach disappears in the many exhortations to simplicity of expression and even the complete abandonment of words. Most important in terms of the basic desire to communicate an exact account of the self is the fact that prayer conveys no new information whatsoever to the Person addressed, or so we may infer from the omniscience of God. This relates prayer in the deepest way to confession: it continues self-examination and the affirmation of Providence, as we shall see. The experience of inexpressibility gradually disappears, not through the verbal resourcefulness of man but as a result of the omniscience of God.

To return to Gower's *Mirour de l'omme*, Oreisoun, or prayer, dwells in the house of Devocioun (10180), the first of the five daughters of Humilité in the *Mirour*. After noting the advantages of praying in secret, Gower sets forth the obligation to speak plainly, a duty incumbent also on the penitent and the lover:

> Q'om doit orer tout plainement
> Senec nous fait enseignement,
> Si dist, qant l'en dieu priera
> Sanz parler curiousement
> Et sanz nul double entendement
> Du plain penser plain mot dirra,
> Car double lange dieus n'orra. . . .   (10225–31)

> (Seneca informs us that a man
> must pray with absolute plainness,
> he says, when a man prays to God
> without speaking elaborately
> and without double meaning,
> he will speak a plain word
> from a plain thought, for God
> will not hear a double tongue.)

This directness of speech in prayer comes to focus immediately and logically on the quality of truth as the crucial condition of effective prayer:

> David tesmoigne bien cela,
> Disant que dieus au toute gent
> Est prest, qant om l'appellera,
> Maisque tout verité serra
> Q'il prie, et nounpas autrement.   (10232–36)

> (David gives effective witness
> that God is well-disposed to everyone,
> when a man calls on him, but
> everything that he prays must
> be the truth and not otherwise.)

So far prayer is treated like any other kind of speech, and this is quite traditional, for Aquinas in his discussion of the subject quotes Isidore's etymology of *oratio* as *oris ratio*.[47] Prayer differs from the other kinds of speech we have been discussing, however, in that it does not need words. In fact, words can be a hindrance:[48]

Mais en priant oultre trestout
Il falt que l'omme en soit devout,
Car meulx valt prier sanz parole
A celluy qui son cuer y bout
Qe vainement a parler moult
Sanz bien penser, du lange sole:
Car sainte lange ove pensé fole
Ne valt ja plus que la frivole,
Que sanz merite dieus debout;
Sicomme l'en fait de la citole,
Dont en descorde la note vole
Et grieve a celluy qui l'escoult.   (10381–92)

(But in praying above all,
a man must be devout
for praying without speech is worth more
to him who has his heart in it
than vainly praying a great deal
with the tongue only without careful thought:
For a holy tongue with a foolish thought
is no more than frivolous
and God dismisses it without merit:
as someone who plays a discordant
note on the zither and grieves the listener.)

The requirement to be devout and the possibility of wordlessness makes us reflect more deeply on the nature of truth in prayer, for the ideal proposes a man completely at one with himself—a harmony of emotions (or heart), speech, and mind:

Cuers q'a sa lange se des*corde*
En sa priere a dieu n'a*corde*;
Ainz l'un ove l'autre ensemblement,
Qant lange son penser re*corde*
Et ly pensiers son *cuer* remorde,
Lors prie a dieu devoutement,
Par si qu'il prie honnestement. . . .   (10394–99; my italics)

(The heart in discord with its tongue,
does not accord with God in its prayer;
if the one together with the other,
when the tongue records its thought
and the thinker fills his heart with remorse
then he prays to God devoutly,
because he prays honestly. . . .)

The aspect of truth in prayer becomes awesome if we consider closely the classic definition, which includes both union and petition: a raising of the mind and heart to God and a request for specific benefits.[49] Anything that does not violate the moral law may be prayed for, but the granting of the request depends on the providential plan for the individual, an element which introduces a new dynamism into our survey. A person coming to prayer with an awareness of the traditional problem posed by medieval thinkers is confronted first of all by a God who already knows what he is going to say.[50] Not only that, a decision about what he is going to ask has already been made and, furthermore, cannot be changed because Providence is immutable. Yet he must still ask, because the decision has been made to a great extent on the basis of whether he was going to ask or not. Aquinas provides a summation of the problems together with the accepted solution:

> We must consider as part of the evidence here that divine providence arranges not only what effects come about but also from what causes and in what order they come about. Among other causes however are the human acts of certain persons. Wherefore men should do certain things in order to fulfill through acts certain effects according to the order disposed by God. And the same thing is true regarding natural causes. And prayer also is like this. For we do not pray that we may change the divine arrangement, but that we may obtain what God has arranged to be fulfilled by the prayers of the saints: that men actually "by asking may merit to receive what almighty God decided to give them before the ages," as Gregory says in the book of the Dialogues. (Bk I, ch. 8, *PL* 77, 188.)[51]

Prayer, then, is a kind of dialogue with one's future: it is acceptable and efficacious—indeed, it eludes absurdity—only if a man accepts what Providence has planned for him. In this context, prayer enforces a self-knowledge which counterpoints the confessional process and which is complete only at the end of the confession. The element of truth that pertains to prayer as a kind of speech, then, extends further in time than is the case in any other kind of speech, and more deeply into the personality of the individual praying.

Since a man ought to pray for everything, prayer is more universal in its aims than any other kind of speech, and hence is relevant to, and occurs in, more sections of the *Confessio Amantis* than does any other kind of speech. Moreover, since prayer obviously brings the mind into play and makes a man reflect on his own nature in terms of his desires, the future, and Providence, it takes on a cognitive and evaluative function.[52] An allusion to prayer in a context of boasting, gluttony, or avarice brings with it a tendency to condemnation of the wrong or inordinate desire. The logical conclusion of this is that the prayer of petition and union finally merge, for a perfect acceptance of the divine will removes the necessity, in one sense at least, for petition. The self-knowledge initiated by confession and reinforced by prayer becomes increasingly a knowledge of the Other, a union with the Divine Will, which in our context of speech and communication is most fittingly described by the tradition of the Verbum.

III

Among the many metaphorical configurations that represent union with God as the goal of the Christian life, the pattern of the Word occupies a unique place.[53] Logos or Verbum is perhaps the most important name given to Christ in the New Testament. The name is used only by John in the prologue to his Gospel, 1:1–18, and in the opening words of his first epistle, but the concept is important in the Epistle of Paul to the Colossians, 1:15–20, and in the Epistle to the Hebrews, 1:1–3. The phrase "word of Yahweh," which for the most part designates the prophetic experience, occurs 241 times in the Old Testament, and "word" itself about three hundred times. The spoken word in ancient Hebrew culture had a power and meaning that the Middle Ages, more thoroughly imbued with the assumptions of a predominantly oral culture than the modern world, would have immediately responded to. Blessings and curses, convenants, promises, threats, wishes, and commands conveyed by the spoken word seemed to release a potent and irrevocable psychic energy.[54]

The central aspects of the configuration of the Verbum described by Christian writers throughout the Middle Ages are first the identification of God with his Word and of Christ, the Word, with his words. When the question arises as to how man's word is like God's Word, a number of similarities and differences are pointed out; in this configuration, a man achieves salvation by a union of his word with the Word, Christ. In a classic passage from St. Augustine, *De Trinitate*, XV, 11, the nature of the relationship between the word of man and the Word of God is described together with the process by which union with the Word is achieved.[55] By *word* Augustine means primarily what in later medieval thought became known as the concept the "verbum mentis," the audible expression of which he compares to the Incarnation.[56] Just as the Eternal Word had to assume flesh in order to be manifest to men, so the mental word of man assumes an articulate sound in order to be manifest. If one searches for a deeper similarity between man's word and the Word of God, however, he must examine the mental word, "that image of God that is not born of God, but made by God."[57] The rhetorical antithesis here juxtaposes the beginning and goal of the process of union: word and Word. Underlying man's mental word is knowledge; when he expresses that knowledge as it really is, the result is truth, not the exterior truth of the Aristotelian virtue, but truth as the means by which union with the Word is achieved: "And so this likeness of the image that is made, approaches as nearly as possible to that likeness of the image that is born, by which God the Son is declared to be in all things like in substance to the Father."[58]

Further, just as God made everything through the Word, so that nothing exists which was not preceded by the Word, "so there are no works of man that are not first spoken in his heart." Truth is once again of central importance:

> But here also, it is when the word is true, that then it is the beginning of a good work. And a word is true when it is begotten from the knowledge of working good works, so that there too may be preserved the "yea, yea, nay, nay;" in order that whatever is in that knowledge by which we are to live, may be also in the word by which we are to work, and whatever is not in the one may not be in the other. Otherwise such a word will be a lie, not truth; and what comes thence will be a sin, and not a good work.[59]

The universal pattern described by the fact that no action of man is performed unless preceded by a word and that no creature exists which has not been created by the Word provides a universal stage for man's imitation and explains why the Son rather than the Father or the Holy Spirit became incarnate:

> There is yet this other likeness of the Word of God in this likeness of our word, that there can be a word of ours with no work following it, but there cannot be any work unless a word precedes; just as the Word could have existed though no creature existed, but no creature could exist unless by that Word by which all things are made. And therefore not God the Father, not the Holy Spirit, not the Trinity itself, but the Son only, who is the Word of God, was made flesh; although the Trinity was the maker: in order that we might live rightly through our word following and imitating His example, i.e. by having no lie in either the thought or the work of our word. But this perfection of this image is one to be made at some time hereafter. In order to attain this, the good master teaches us by Christian faith, and by pious doctrine, that "with face unveiled" from the veil of the law, which is the shadow of things to come "beholding as in a glass the glory of the lord," i.e., gazing at it through a glass, "we may be transformed into the same image from glory to glory, as by the Spirit of the Lord. . . ."[60]

Man's union with God through Christ, the Word, rests on, as it were, a linguistically ontological similarity. This process constitutes the paradigm which, in varying degrees of explicitness, similarity, and contrast, is illustrated in the stories from the *Confessio Amantis* that I will discuss. The important literary fact about the theological tradition of the Verbum is that it provides and climaxes a metaphorical universe: that is, *word* is used as one member of a metaphorical predication that includes virtually all the categories of being. To recapitulate from the point of view of the medieval moral handbooks, for example, all human action can be divided into thought, word, and deed. In the passage previously quoted, Augustine refers to the thinking of a word and the doing of a word, whereby he makes the word both the central member of a triad and a synecdochic substitute for each of the other two. As a result, an action performed by someone can be referred to as a word, as can the thought of that action and, of course, its verbal expression.

In addition to the fact that any human activity can be referred to as a *word*, any event or thing can be used by God to communicate with man and hence can be designated as a medium of speech. Augustine cites as examples of this an element of the world such as the star of the Magi, the casting of lots, the human soul of a prophet, an angel, a mysterious voice that seems to come from nowhere, dreams, and ecstasy.[61] More precisely metaphorical is a remarkable catalogue of the effects of God's Word in Vincent of Beauvais, who enumerates no less than twenty-four items, almost all of which are supported by several quotations from scripture. The word of God nourishes, inebriates, builds, makes fertile, heals, gives life, saves from material and spiritual mishap, penetrates as a sword, enriches, inflames, softens the heart, illuminates, delights and sweetens, informs, arms, fights against evil will, cleanses, strengthens, delivers man from the danger of death, conquers, transforms, brings salvation, fructifies, and finally obtains grace in the present and glory in the future. The difference between saying that God speaks through food and that the Word of God nourishes is that the first statement is literal theological truth and the second is metaphor, but even metaphor in this context strains the limits of purely figurative expression.[62]

Complementing the role of the Word in the spiritual fulfillment of the individual are the social and public means by which the Word is manifested.[63] Although every spoken word is ontologically rooted in the Word, speech which is directly related to the Christian message has a more explicit proximity to its divine archetype. Gregory the Great refers to the justly speaking man as the mouth of the Lord, and Pierre Bersuire asserts that speech which edifies is in reality the speech of God Himself.[64] Rabanus Maurus, although he does not equate edifying speech with the speech of God, insists that the Christian should speak with the purpose of building up the faith of the hearers. Whatever speech does not have this function grieves the Holy Spirit. How much more grieved is the Holy Spirit, he adds, if speech not only does not increase the faith of the hearers, but also does spiritual injury to the mouth of the speaker and the ear of the hearer, as do lying, detraction, cursing, and the like.[65]

The redeemed faculty of speech, by virtue of the Verbum, brings about peace and unity as opposed to "divisioun," which is Gower's main term for evil in the *Confessio Amantis*. The chaos or "divisioun" that Gower finds in contemporary society can be remedied by truth. The lover in his conversation, the penitent in confession, and the Christian in prayer seek to obtain love by a devout, precise expression of their thoughts. This expression in itself effects a union whose stability is proportionate to the truth it manifests. Although the remedy for "divisioun" is love and charity, the means of obtaining the remedy is truthful speech. But peace and unity in a state are dependent on those qualities in private individuals, and here again the Verbum is an ultimate criterion and an efficacious influence. Without the Word made Flesh, "de nouveau la Parole de Dieu se fragmente en 'paroles humaines'; paroles multiples, non pas seulement nombreuses, *mais multiples par essence, et sans unité possible,*—car, ainsi que le constate Hugues de Saint-Victor, 'multi sunt sermones hominis, quia cor hominis unum non est.' "[66] This last quotation from Hugh of St. Victor focuses empirically on human speech and finds man's essential limitation in the very multiplicity of verbal expression. The Word of God is one with the Father, but man "is divided, and made another, and he is not one whole."[67]

In his *Sermones de Diversis,* Bernard of Clairvaux expatiates on the paradoxical theme that man's speech is at once the vital bond of an orderly society, a bulwark against "divisioun," and the conclusive proof of his intrinsic disunity. Ruefully philosophizing on the discursive nature of human thought, Bernard laments that man must even talk to himself and characteristically proceeds from an examination of this internal colloquy to an exhortation to the unity made possible by the Word which is always One. The section is entitled "Concerning the address of man to himself, or to his soul."

> How great is our misery and how multiple is our need! We have need even of words. Our situation is miserable from any point of view, but it is not remarkable that we have this need in regard to each other. It is indeed remarkable that we have the need even towards ourselves. *No one knows what things are in man except the spirit of man that is in him* (1. Cor. 2:11). A great chaos would be established among us unless a certain crossing over of our hearts in the communication of thoughts took place by the intervening instrument of words. Who does not know that words have been invented for this need. Yet truly we must address even ourselves with words. *Will you not submit to God, my soul?* says the prophet, *for from him is my salvation* (Ps. 61:1). And who does not often need to call back his soul, to call for the opinion of his reason, to call together his affections? Who must not frequently collect himself with words, chide himself with threats, bestir himself with warnings, drive himself with accusations? Indeed it is helpful to persuade with reasons; as for example, *From him is my salvation;* or sometimes to console according to this verse, *Why are you sad, my soul, and why do you trouble me* (Ps. 145:1); and occasionally to remember, more diligently, necessary duties, as *Bless*

the Lord, my soul, and do not forget his constant gifts (Ps. 102:2). To be sure, my heart has abandoned me and I must talk to myself, and worse, to myself as another. And this I must do all the more, the less I have returned to my heart, returned to myself, and finally, been united to myself. For we will not have to use words even to each other where we will all run together into one perfect man. Fittingly therefore tongues shall cease; nor shall a mediating interpreter be required, where that unique Mediator shall by charity have done away with absolutely every middle term, that we also may be made one in them who are truly and eternally one, God the Father and the Lord Jesus Christ Himself. [68]

The guiding principle of my use of Gower as exemplum, then, is based on the perennial human desire for perfect verbal communication and the equally persistent realization of its impossibility. The most perfect communication known to the medieval world was the Father's communication of Himself in the Person of the Word. Medieval love poetry provides conventions which pungently illustrate this desire for perfect communication; the sacrament of confession is in one sense an application of the redemption precisely to the ability to disclose one's inmost self, and in prayer man engages, from the medieval point of view, in the most perfect communication of which he is capable. The pagan god Mercury, as we shall see, was interpreted not only as a symbol of rhetoric and of elegant speech throughout the Middle Ages, but also as the Word Himself. Quite remarkably, there are a number of uses of the figure of Mercury in the *Confessio Amantis*, at least one for three of the four kinds of conversation which, to me, satisfactorily encompass the examples of speech in the poem. In the subsequent chapters, we will show just how spiritual fulfillment in the Word is the resolution of the many conflicts arising out of the nature of human speech in the *Confessio Amantis*. Every use of words that involves an awareness of their inadequacy operates on a model of perfect expression, which becomes present to the lover of the poem as the Word—implicitly through the experience of amorous persuasion, confession, and prayer and explicitly through allusions to Mercury and the Annunciation, stories involving mysterious voices of divinely authoritative origin, and the identification of the image of God in man's nature with his faculty of speech.

2

The Annunciation Pattern in Amorous Persuasion

Knowing that words are inadequate can tempt a lover to guarantee an apparent perfect expression by pretending a divine message. Such a lie, however, also serves to dramatize the Word as the final cause of all the verbal causes. The most famous passage on the Word in Christian literature is, of course, the beginning of the Gospel of John, fourteen verses in which a favorite notion of Greek philosophy is fused with fulfillment of God's revelation in the person of his Son. The passage enjoyed considerable favor in medieval times and was given memorable literary permanence in Chaucer's comment on the friar:

> For thogh a widwe hadde noght a sho,
> So plesaunt was his "In principio,"
> Yet wolde he have a ferthyng, er he wente.　　(I [A] 253–55)

Some time ago, J. S. P. Tatlock recounted briefly some uses of the friar's salutation. The first three verses of St. John's Gospel were employed "with various ceremonies as a charm against fever by the Anglo-Saxons." Hugh of Lincoln "is said to have cured a demoniac by the use of holy water" and by reciting the first fourteen verses.[1] Seán Ó'Súilleabháin refers to a custom in Ireland of hanging a portion of the Gospel of John, the *Leabhar Eoin*, "around a lunatic's neck for curative purposes."[2] In a lengthier discussion of the friar's "In principio," Robert Adger Law concludes that the phrase meant all of John 1:1–14, and not just the first verse, just as *pater noster* refers to the whole prayer. He further concludes that the friar used this not as a greeting, but as a favorite devotion after he entered the widow's house. The most important sentence in these verses is "Et Verbum caro factum est," which, according to Law, combats "four formidable heresies": the Arian, Apollinarian, Eutychian, and Nestorian.[3]

The circumstances under which the Word was made flesh, the message of the angel Gabriel to the Virgin, is usually designated as the Annunciation, the most important paradigm for our thesis about speech and human love. The sexual laxity of many friars, coupled with the widespread use of this greeting, suggests a topical basis for Gower's use of the Annunciation motif in a seduction scene.[4]

If we look at one use Gower makes of the Annunciation allusion from a purely secular point of view and attempt to classify it as a narrative motif, it belongs to Stith Thompson's "Seduction by posing as a god" (K 1315.1).[5] Since Gower tells many stories about the amorous adventures of gods and goddesses, we might expect a plethora of this type in the *Confessio Amantis*. Such is not the case; as a matter of fact, there are only three examples, and their occurrence is structurally significant. The first example of this kind of story comes as the first illustration of the heart of the poem, of the first and greatest sin, Pride. The second example occurs at the end of Book I in the treatment of the opposing first virtue, Humility. The third and final example of the Annunciation motif occurs as virtually the last story in Book VI and provides the rationale for the lengthy encyclopedic digression of Book VII.

To see the purpose of this allusion, it will help us to look into the mainstream of commentaries on the Annunciation. The texts I have gathered illustrate three main points. First, the potentially seductive overtones of the Annunciation *mise en scène* are noticed very early in the tradition and it is this which paves the way for Gower's specific use of the motif. Second, the application to the life of the individual Christian is usually an exhortation of some kind to receive the Word as Mary did, some commentators going so far as to speak of the individual soul becoming the mother of God. Finally, if I may be permitted the cliché, the "medium becomes the message." A connection is made between the words of Gabriel and the incarnation of the Word which he is sent to announce.

The appearance of a strange man with an extraordinary salutation in the private chamber of a young woman suggests an inevitable moralization. A warning initiated by Ambrose and found verbatim in Bede brings out this potential seduction motif, which is found in later medieval parodic uses of the Annunciation:

> Learn to be a virgin in manners, learn to be a virgin in modesty, learn to be a virgin from this oracle, learn from this mystery. It is the duty of virgins to dread, to fear the approach of every man, to be wary of the speech of every man. Let women imitate this example of modesty. Alone in her chambers whom no man should see, the angel alone discovered her, alone without companion, alone without witness, lest she be debased by improper emotion, she is greeted by the angel. Learn, virgin, to avoid the lustfulness of speech.[6]

Ambrose's observation implies a praise of the Virgin's caution as well as denunciation of a naïve eagerness for conversation. The important point about this passage, for our own purpose of showing the relevance of

Annunciation exegesis to parts of the *Confessio Amantis,* is that Gabriel's speech can suggest not only the Word of God but also seductive verbal persuasion. Conversely, Gower's use of seductive speech in an Annunciation context ironically suggests the Word of God.

The potentially seductive connotation of the sacred event is vividly illustrated in vernacular literature by the York play of Joseph, who even in the biblical account needed angelic reassurance about his wife's fidelity. The expression of his suspicion describes the basic plot elements that Gower uses:

> Þanne se I wele youre menyng is,
> Þe Aungell has made hir with childe;
> Nay, som man in aungellis liknesse
> With somkyn gawde has hir begiled,
>   And þat trow I.[7]   (ll. 134–38)

In typically medieval fashion, the fidelity of Mary's conversational response is contrasted to the disastrous consequences of Eve's speech with the serpent. The interesting thing is that this fecund source of contrasting theological imagery, the fall of man, gets particularized as a sin of speech. The Annunciation is thus seen as a rectification of Eve's specifically conversational fall from grace. The existence of this exegetical diptych prepares the way for a literary use of a seduction scene with an Annunciation backdrop by which the victory and proper response of Mary is contrasted to the archetypal and hence figuratively repeated failure of Eve. An early statement by St. Justinus particularizes the parallel between Mary and Eve by having the latter conceive the word of serpent:

> Eve, though she was a virgin and incorrupt, having conceived the word of the serpent, brought forth inobedience and death. But the Virgin Mary, when she had perceived faith and joy, the angel Gabriel announcing the joyful message, that the Spirit of the Lord would come over her and the power of the most high would overshadow her, and that therefore He who would be born of her would be the holy Son of God, answered: *Be it done to me according to your word.*[8]

St. Ephraem describes this primary event in the history of the redemption in terms of a properly ordered conversation between the angel and the virgin in contrast to the conversation between Adam and the serpent:

> Adam, at the serpent's persuasion, made himself a debtor to justice, and the penalty of the crime was transmitted to all generations. The angel and the girl properly disposed themselves, spoke together and listened and paid the debt. . . . God established as mediators the angel and the girl that through their words the matter should be settled, reconciliation effected, and the mark of the debtors be blotted out in heaven and on earth.[9]

In a sermon of Jacobus de Voragine, the speech of Gabriel to Mary is contrasted to that of the serpent to Eve in terms of salutation, assertion, and promise:

> The Angel Gabriel was sent by God into a city of Galilee, etc. Once the devil was sent to Eve bearing an evil suggestion, a lying assertion, and a false promise. But today the Angel is sent to the Virgin offering a reverent salutation when he said: Hail, full of grace; a true assertion when he said: For you have found grace with the Lord; a useful promise when he said: Behold you shall conceive.[10]

In the *Ancrene Riwle*, the eagerness of Eve to converse is contrasted to the caution of the Blessed Virgin:

> Eue heold ine parais longe tale mid te neddre. tolde hire al lescun god hire hefde ilered adam of þen epple. so þe ueond þuruh hire word understod anonriht hire wocnesse. i vond wei touward hire of hire uorlorenesse. vre lefdi seinte marie dude al an oðer wise. ne tolde heo þen engle none tale. auh askede him þing scheortliche he ne kuðe. e mine leove sustren uolewe ure lefdi nout þe kakele eue. . . . eue wiðute drede spec mit te neddre. vre lefdi was ofdred of Gabrieles speche.[11]

Apparent through all these texts is the relevance of Mary's conduct at the Annunciation to the figural loquacity of Eve. In view of this tradition, we might say that an allusion to the Annunciation in a seduction scene would neither shock nor surprise a medieval audience. The meaning of such an allusion is likewise apparent. It is both a reminder of the primal sin and the means by which temptation to a similar conversation is to be overcome. By contemplating the significance of the Annunciation, one chooses the *word* of God and rejects seductive speech.

To proceed to our second point, the application of the Annunciation to the moral life of the individual Christian consists also of an exhortation to receive the Verbum in the manner of the Blessed Virgin. Hugh of St. Victor described the divine motherhood as an example to be followed by all:

> We ourselves, bretheren, ought to be the mother of Christ. . . . We ought to conceive Christ, to have the pains of labor, to give birth to Christ, to possess Christ born. . . . So it is in spiritual generation, in which God is male and the soul female. When God himself is joined to the soul, the soul conceives Christ through faith.[12]

Hildebert extends the Annunciation allegorically to refer to the situation of a faithful soul fruitfully receiving the words of a preacher:

> For the Virgin Mary has become the Church, or any faithful soul, which through the chaste incorruption of the will and sincerity of

faith is a virgin. Whence the Apostle "I have betrothed you to one husband, a chaste virgin to show to Christ (2 Cor. 11:2)." The angel announcing that Mary has conceived is a preacher of the truth, at whose preaching of the gospel the faithful mind conceives the Word of God; and then gives birth.[13]

Guérric d'Igny makes a similar application of the mystery:

And you should fully know that the conception of the Virgin is not only mystic, but moral; that which is a sacrament for redemption is also an example for your imitation; that you may openly make void in yourself the grace of the sacrament, if you do not imitate the force of the example. For she who conceived God in faith, if you have faith, promises the same to you, that, plainly if you will receive the word faithfully from the mouth of the heavenly messenger, God, whom the whole world cannot grasp, you can yourself conceive. Conceive not only in the heart, but also in the body, though not in bodily fact or appearance, yet plainly in your body; when indeed we are ordered to glorify and carry God in our body (1 Cor. 6:20).[14]

This inducement to a physical experience of the doctrine of the Annunciation shows its relevance to the erotic connotations. Passages of this sort show the power of the Annunciation as a cure for the fault the situation can suggest. This physical aspect is developed even more remarkably in the following quotation:

Attend therefore, as it is written, diligently to your hearing, for faith is from hearing, but hearing is through the Word of God (Rom. 10:17); for without doubt the angel of God speaks the gospel to you, when with his fear or love a faithful preacher deals with you, who, you dare not doubt, is named and is the angel of the Lord of hosts (Mal. 2:16, 17). How blessed are they who can say: From your fear, O Lord, we have conceived and labor with the spirit of salvation (Isa. 26:17, 18)! who indeed is none other than the spirit of the savior, than the truth of Jesus Christ. See the unspeakable condescension of God and at once the power of incomprehensible mystery; He who created you is created in you; and, as if it were too little to have you as a father, wants you also be become his mother. *Whoever*, He said, *does the will of my father, he is my brother, and sister and mother* (Matt. 12:50). O faithful soul, expand your breast, enlarge your affections, do not be narrow in your entrails, conceive Him Whom creation cannot grasp. Open to the Word of God the ear of hearing, that is, the way to the womb of the heart to conceive the spirit, thus are the bones of Christ constructed, virtues in the belly of the pregnant.[15]

In Gower, the antithesis between the Annunciation allusion and the erotic story is resolved in a process which Angus Fletcher calls "isomorphic imitation," an extreme similarity in artistic representation between two events or images.[16] The texts we have cited illustrate this principle, especially those juxtaposing the response of Adam and Eve in the garden with that of Mary to the angel. The redemption of mankind begins with a recapitulation of the particulars of the Fall. One can undo a wrong thing only by going back as much as is possible to the original event and doing it over correctly. The similarity in particulars between the virtue of the Annunciation and the vice of seduction points hopefully to a final unity in the person, the triumph of the virtue. The similarity of the vice to the virtue suggests the ontological substratum of goodness even in an evil person or event. The similarity of the virtue to the vice is a talisman of being which reinforces and draws out this potentiality for goodness.

This unity is ritually accomplished, primarily by a kind of repetition that our third series of texts demonstrates. Peter Chrysologus, concluding a sermon on the Annunciation, relates the speech, or word, of Gabriel to the Verbum. The Virgin's appropriate response to the words of the heavenly messenger merits her the conception of the Word:

> *Be it done to me according to your word.* She who believed the word, rightly conceived the Word: In the beginning was the Word, and the Word was with God (John 1); and she possessed the whole reality who consented in listening to the secret of faith. How much the heretic sins, who after the fact does not believe, when he sees how much she believed before the fact.[17]

In a similar passage from a sermon by Abelard, *verbum,* in Luke 1:38, tends to be identified with the Verbum: *"Let it be done to me according to your word.* That is, that I may chastely conceive the Word of God Himself [ipsum Dei Verbum] according to the word of your promise, and give birth incorruptly."[18] In the same sermon, Abelard interprets *verbum* in Luke 1:37, where its primary meaning is clearly an action referred to or described in words, as the eternal Word of God:

> *Because no word will be impossible with God.* The word of God here is the divine speech itself, which is described by the blessed Augustine, a divine ordering not having a clattering sound, but a force remaining forever. No word of God therefore will be impossible to Him, since whatever he disposes to do cannot be opposed by any accident.[19]

The relationship between the speech of Gabriel and the message it contains is more explicitly elaborated in a sermon by Guérric d'Igny. The message of Gabriel becomes the fulfillment of a text in Proverbs concerning the effect of kind speech on a sorrowful heart:

So indeed you have a text: *Sorrow in the heart of a man will humble him; and he will be made glad by good conversation.* [sermone bono] (Prov. 12:25). Truly a good conversation, a faithful conversation, and one worthy of every acceptance, is the Gospel of our salvation; which the angel sent today by God preached to Mary, and the joyful word of the Incarnation of the Word, the day of the day, that the Angel announced to the Virgin. That conversation, while it offers a Son to a Virgin, promises forgiveness to the guilty, redemption to the captive, an opening to the enclosed, life to the buried. That conversation, while it preaches the kingdom of the Son, announces also the glory of the just; terrifies Hell, gladdens Heaven; and, as by the knowledge of mysteries, so also by the newness of joys, increases the perfection of the angels. Whom then would that good conversation not cheer in affliction, whom would that word not console in his humiliation.[20]

Finally, at the end of the sermon, he identifies this speech of Gabriel with the Divine Speech: "Bonus plane sermo et consolatorius omnipotens Sermo Tuus, Domine. . . ."

The wordplay on *verbum* characteristic of the traditional reflections on the Annunciation is virtually repeated in the following stories from the *Confessio Amantis.* What was homophonic repetition and grammatical variation in the exegetes becomes in these stories a repetition of the functions of speech which keeps the reader aware of the divine Prototype of the faculty of speech that false lovers employ seductively. Just as the constant uses of *verbum* in the commentaries culminate in the Verbum and diffuse the power and grace of his implied presence, so the different uses of the faculty of speech point finally to the principal Annunciation allusion in each story. The Annunciation themes recall a climactic and timeless center in redemption history which various uses of human conversation approximate in varying degrees of similarity and perfection insofar as the characters of a story exercise their faculty of speech in accordance with the angelic message. Seductive speech in love is thus given a typological significance in relation to the fall of Eve and the salutary response of Mary.[21]

I

The first story in the *Confessio Amantis* (the first illustration of the sin of Pride, manifested in religious hypocrisy) is prefaced by a number of references to imperfect speech. The introductory Latin verses decry the hypocritical speech of deceitful lovers. Speech as the word of God is present by way of a reference to the clergy's failure to act on their own preaching—a frequent theme in Gower—and the common duplicity of all Christians in prayer. Hypocrisy in lovers' speech is denounced again in English. The progression from words to Word noticed in the commentaries appears dramatically in the central part played by Mundus's disguise as Anubis, the Egyptian god of speech who was equated with Mercury in the Latin tradition. Before having recourse to this mythographical material, however, we will see how the story itself shows an allegorical drift.

The Latin verses that introduce the section emphasize the role of speech in the hypocrisy by which women are seduced:

> Laruando faciem ficto pallore subornat
> Fraudibus Ypocrisis mellea verba suis.
> Sicque pios animos quamsepe ruit muliebres
> Ex humili verbo sub latitante dolo.

> (By masking the face with feigned pallor,
> Hypocrisy provides honeyed words with fraud.
> And thus often brings down the pious souls of women
> Through the hidden deceit of a humble word.)

A reference to the specific function of the clergy's speech begins the theme of the word of God. The religious hypocrisy of the clergy is manifested principally in the discrepancy between their words and actions:

> For now aday is manyon
> Which spekth of Peter and of John
> And thenketh Judas in his herte.   (I.655–57)

In addition to hypocrisy in preaching the word of God, duplicity in prayer is mentioned (I.661–72). The discussion of religious hypocrisy manifested in speech forms a logical transition to hypocrisy in amorous conversation. The emphasis on speech continues in reference to the false lover:

> For whanne he hath his tunge affiled
> With softe speche and with lesinge. . . .
> He wolde make a womman wene
> To gon upon the faire grene,
> Whan that sche falleth in the Mir.   (I.678–83)

Such a deceiver "halt no word of covenant." Amans disclaims any guilt for this fault of speaking as if he were in love when he was not:

> For that thing schal me nevere asterte,
> I speke as to my lady diere,
> To make hire eny feigned chiere.   (I.722–24)

By way of beginning the first story of the main part of the *Confessio*, Genius enunciates the following general principle, which embodies the theme I consider central to the poem:

> Mi Sone, it sit wel every wiht
> To kepe his word in trowthe upryht
> Towardes love in alle wise. (I.745–47)

With this emphasis on speech in mind, let us examine the story.[22] Mundus, a knight of Rome, attempts to seduce a young, beautiful wife, named Pauline. She rejects him. While thinking of the various ways in which he can deceive her, he reflects

> How that ther was in the Cite
> A temple of such auctorite,
> To which with gret Devocioun
> The noble wommen of the toun
> Most comunliche a pelrinage
> Gon forto preie thilke ymage
> Which the godesse of childinge is,
> And cleped was be name Ysis. . . . (I.799–806)

The temple of Isis provides the erotic setting for the seduction. Io, one of Jove's mistresses, was said to have been changed into Isis after her liberation from the monster Argus by Mercury.[23] The fact that Boccaccio interprets the change from Io to Isis as the damnation of the soul gives the temple in Gower's story a nefarious aspect. The theme of speech is interestingly reinforced by the use of the image of the sacrament of confession to describe the manner in which Mundus bribes the priests of the temple to aid him in the seduction of Pauline:

> To ech of hem yaf thanne a yifte,
> And spak so that *be weie of shrifte*
> He drowh hem unto his covine,
> To helpe and schape how he Pauline
> After his lust deceive myhte. (I.817–21; my italics)

Mundus persuades the priests to accept his plan. The sacrament of confession is used as a metaphor of effective persuasion. He does manifest to them his evil desire, not to acknowledge his guilt, but to actuate his intentions. Mundus and the priests decide to use the god Anubis as the means of deceiving Pauline. The priests approach her:

> Feignende an hevenely message
> Thei come and seide unto hir thus:
> 'Pauline, the god Anubus
> Hath sent ous bothe Prestes hiere,
> And seith he woll to thee appiere
> By nyhtes time himself alone,
> For love he hath to thi persone. . . .' (I.834–40)

The "hevenely message" invites comparison between the plot being laid for Pauline and the plan of redemption proclaimed to the Blessed Virgin by Gabriel. This analogy is made more probably an intentional part of Gower's telling of the story by the submission of Pauline to what she thinks is the Divine Will and by her concomitant joy. Like the Christian God, Anubis, according to the priests, will do nothing without the free consent of the human agent concerned. As C. S. Lewis observed some years ago,[24] Pauline resembles Mary in her total attitude:

> Glad was hire innocence tho
> Of suche wordes as sche herde,
> With humble chiere and thus answerde,
> And seide that the goddes wille
> Sche was al redy to fulfille. . . . (I.852–56)

The fact that Mundus, by pretending to be Anubis, becomes almost a personification of speech (as we will shortly demonstrate) introduces a parallel in the story with the Word made flesh. The passage just quoted, with its reference to "wordes" together with the religiously submissive attitude of Pauline, constitutes a paraphrase of the biblical "Fiat mihi secundum verbum tuum." Pauline believes that she has been especially chosen and asks by what observance she can best prepare for the divine visit:

> And thei hire bidden forto slepe
> Liggende upon the bedd alofte,
> For so, thei seide, al stille and softe
> God Anubus hire wolde awake. (I.884–87)

Mundus's deceitful assumption of the appearance of Anubis, we must remember, is characterized specifically as religious hypocrisy. He is to be identified with the angel Gabriel in the Annunciation scene but also as the Verbum, who is the summation of Gabriel's words. We are forced to recall in the actions of Mundus the most edifying of all speech and how Christ as the Verbum is the final cause of speech as a providentially constituted faculty:

> And he, that thoghte to deceive,
> Hath such arrai upon him nome,
> That whanne he wolde unto hir come,
> It scholde semen at hire yhe
> As thogh sche verrailiche syhe
> God Anubus, and in such wise
> This ypocrite of his queintise
> Awaiteth evere til sche slepte. (I.900–907)

The verbal persuasiveness of Mundus, disguised as Anubis, is especially emphasized. Pauline is startled at his approach:

Bot he with softe wordes milde
Conforteth hire and seith, with childe
He wolde hire make in such a kynde
That al the world schal have in mynde
The worschipe of that ilke Sone;
For he schal with the goddes wone,
And ben himself a godd also.
With suche wordes and with mo,
The whiche he feigneth *in his speche,*
This lady wit was al to seche,
As sche which alle trowthe weneth:
Bot he, that alle untrowthe meneth,
With blinde tales so hire ladde,
That all his wille of hire he hadde.   (I.915–28; my italics)

The emphasis on words and the message of a divine child unerringly bring the story into focus with the Annunciation. Mundus departs as stealthily as he came and waits for Pauline to come out of the temple. He taunts her with her devotion to Anubis:

'The myhti godd which Anubus
Is hote, he save the, Pauline,
For thou art of his discipline
So holy, that no mannes myht
Mai do that he hath do to nyht
Of thing which thou hast evere eschuied.
Bot I his grace have so poursuied,
That I was made his lieutenant. . . .'   (I.940–47)

The cruel irony of this remark focuses on Pauline's susceptibility to what was in reality a kind of blasphemous flattery. The emphasis on Anubis throughout the passage is like a rhetorical repetition of *verbum,* in that Anubis is the Egyptian god of speech usually identified with the Roman Mercury. The climactic irony of this speech of Mundus lies in the fact that what seemed to Pauline a divine incarnation turned out to be more like the fall of Eve.

Apart from the extreme probability given by the context that Anubis represents the Verbum, there is a mythographical tradition that leads to this significance by way of his identification with Mercury. The Roman religion, in the course of its development, became highly syncretistic and had absorbed many barbarian cults.[25] Anubis was generally understood to be the Egyptian Mercury. Servius, commenting on the *Aeneid,* VIII. 698, makes the following observation: "*Barker Anubis,* because he is painted with a dog's head, they intend him to be Mercury, because nothing is more cunning than a dog."[26] Robert Holcot, in the course of analyzing the religious practices of the Egyptians and Channanites, says that "they worshiped Jove in the appearance of a ram and Mercury in the appearance of a dog."[27] This resemblance to a dog is an aspect of the traditional "painting" of Mercury that occurs frequently in the mythographers. Mythographus Primus says of Mercury, "He is painted with a dog's head (whence he is called Anubis), for nothing is known more cunning than a dog."[28] Bersuire in his discussion of Mercury couples the dog aspect with the name of Anubis: "For some, as Rabanus says, painted him with a dog's head: whence Ovid: and you Anubis, the barker."[29] Bersuire interprets this canine appearance as a symbol of eloquence: "wherefore he has a dog's head because it signifies the barking of eloquence"; which eloquence of the Mercury-Anubis figure is the eloquence of "preaching and refuting."[30] If we recall that the tropological level of the Annunciation is to conceive the Verbum in our souls with the help of a preacher, the interpretation of Anubis by Bersuire has an ironic appropriateness to the plight of Pauline.

After telling the story, Genius makes the following application:

> . . . men scholde noght
> To lihtly lieve al that thei hiere,
> Bot thanne scholde a wisman stiere
> The Schip, whan suche wyndes blowe:
> For ferst thogh thei beginne lowe,
> At ende thei be noght menable,
> Bot al tobreken Mast and Cable,
> So that the Schip with sodein blast,
> Whan men lest wene, is overcast. . . .   (I.1062–70)

The explicit comparison of deceitful speech to dangerous winds and the image of a ship recalls the story of Ulysses with its emphasis on resistance to the seductive eloquence of the sirens.[31] Since the Ulysses story immediately preceded the story of Mundus and Pauline, the ship-storm image frames this illustration of religious hypocrisy in a context of harmfully erotic speech.

To sum up, the story of Mundus and Pauline is clearly connected with the admonition to guard the sense of hearing with its corollary emphasis on speech. The particular application of the story made by the confessor directs the meaning of the story to the necessity of not believing the smooth talker. Moreover, the fact that Mundus accomplishes the seduction of Pauline by pretending to be the Egyptian god Anubis—explicitly identified with the Christian preacher, with Mercury the god of speech, and hence inevitably with the Verbum—coincides with the application made by the confessor and ironically places the story in the Annunciation context.

II

Righting the balance at the very end of Book I, just as Humility reverses Pride, is a more positive, hopeful illustration of the relationship of the

Annunciation to love between man and woman. Instead of a devious seduction, there is a royal proposal, and in the place of the expectation of a divine son, there is a courageous venture on behalf of a very human father. The allusion to the Annunciation results from two separate but causally connected incidents in the story. Just as the Annunciation in some of the commentaries we have looked at is seen to remedy a specifically verbal fall from grace, so the story of Peronelle and the Three Questions begins with her father's loss of the king's favor through a sort of conversational hubris.

The events of the story are set in motion by a precipitous quality in the speech habits of Peronelle's father. The king is particularly fond of posing difficult questions, and the father is annoyingly quick with the right answers. The king

> . . . wolde in sondri wise
> Opposen hem that weren wise.
> Bot non of hem it myhte bere
> Upon his word to yeve answere,
> Outaken on, which was a knyht;
> To him was every thing so liht,
> That also sone as he hem herde,
> The kinges wordes he answerde;
> What thing the king him axe wolde,
> Therof anon the trowthe he tolde.   (I.3073–82)

"Trowthe" here is incomplete because the imprudence of its expression angers the king, and he puts to the knight three formidable questions which he must answer under penalty of forfeiture of his goods and death. The first question is, What has least need and is helped most? The second, What is worth most and costs least? The third, What costs most, is worth least, and is lost? Despairing of a solution to the riddle, the knight is persuaded by his fourteen-year-old daughter to let her speak on his behalf. She is beautiful, gracious, and "of goodli speche . . ." (I.3137). She counsels her father to inform the king that he has delegated his word to his daughter:

> . . . telleth him, in such degre
> Upon my word ye wole abide
> To lif or deth, what so betide.
> For yit par chaunce I may pourchace
> With som good word the kinges grace,
> Your lif and ek your good to save. . . .   (I.3200–3205)

The acceptance of a woman's counsel, as we shall see in the tale of Florent, extends to the point of making her words one's own. In both the daughter's counsel and the knight's speech to the king, the total delegation of his power of speech is emphasized:

And to the king knelende he tolde
As he enformed was tofore,
And preith the king that he therfore
His dowhtres wordes wolde take,
And seith that he wol undertake
Upon hire wordes forto stonde.   (I.3228–33)

The appropriation of her father's right to speak and the implied union between them anticipates the structure of her later claim on the king's promise of marriage. The daughter takes on the role of advocacy or intercession and a new bond is created between father and daughter. We should recall here also how in a sense the Blessed Virgin at the Annunciation represents all mankind in her conversation with the angel and her acceptance of the Word. The wisdom of the daughter is shown in her answer. The earth, which has the least need of aid but receives most, is the solution to the first question. Pride, which costs most and is worth least, answers the third question. In answering the second question, the daughter alludes to the love of God for the Blessed Virgin in making her the mother of his Son and describes a pattern for the final and most important use of speech in the story. Humility costs least and is worth most:

I seie it is Humilite,
Thurgh which the hihe trinite
As for decerte of pure love
Unto Marie from above,
Of that he knew hire humble entente,
His oghne Sone adoun he sente,
Above alle othre and hire he ches
For that vertu which bodeth pes. . . .   (I.3275–82)

Just as the humility of the Virgin causes love in God, the humble speech of the knight's daughter wins the affection of the king. He forgives her father and makes a conditional proposal of marriage:

And if thou were of such lignage,
That thou to me were of parage,
And that thi fader were a Pier,
As he is now a Bachilier,
So seker as I have a lif,
Thou scholdest thanne be my wif.   (I.3335–40)

Through her own humble speech, the girl has redeemed her father's error. As part of the remuneration granted to the knight, he receives an earldom. Balancing her humility with a laudable boldness, the daughter once more speaks up, this time on behalf of love, and appeals to the promise of marriage contained in the king's inviolable word:

'Mi liege lord, riht now tofore
Ye seide, as it is of record,
That if my fader were a lord
And Pier unto these othre grete,
Ye wolden for noght elles lete,
That I ne scholde be your wif;
And this wot every worthi lif,
A kinges word it mot ben holde.   (I.3362–69)

This evocation of the king's word, which manifests the inherent superiority of his royal person, as a claim to marriage cannot fail to remind us of Peronelle's own allusion to the Blessed Virgin's conquest of divinity. Coming as it does to counterbalance a sin of speech, this ritually verbal exchange between maiden and king must be seen as a variation on the pattern of the conception of the Word as described in the commentaries cited. Peronelle's assimilation of what the king has said can be described as a mental conception of his word. Her acceptance of his implied promise is a verbal confirmation, a "fiat mihi secundum verbum tuum."

The many references in the story to *grace* are an additional corroboration of the Annunciation allusion. After the maiden has answered the three questions, for example, the king is said to find her in "so mochel grace,/ That al his pris on hire he leide . . ." (I.3328–29). She is later described by Genius as "full of grace . . ." (I.3397), which is, of course, an exact translation of the Angel's phrase, *gratia plena,* as reported in Luke 1:28. In the conclusion, Pride, here a personification representing Satan, is described as one "To whom no grace mai betide . . ." (I.3406). Amans is told that if he practices humility, "The more of grace" (I.3425) he will receive. The remark to Amans presumably has an amorous reference, but theological overtones are not out of place.

In view of the Annunciation overtones of the whole story, Peronelle's invocation of the solemnly binding and magically efficacious power of the king's word clearly evokes the connotations of the Verbum. The elevation in the social scale obtained by the girl and her father parallels the increase in spiritual dignity accompanying sanctifying grace and the acceptance by the Virgin of a role in the Redemption.

III

Because of the diffusiveness of the *Confessio Amantis,* critical discussion of the Nectanabus story poses a tactical problem: we must skip from Book I to Book VI to treat this story. The location of the first two Annunciation stories already discussed—the first and last stories of Book I, exemplifying respectively Pride and Humility—has an obvious importance. Virtually the last story in Book VI, the tale of Nectanabus is the *raison d'être* for Book VII and gives an Annunciation framework to this principal encyclopedic section of the poem. As the *Confessio Amantis* is intended primarily for a king, citing Aristotle's teaching of Alexander has an obvious and conventional appropriateness. Like Mundus in Book I, Nectanabus seduces Olimpia by persuading her that she has won the love of a god. Up to this point, the story is a false Annunciation, but an evil from which good flows, for the son of their union is Alexander, the greatest example of chivalry known to the Middle Ages. Having narrated the birth of Alexander, Genius has an excuse to describe his education for the whole of Book VII, a digression of presumed utility to the royal reader and to everyman, who has the kingdom of his own life to govern. Book VII, then, is the doctrinal legacy of a chivalric hagiography. Even though Olimpia succumbed to a false Annunciation, the fact that her offspring was a "god of earth" (VI.1935–40) elicits from this "fall of Eve" its redemptive antithesis, albeit in a somewhat secularized form. In addition to seduction by pretended divinity, the story illustrates the power of speech in terms of simple persuasion and also in terms of the ontological power of speech as used in natural magic. The order of precedence in natural magic given in Book VII places paramount importance on the spoken word (VII.1545–71), which, we will see, is crucial in the seduction of Olimpia.

Nectanabus, a famous magician driven from his kingdom in Egypt, arrives in the chief city of Macedonia. The king is at war and the queen is celebrating the feast of her nativity with a tournament. Nectanabus draws near her at the playing field and fixes his gaze on her. She becomes aware of his presence, beckons him, and asks him what he wishes. He pretends to have a message which can be communicated only in private conversation. She invites him to visit her alone in her room in the evening, a situation which parallels that of the Blessed Virgin when visited by Gabriel. This kind of situation is also explicitly inveighed against by commentators on the Annunciation, it will be remembered. Lacking the caution and restraint of the Virgin, the queen is completely absorbed in what he says:

> And sche with gret affeccion
> Sat stille and herde what he wolde:
> And thus whan he sih time, he tolde,
> And feigneth with hise wordes wise
> A tale and seith in such a wise. . . .   (VI.1898–1902)

The message of Nectanabus, that the queen is loved by a god who wishes to beget upon her a divine child, is referred to as a "word" and has an immediately mollifying effect:

> On of the goddes hath me bede
> That I you warne prively,
> So that ye make you redy,

> And that ye be nothing agast;
> For he such love hath to you cast,
> That ye schul ben his oghne diere,
> And he schal be your beddefiere,
> Til ye conceive and be with childe.'
> And with that *word* sche was al mylde. . . .   (VI.1910–18;
>   my italics)

The impact that this unique child is to have on the world and history, in addition to the value his life will have as an example to subsequent generations, increases his resemblance to Christ and hence the probability of an Annunciation allusion.

> 'He schal a Sone of you begete,
> Which with his swerd schal winne and gete
> The wyde world in lengthe and brede;
> Alle erthli kinges schull him drede,
> And in such wise, I you behote,
> The god of erthe he schal be hote'   (VI.1935–40)

The fact that this story introduces Book VII, which purportedly contains the knowledge that Aristotle imparted to Alexander, emphasizes the imitative value of his life.

Nectanabus compounds the evil of his lie by employing means which, in this situation, are considered especially offensive to the truth of the Christian faith. By sorcery—in which, as Gower points out in Book VII, speech plays an important part—Nectanabus causes Olimpia to have a dream in which the god Amos appears to her in the form of a dragon, changes to the shape of a man, and makes love to her, causing her to conceive. The dream is sustained by the vocal incantation of Nectanabus:

> Nectanabus, which causeth al
> Of this metrede the substance,
> Whan he sih time, his nigromance
> He stinte and nothing more seide
> Of his carecte, and sche abreide
> Out of hir slep. . . .   (VI.2002–7)

Olimpia later relates the dream to Nectanabus and takes its marvelous elements as evidence of the truth of his speech:

> Sche tolde him pleinly as it was,
> And seide hou thanne wel sche wiste
> That sche his wordes mihte triste. . . .   (VI.2020–22)

Nectanabus carries out his scheme and possesses the queen. The deception of Olimpia, however, is a kind of *felix culpa,* in that a great benefit is derived from her infidelity:

> Althogh sche were in part deceived,
> Yit for al that sche hath conceived
> The worthieste of alle kiththe,
> Which evere was tofore or siththe
> Of conqueste and chivalerie. . . .   (VI.2085–89)

Nectanabus is finally punished by dying through the agency of his own son, Alexander. The moral drawn by Genius decries the use of sorcery against innocent women who assume the truth of what is spoken to them:

> Bot every man mai understonde,
> Of Sorcerie hou that it wende,
> It wole himselve prove at ende,
> And namely forto beguile
> A lady, which withoute guile
> Supposeth trouthe al that sche hiereth. . . .   (VI.2280–85)

The analogous warning of Ambrose in regard to false Annunciations, we will recall, is less gallant: "Learn, maiden, to avoid the lustfulness of speech."

The positive aspect of the seduction of Olimpia, as I have suggested, is not neglected by Gower, for had Nectanabus not fathered Alexander, the history of knighthood and good rulers would be the poorer. We noticed that one group of commentaries on the Annunciation extended the conception of Christ as a spiritual possibility for all the faithful. The assimilation of the education of Alexander is the secular counterpart and extends the hortatory structure of the Annunciation in a secularized way to the whole of Book VII, making the examples of Christ and Alexander of complementary relevance. This fact, together with the placing of the stories of Mundus and Pauline and of Peronelle in Book I as respectively illustrative of Pride and Humility, makes the Annunciation relevant to the whole poem in a way that connects the theme of speech with amorous conversation, the Verbum, and the purpose of the work as a piece of counsel for Richard II and Henry IV. In a poem concerned mainly with love, the most appropriately explicit form that the model of perfect expression (implicit in an awareness that words can be morally as well as semantically inadequate) can take is the Annunciation—as I hope to have shown.

3

Amorous Persuasion and Prayer

Although an immediate corollary of treating love as a religion is treating prayer as a metaphor for amorous persuasion, the analogy presents an obvious difficulty for a medieval didactic poet. On the one hand, sexual experience is Christianized by envisioning prayer as the criterion of authentic human love-conversation; on the other hand there is a danger that amorous persuasion will mistakenly be identified with prayer. In the *Confessio Amantis*, the final stage of the interaction between the two kinds of speech presents a rejection of amorous persuasion in favor of Christian prayer, but the journey to this goal is by no means narrowly moralistic. A whole range of possible relationships between the two kinds of speech is suggested, mutual illumination and reinforcement as well as ironic contrast and humor. Explicit, precise comparisons alternate with allusive, subtle juxtapositions. The distinctiveness of the various subdivisions of a vice with their corresponding virtues presents the relationship between the two modes of discourse in fresh and sometimes startling aspects.

The requirement of truthful speech in the sacrament of confession, as I pointed out in the first chapter, is the standard by which the speech of a lover is judged and which makes the sacramental framework an effective metaphor for a sincere declaration of love. The equal importance of truth in prayer was pointed out in the first chapter. It is impossible to deceive God, and the purpose of prayer is not to convey information but to effect a union with God based on a man's realization of what he is in the divine plan. The truth required and given in prayer, then, is a profound self-knowledge. The first section of this chapter makes use of the Aristotelian-Thomist virtue of truth to examine the stories of Albinus and Nebuchadnezzar, and the discussion of Cheste, or contentiousness, in Book III of the *Confessio Amantis*. The first two stories show how prayer remedies the vice of boastful speech, which is opposed to the virtue of truth by excess. The discussion of Cheste shows how prayer indirectly remedies the vice of *ironia* or false modesty, which is opposed to the virtue of truth by defect. More obviously, Cheste opposes the virtue of friendship by denigrating the value of the person spoken to and thus denying the truth about that person. Cheste is seen as a remedy for the fear of the conventional lover to declare himself or the truth of his affection. More precisely, his fear is that such a truthful declaration will become Cheste and make his lady angry. The right of the Christian to speak openly to God without the imputation of Cheste is invoked as sufficient reason for similar open speech to a lady. In regard to the virtue of friendship, Cheste is the extreme opposed to flattery—the more usual sin of speech found in a lover—and, in a sense, a wholesome antidote to that vice.

Prayer as a means of reverential union with divinity is the basis of the second section of this chapter. Since in the religion of love, the lady herself partakes of divinity, prayer is a conventional metaphor of amorous persuasion. Gower's ambiguous handling of this convention is one of his most interesting achievements. In a context of apparent acceptance of this conventional meaning of prayer, there is an undertone of its Christian meaning which is opposed to the amorous metaphor. As a result there is an increasing ironic awareness that Amans must abandon amorous persuasion in favor of Christian prayer. The main illustrations in this section are taken from Book IV of the *Confessio Amantis,* where the vice under discussion is Sloth, for which prayer is a traditional remedy. In order to clarify the analogy between prayer and amorous persuasion, however, I depart from the order of the stories in the poem itself. Thus before I examine Book IV, I discuss stories from Books I, III, V, and VI. The story of Paris and Helen in Book V makes a clear distinction between the two kinds of speech, which are elsewhere handled ambiguously. This distinction is based on the existence of an appropriate place for prayer as opposed to amorous persuasion. The persuasion and abduction of Helen by Paris takes place in church, where the appropriate speech is prayer. The value of this story in the development of the theme is the explicit statement of the radical difference between the two kinds of speech. By means of this story Amans and the reader of the poem should realize that the ambiguous treatments of the similarity between the two kinds of speech have the pedagogical and psychological purpose of leading the medieval lover up the ladder of amorous experience to the love of God. The story of Bacchus in the desert, which appears in Book VI, contains an ambiguous handling of the analogy and resolves the ambiguity in favor of prayer. To refer once more to Book IV of the poem, the ambiguity and its resolution are epitomized in the last story, where the figure of Mercury represents simultaneously the danger of amorous persuasion and the role of the Word in human speech.

I

The first two stories which we will examine are adjacent in Book I of the *Confessio* and form a unity based on their concern with falsely proud speech, the first in reference to love and the second in reference to royal power. Prayer as humble speech is the remedy for this vice and at the same time implies man's supernatural dignity.

The subtle comedy of our first illustration demands emphasis. Of all the ways in which a medieval lover could win a lady, the display of brute prowess is least relevant to the infirm and impotent Amans. Halfway through the introduction to the story, Amans meekly suggests that for reasons of repeated failure, boasting is no problem for him, but Genius goes on blithely to warn him against a kind of savage egoism that is quite distant from whatever modest self-assertion he is capable of.

The introductory Latin verses clearly relate boasting as a sin of speech to a lack of self-knowledge, a defect which Amans and Alboin, who is the main character in the first exemplum, share in only the most general way:

> Magniloque propriam minuit iactancia lingue
>   Famam, quam stabilem firmat honore cilens.
> Ipse sui laudem meriti non percipit, unde
>   Se sua per verba iactat in orbe palam.

> (The boasting of a magniloquent tongue lessens
> the proper fame that silence makes sure with honor.
> Such a one does not perceive the praise of his own merit,
> whence he boasts openly in the world through his own words.)

Objectively, the error of the vice lies in the overstatement of a legitimate achievement:

> That ferst was wel is thanne mis,
> That was thankworth is thanne blame,
> And thus the worschipe of his name
> Thurgh pride of his avantarie
> He torneth into vilenie.   (I.2404–8)

The whole thrust of this section depends on the play between such conventions as secrecy, self-knowledge, and friendship, and their comic and obliquely revealing relevance to Amans. In itself, boasting can diminish the worth of the friend, or beloved, by destroying the necessary sense of equality, or, in the case of the lady, superiority. The convention of secrecy, or "derne love" occurs when Genius asks Amans if he has made known the reception of some token—a ring, a letter, a "goodly word"—from his lady. An imprudent disclosure tends to cheapen and diminish the value of an intimate exchange and the consequent embarrassment of the lady is the precise damage of boasting:

> Estque viri culpa iactancia, que rubefactas
>   In muliere reas causat habere genas.

> (A fault of the man is boasting,
> which makes a woman blush.)

So much for the convention, but we can understand how the lady would be embarrassed to have Amans as a lover.

Amans then is amusingly innocent of boasting; his departure from the virtue of truth is to the extreme of *ironia,* or excessive modesty, in a morally dangerous sense, as we shall see. He has never received anything to boast about:

> Noght of so mochel that sche sende
> Be mowthe and seide, 'Griet him wel:'
> And thus for that ther is no diel
> Wherof to make myn avant,
> It is to reson acordant
> That I mai nevere, bot I lye,
> Of love make avanterie.   (I.2432–38)

Underlying his absurd ineffectuality is the serious need to discover that the real value of his person exists apart from the court of human love. He does go on to imply that success would have made him guilty of Avantance (I.2439–42), but even a hypothetical aspiration that would lead him to see Alboin as relevant to his own situation further dramatizes his absurdity.

The story itself has a grisly effectiveness and tells of a violation of truth brought about by a ghastly humiliation of the lady involved. Albinus (Alboin), having defeated Gurmond and accomplished his resolve to have a cup made of his enemy's head, falls in love with and eventually marries Gurmond's daughter, Rosemund. Their union is temporarily successful and peaceful. At a feast which he prepares to honor his wife, however, the contemplation of his own splendor comes to focus unluckily on Gurmond's head:

> The king himself began to glade
> Withinne his herte and tok a pride,
> And sih the Cuppe stonde aside,
> Which mad was of Gurmoundes hed. . . .   (I.2532–35)

The disguise of the cup's nature is so complete that "no signe of the Skulle is sene . . ." (I.2544). Arrogantly, Albinus orders his wife to drink from the cup. Although whether Rosemund knows the origin of the cup or not is obscure, she obeys. What follows certainly shames her:

> . . . and thanne al oute
> The kyng in audience aboute
> Hath told it was hire fader Skulle,
> So that the lordes knowe schulle
> Of his bataille a soth witnesse,
> And made avant thurgh what prouesse

> He hath his wyves love wonne,
> Which of the Skulle hath so begonne.   (I.2555–62)

The last line asserts that Albinus in his boastful lapse from truth has claimed that the military prowess enshrined in the gruesome memorial of the cup won Rosemund's love. It is important to note a correlative antithesis between the excessive departure from one virtue, truth, and the defective departure from the other, friendship:[1] the boast of Albinus is unflattering in the extreme. By exalting himself, he degrades his wife and induces a murderous anger in her. Revolted by his perversion of truth and the nature of their love, she revenges herself by taking a lover who helps to poison Albinus.

The confessor's application is appropriate to the subject matter, but not to the penitent:

> Good is therfore a man to hide
> His oghne pris, for if he speke,
> He mai lihtliche his thonk tobreke.
> In armes lith non avantance
> To him which thenkth his name avance
> And be renomed of his dede:
> And also who that thenkth to spede
> Of love, he mai him noght avaunte;
> For what man thilke vice haunte,
> His pourpos schal fulofte faile.
> In armes he that wol travaile
> Or elles loves grace atteigne,
> His lose tunge he mot restreigne
> Which berth of his honour the keie.
>   Forthi, my Sone, in alle weie
> Tak riht good hiede of this matiere.   (I.2648–63)

Amans doubtless finds the admonition too flattering not to comply with:

> I thonke you, my fader diere,
> This scole is of a gentil lore;
> And if ther be oght elles more
> Of Pride, which I schal eschuie. . . .   (I.2664–67)

Although the character of Amans and the need for the framework to include heroic instances necessitate a frequent disparity between story and application, the distance here seems amusingly quixotic—in a literal sense.

The remedy of prayer guides the details of the next exemplum, which is a religious variation on the fault of Alboin. The rubric is Vain Glory, manifested principally in, and therefore essentially a continuation of, the immediately preceding vice of boasting. Similarity of subject matter and closeness in the text tend to make the reader see the two stories as a unit, with the religious solution of the second applying also to the first. Flattery is seen not only as a product of the Vain Glory of the flatterer but also as the best means of pleasing a vainglorious person. The Latin verses that introduce the section emphasize the necessity of flattering speech in gaining the favor of those who are vain:

> Eius amiciciam, quem gloria tollit inanis,
>> Non sine blandiciis planus habebit homo;
> Verbis compositis qui scit strigilare fauellum,
>> Scandere sellata iura valebit eques.
> Sic in amore magis qui blanda subornat in ore
>> Verba, per hoc brauium quod nequit alter habet.

> (A plain man will not have the friendship
> of a vainglorious person without flattery.
> A knight who knows how to curry favor with ordered words
> will be able to rise on mounted rights.
> So in love it is rather he who employs flattering words
> who will thus have the prize that another cannot.)

Even though the story of Nebuchadnezzar, which illustrates Vain Glory, has a religious emphasis, the amorous theme is evident in the preceding verses and continues in the lines introductory to the story. The similarities between speech to a lady and prayer are thus highlighted. A violation of the virtue of truth is suggested by the fact that the lover exults in a fine appearance and the composition of songs for his lady to the point of forgetting his mortal nature and heavenly destiny. This is evidenced by a preoccupation with changes in bodily form and external appearance which foreshadow the metamorphosis of Nebuchadnezzar:

> I trowe, if that he myhte make
> His body newe, he wolde take
> A newe forme and leve his olde:
> For what thing that he mai beholde,
> The which to comun us is strange,
> Anon his olde guise change
> He wole and falle therupon,
> Lich unto the Camelion,
> Which upon every sondri hewe
> That he beholt he moste newe
> His colour, and thus unavised
> Fulofte time he stant desguised.   (I.2691–2702)

Amans once again is comically free from this vice insofar as success is necessary to Vain Glory. As verbal persuasion, the lyrics of his songs seem particularly ineffectual:

> And also I have ofte assaied
> Rondeal, balade and virelai
> For hire on whom myn herte lai
> To make, and also forto peinte
> Caroles with my wordes qweinte,
> To sette my pourpos alofte. . . .   (I.2726–31)

> Bot yit ne ferde I noght the bet.
> Thus was my gloire in vein beset
> Of al the joie that I made;
> For whanne I wolde with hire glade,
> And of hire love songes make,
> Sche saide it was noght for hir sake,
> And liste noght my songes hiere
> Ne witen what the wordes were.   (I.2735–42)

The lady, it seems, suspects Amans's "trouthe." In addition to comic inadequacy, we should remember here that the speech of Amans as a penitent confessing his sins and admitting his rhetorical failure contrasts significantly to the triumphant amorous speech being indicted by the confessor. Amans's vainglorious response to speech about his lady contrasts to the obligation of accepting truthful, realistic counsel, a duty which in the accompanying exemplum Nebuchadnezzar neglects:

> And natheles I wol noght say,
> That I nam glad on other side;
> For fame, that can nothing hide,
> Alday wol bringe unto myn Ere
> Of that men speken hier and there,
> How that my ladi berth the pris,
> How sche is fair, how sche is wis,
> How sche is wommanlich of chiere;
> Of al this thing whanne I mai hiere,
> What wonder is thogh I be fain?   (I.2750–59)

Genius absolves him of this and proceeds to the story of Nebuchadnezzar, which is the only narrative illustration of the vice. After an introductory description of his wealth and power, the idea of Vain Glory manifesting itself to God as sinful speech occurs in the metaphor of his speaking thoughts:

> The privetes of mannes herte
> Thei speke and sounen in his Ere
> As thogh thei lowde wyndes were. . . .   (I.2806–8)

Speech as counsel by the voice of God is illustrated in Nebuchadnezzar's dream of the punishment he will receive if he does not listen to this voice. In his dream he beholds in the middle of the earth an enormous tree covered with leaves and sufficient fruit to nourish all men. Numerous birds and beasts are feasting in and around it.

> As he this wonder stod and syh,
> Him thoghte he herde a vois on hih
> Criende, and seide aboven alle:
> 'Hew doun this tree and lett it falle. . . .'   (I.2831–34)

The theme of counsel is continued in the explanatory advice of the prophet Daniel. The stature and fertility of the tree represent the political wealth and power of Nebuchadnezzar. The use of an isolated voice of obviously divine origin in the dream and the use of "word" to refer to a message of compellingly personal application suggest the model of the Verbum and anticipates the verbal nature of both his sin and his punishment:

> And of the vois thou herdest speke,
> Which bad the bowes forto breke
> And hewe and felle doun the tree,
> That *word* belongeth unto thee. . . .   (I.2901–4; my italics)

The cutting down of the tree and the binding of its root for seven years predicts the punishment that will befall Nebuchadnezzar if he refuses the counsel of God's word. He must respond by good words but particularly by prayer:

> Besech and prei the hihe grace,
> For so thou myht thi pes pourchace
> With godd, and stonde in good acord.   (I.2937–39)

Nebuchadnezzar, ignoring the exhortation to prayerful speech, exhibits his preference for Vain Glory and boastful words:

> His herte aros of veine gloire,
> So that he drowh into memoire
> His lordschipe and his regalie
> *With wordes of Surquiderie,*
> *And whan that he him most avaunteth,*
> *That lord which veine gloire daunteth,*
> Al sodeinliche, as who seith treis,
> Wher that he stod in his Paleis,
> He tok him fro the mennes sihte. . . .   (I.2957–65; my italics)

For seven years, through "the myhti goddes lawe," which "dede him transforme/ Fro man into a bestes forme" (I.2970–72), he eats grass and sleeps on the ground. Just as forgetfulness of his true nature causes the vainglorious lover to desire a different form and body (I.2691–2702), Nebuchadnezzar's boastful lapse from truth results in a bestial transformation.

Later, when he regains human consciousness, his inability to speak is the appropriate punishment for his boastful words. As sinful speech caused the bestial transformation and speechlessness is a significant result, the proper use of human speech, in conformity with the virtue of truth, becomes synecdochally the essence of human nature. Finally realizing his dependence on God, he attempts to pray:

> *Thogh he no wordes myhte winne,*
> Thus seide his herte and spak withinne:
> 'O mihti godd, that al hast wroght
> And al myht bringe ayein to noght,
> Now knowe I wel, bot al of thee,
> This world hath no prosperite:
> In thin aspect ben alle liche,
> The povere man and ek the riche,
> Withoute thee ther mai no wight,
> And thou above alle othre miht.'   (I.3003–12; my italics)

His inability to achieve human speech is the continuing mark of his previous failure in truth:

> And so thenkende he gan doun bowe,
> And thogh him lacke vois and speche,
> He gan up with his feet areche,
> And wailende in his bestly stevene
> He made his pleignte unto the hevene.
> He kneleth in his wise and braieth,
> To seche merci and assaieth
> His god. . . .   (I.3022–29)

The most vivid contrast to the boastful words which caused his transformation occurs in the humiliating animal noises he now makes, and the truth of his dependence upon God is proclaimed in the simulated speech of bestiality. By this prayer, which is the repudiation of his former boasting, he regains his human form. The model of perfect expression, implicit in Nebuchadnezzar's falsely inadequate vainglorious speech, becomes explicit in the divinely authoritative voice, which, interpreted by a prophet, deprives him of his faculty of speech and finally provides the opportunity for wordless prayer.

Since the stories of Albinus and Nebuchadnezzar both illustrate proud speech, and the theme of love which is central in the first story is extended to the introduction of the second, the achievement of truth by prayer is relevant in both cases. Although the truth of man's dependence on God has had a humiliating effect on Nebuchadnezzar, the final effect of such a realization is a sense of dignity and confidence, as we will see in the next section.

In Book III of the *Confessio Amantis,* prayer is used again as the touchstone of truthful communication. The truth of prayer as opposed to boasting, as we have seen, consists in the humble acknowledgment of the real human condition in relation to the creator. The sin of Cheste, corresponding to *litigium*, or quarrelsomeness, is considered primarily as an effect on the listener.[2] It violates the virtue of friendship, like its opposite extreme, flattery, and causes anger or wrath in the listener. The precise definition of Cheste given by Genius, from the point of view of the speaker, is complete lack of restraint in speech. The vice, so considered, is exactly the opposite of that treated in Book IV under Sloth, where the problem is extreme reluctance to speak. From another point of view, Cheste can be a means of overcoming *ironia*, an excessive self-dispraisal, which prevents a truthful self-revelation. Since the reason for Amans's fear of offending his lady by Cheste is a lack of "trouthe" due to his extreme diffidence, the purpose of the allusion to prayer in this section is to restore a sense of dignity. Prayer then has a kind of similarity to Cheste in that it represents a particularly free speech. The Old and New Testaments are full of people who freely harangue, question, complain, and demand in their relationship with God. The treatment of Cheste anticipates in some measure the extensive treatment of the relationship between the lord and subject in regard to counsel, where the great danger is flattery and a certain kind of Cheste is recommended as an antidote, particularly in the story of the Roman Triumph (VII.2355–2411).

In his character as a conventional lover, Amans is fully aware of how Cheste opposes love. *Litigium*, which is the same as Cheste, we should remember, opposes the virtue of friendship by defect. In the course of asserting his innocence of this vice, he exhibits the strain upon truth that the avoidance of Cheste can produce. He becomes defensive about his occasional lapses into the vice, and in pathetic exasperation, he appeals to the right of man to pray. Then he tells how carefully he examines himself upon the tone of his speech to his lady and confesses a mood of Cheste toward himself. Since Cheste is so clearly opposed to love and Amans commits the sin against himself, this sin indicates the loss of self-respect or dignity experienced by the lover. His appeal to the freedom of speech in prayer is an assertion of dignity which, ironically, he fails to assimilate at this stage in his confession. The impossibility of his rhetorical ideal in amorous persuasion is contrasted to the ease of prayer as the speech of divine love.

The first metaphor used to describe Cheste is "wyndes of tempeste," which terrify with sudden blasts those who desire peace and rest. His mouth is ever "unpinned" and his lips "unloke." Everything in the mind of a contentious person "springeth up as doth a welle,/ Which may none of his stremes hide . . ." (III.428–29).

> So buillen up the foule sawes
> That Cheste wot of his felawes:
> For as a Sive kepeth Ale,
> Riht so can Cheste kepe a tale. . . .
> As a Cite withoute wal,

> Wher man mai gon out overal
> Withouten eny resistence,
> So with his croked eloquence
> He spekth al that he wot withinne:
> Wherof men lese mor than winne. . . .   (III.431–42)

Cheste makes war in the bedroom, and his bow is always bent to use the tongue as an arrow. His tongue is like a bell whose noise is more frightening in a town than thunder. The tongue of Cheste is a sturdy weapon:

> For men sein that the harde bon,
> Althogh himselven have non,
> A tunge brekth it al to pieces.   (III.463–65)

In his claim to innocence of this fault, Amans exhibits a sensitivity to the techniques of speech in courtly love. Quarrelsome speech in a lover would be particularly stupid, and if he were guilty of such a fault, he would deserve to be thwarted in love. His lady, he asserts, can witness his avoidance of Cheste, which involves an implication of a higher status in her estimation than he has. Here again we have the idea that human love removes from a man the truth about himself. In this case, he thinks less of himself than he really is. Cheste, we might say, implies that the speaker has confidence in his own worth in relation to the listener:

> And if it scholde so betide
> That I algates moste chide,
> It myhte noght be to my love:
> For so yit was I nevere above,
> For al this wyde world to winne
> That I dorste eny word beginne,
> Be which sche mihte have ben amoeved
> And I of Cheste also reproeved.   (III.491–98)

Amans is keenly aware of the necessity of careful speech toward his lady, in the selection of his words and the effect he intends by them:

> Bot rathere, if it mihte hir like,
> The beste wordes wolde I pike
> Whiche I cowthe in myn herte chese,
> And serve hem forth in stede of chese,
> For that is helplich to defie;
> And so wolde I my wordes plie,
> That mihten Wraththe and Cheste avale
> With tellinge of my softe tale.   (III.499–506)

He does admit to saying too much at times:

> This seie I noght, that I fulofte
> Ne have, whanne I spak most softe,

> per cas seid more thanne ynowh;
> Bot so wel halt noman the plowh
> That he ne balketh otherwhile,
> Ne so wel can noman affile
> His tunge, that som time in rape
> Him mai som liht word overscape,
> And yit ne meneth he no Cheste. (III.511–19)

The characteristic defensiveness of his admission that he sometimes says too much betrays his conviction that he has a right to reveal all his thoughts whether or not they please the listener:

> Bot that I have ayein hir heste
> Fulofte spoke, I am beknowe;
> And how my will is, that ye knowe:
> For whan my time comth aboute,
> That I dar speke and seie al oute
> Mi longe love, of which sche wot
> That evere in on aliche hot
> Me grieveth, thanne al my desese
> I telle, and though it hir desplese,
> I speke it forth and noght ne leve:
> And thogh it be beside hire leve,
> I hope and trowe natheles
> That I do noght ayein the pes;
> For thogh I telle hire al my thoght,
> Sche wot wel that I chyde noght. (III.520–34)

This impassioned assertion of and plea for freedom of speech in love is climaxed by a declaration of the complete affability of God:

> Men mai the hihe god beseche,
> And he wol hiere a mannes speche
> And be noght wroth of that he seith;
> So yifth it me the more feith
> And makth me hardi, soth to seie,
> That I dar wel the betre preie
> Mi ladi, which a womman is. (III.535–41)

The point of the comparison is clearly the more total and immediate self-revelation possible in prayer. The lack of Amans's peace of mind is directly related to the anxiety about success present in the human speech of amorous persuasion. Whenever he is alone, he is guilty of Cheste towards himself. He rehearses every word he said to his lady. First he examines himself as to whether he has spoken excessively:

> And thanne, if that I finde a lak
> Of eny word that I mispak,

> Which was to moche in eny wise,
> Anon my wittes I despise
> And make a chidinge in myn herte,
> That eny word me scholde asterte
> Which as I scholde have holden inne.   (III.561–67)

Concerning the extreme of defect, he wonders if he has left anything out:

> And thanne, if I mai seche and finde
> That eny word be left behinde,
> Which as I scholde more have spoke,
> I wolde upon miself be wroke,
> And chyde with miselven so,
> That al my wit is overgo.   (III.571–75)

The fact that in prayer man says exactly what is on his mind, without the anxiety involved in the desire for precise expression, makes it the appropriate remedy of Amans's present condition.

In the first two sections of this chapter, we have seen how prayer, itself an intense mode of speech, can provide Amans with a balanced sense of "trouthe" in two ways. Based on the humble relationship of creature to creator, prayer can keep him from the sins of boasting and vainglorious speech which are inimical to both human and divine love. On the other hand, Cheste, which is opposed to love, contains similarities to straightforward, honest speech, which is always possible with God. Cheste, for Amans, would be a healthy rebellion against the un-Christian sense of unworthiness that cripples a human lover. His discovery, significantly made while he is engaging in the truthful speech of confession, that he can legitimately, in a sense, commit Cheste against God raises in him a conviction of worthiness as important to his "trouthe" as the virtue of humility. Fear of the lady's anger has made Amans realize how difficult it is to choose the right words, but again the implied model of perfect expression reminds him of prayer and that a man may say exactly what he thinks to God and not fear Cheste. The affability of God, an attribute of the Word, eases the speech of man in prayer. The Word, even by implication, is the cause of all the verbal causes.

II

As suggested earlier, a medieval poet wanting to exploit the conventions of love as a religion for didactic purposes must distinguish in some fashion between the analogy and the reality. The juxtaposition of prayer and amorous persuasion in the story of Paris and Helen in Book V explicitly condemns any confusion of the two. In fact, a terminal rather than a transitional fusion of prayer and amorous persuasion simply does not occur in the *Confessio*

Amantis. Happy unions in the romance convention, which result in more or less ideal societies, come from a submission of the lover to the lady's rhetoric rather than vice versa. When the two suitors of Constance in Book III attend to her, they receive Christianity and, in the case of Alla of Northumbria, temporal order and prosperity. More important for the whole poem, attention to the philosophy propounded by Venus in Book VIII would result in such an ideal society. The story of Paris and Helen, on the other hand, shows what happens when the lover's speech completely supplants prayer. Gower specifically opposes the antithetical rhetorics of church and chamber, the latter of which, in the case of Paris and Helen, results in the disruption of society as a whole. The foolish advice of Paris in favor of vengeance, opposed to Hector's appeal for patience, foreshadows the improper substitution of amorous rhetoric for prayer in church, and results in the Trojan War.

The particular species of Avarice under discussion is Sacrilege, or robbing churches, and the contrast of such theft to prayer is stated early in the section:

> Wher that he scholde bidde his bede,
> He doth his thefte in holi stede. . . .   (V.6985–86)

After a mention of Antiochus and Nabuzaradan and a brief summary of Nebuchadnezzar's theft of the holy vessels, Genius goes immediately into the theme of the lover's sacrilege:

> And riht so, forto telle soth,
> In loves cause if I schal trete,
> Ther ben of suche smale and grete:
> If thei no leisir fynden elles,
> They wol noght wonden for the belles,
> Ne thogh thei sen the Prest at masse;
> That wol thei leten overpasse.
> If that thei finde here love there,
> Thei stonde and tellen in hire Ere,
> And axe of god non other grace,
> Whyl thei ben in that holi place;
> Bot er thei gon som avantage
> Ther wol thei have, and som pilage
> Of goodli word or of beheste. . . .   (V.7032–45)

The tone here is something between earnest and game: part of its charm comes from treating what is, even from a serious moral viewpoint, only a peccadillo, as the heinous crime of robbing churches. The sense of sight gets its lengthy treatment here also, but the lover's confession focuses on prayer to win the lady:

> And if so falle that I preie
> Unto mi god, and somwhat seie

> Of Paternoster or of Crede,
> Al is for that I wolde spede,
> So that mi bede in holi cherche
> Ther mihte som miracle werche
> Mi ladi herte forto chaunge. . . .   (V.7117–23)

Although a completely permissible prayer, it is only incidental to the distractions caused by the lady. The lover's sacrilegious theft of "A glad word" (V.7138) parallels the gift of prayerful speech that he should offer. The opposition of amorous speech to prayer is implied again by the phrase "a good word eke" (V.7147) and the assertion:

> No Sacrilege of hire I tok,
> Bot if it were of word. . . .   (V.7165–66)

The whole discussion preceding the exemplum is epitomized in a couplet spoken by Genius:

> The cherche serveth for the bede,
> The chambre is of an other speche.   (V.7188–89)

The story as a whole echoes the theme of Avarice and war that introduces Book V (V.1–20). Hercules and Jason are treated inhospitably by the Trojans and for vengeance destroy Troy and steal the king's daughter, Esiona. The fallen king's son, Priam, rebuilds the city and sends Anthenor to ask for the return of Esiona. He is refused, and a lengthy council scene follows, in which Hector points out the unlikelihood of victory in a war against the Greeks. Paris, on the basis of a dream in which he is offered the disposition of the famous golden apple and promised the fairest woman on earth, persuades the Trojans to answer theft with theft. Important for the emphasis on speech, the true prophecy of disaster made by Cassandra, identified by Genius as the Sibyl (V.7454), is rejected by the Trojans.

Both the first meeting and the theft of Helen take place in church, Venus's temple, to be more exact, a fact which continues and complicates the context of sacrilege, or church robbery. Within the compass of a few lines, Genius juxtaposes prayer, amorous persuasion, and sacrilege:

> Forth comth Paris with glad visage
> Into the temple on pelrinage,
> Wher unto Venus the goddesse
> He yifth and offreth gret richesse,
> *And preith hir that he preie wolde.*
> And thanne aside he gan beholde,
> And sih wher that this ladi stod;
> And he forth in his freisshe mod
> Goth ther sche was and made hir chiere,
> As he wel couthe in his manere,

> *That of his wordes such plesance*
> *Sche tok,* that al hire aqueintance,
> Als ferforth as the herte lay,
> He stal er that he wente away.
> So goth he forth and tok his leve,
> And thoghte, anon as it was eve,
> He wolde don his Sacrilegge,
> That many a man it scholde abegge. (V.7505–22; my italics)

The sacrilegious theft of Helen, the principal ornament of Venus's temple, takes place fittingly while she is in prayer:

> So fell it, of devocion
> Heleine in contemplacion
> With many an other worthi wiht
> Was in the temple and wok al nyht,
> To bidde and preie unto thymage
> Of Venus, as was thanne usage. . . . (V.7537–42)

The disaster of the Trojan war ensues and Genius makes the application:

> And so it fell, riht as thei sein,
> The Sacrilege which he wroghte
> Was cause why the Gregois soughte
> Unto the toun and it beleie,
> And wolden nevere parte aweie,
> Til what be sleihte and what be strengthe
> Thei hadde it wonne in brede and lengthe,
> and brent and slayn that was withinne.
> Ne se, mi Sone, which a sinne
> Is Sacrilege in holy stede:
> *Be war therefore and bidd thi bede,*
> And do nothing in holy cherche,
> Bot that thou miht be reson werche. (V.7578–90; my italics)

Although the antithesis between prayer and amorous persuasion is not precise in all its details, the intent of context, exemplum, and application is clear. Paris progresses from praying to obtain the lady, to amorous persuasion in church, and finally to the prevention of prayer, by stealing Helen while she is in prayer. Amans has been guilty of the first two literally, but of the third only in the sense of preventing prayer. The fact that the substitution of amorous rhetoric for prayer resulted in the most famous war of antiquity overshadows the ambiguous role of Venus, who is both responsible for and dishonored by the sacrilege. The point is that Genius is here consistent with his role of both seeming to endorse and simultaneously condemning a certain kind of love religion. The total effect here is of condemnation.

The exemplum of Bacchus in Book VI explicitly dramatizes the success of a prayer to Jove asking for the means necessary to complete a journey to a lady. In the confessional application, the fact that the nature of the person to whom Amans is urged to pray is not clearly specified but only tantalizingly hinted at gives this section its poetic power. Genius exhorts Amans to prayer; but whether this is prayer to Jove also, to Venus, Cupid, the lady as deity, or the Christian God, remains unexpressed.

After a rather lengthy passage containing a description of love-drunkenness (VI.76–111), together with Amans's admission to the vice (VI.112–324), Genius introduces an allusion to Jupiter's two tuns with an assertion of the dependence of love on fortune and providence:

> For the fortune of every chance
> After the goddes pourveance
> To man it groweth from above,
> So that the sped of every love
> Is schape there, er it befalle.   (VI.325–29)

The allusion to providence is not explicitly Christian, but it is particularly appropriate to the context of prayer.[3] Genius next introduces the convention of the two casks of love-drink in the cellar where Cupid is the bottler. A drink from either cask brings drunkenness, but of two different kinds: one, sweet, signifies successful love; the other, bitter, signifies unsuccessful love. The blind Cupid does not dispense his potions fairly, and the deserving are often drunk on the bitterness of failure. Since the generic vice under discussion is Gluttony, Genius appropriately condemns any kind of love-drunkenness. Amans has clearly drunk of the bitter tun, as his desperate condition indicates. Somewhat surprisingly, the alternative suggested by Genius is not a draught from the sweet but presumably abstinence.

> For wel I knowe be thi tale,
> That thou hast drunken of the duale,
> Which biter is, *til god the sende*
> *Such grace that thou miht amende.*   (VI.387–90; my italics)

Thus the first use of "grace" in this section is associated with repentance, rather than amorous success. Next comes the exhortation to pray, but with a seemingly unresolvable ambiguity:

> Bot, Sone, thou schalt bidde and preie
> In such a wise as I schal seie,
> That thou the lusti welle atteigne
> Thi wofull thurstes to *restreigne*
> Of love, and taste the swetnesse;
> As Bachus dede in his distresse,
> When bodiliche thurst him hente
> In strange londes where he wente.   (VI.391–98; my italics)

Although one can conceivably "restreigne" thirst by drinking, the import of the preceding lines (389–90) suggests the attainment of a "lusti welle" which will enable him to "restreigne" love itself.

The story itself illustrates the value of prayer and may have allegorical overtones which further specify the "welle" which the ambiguity of "restreigne" suggests. My interpretation is corroborated by the possibility of such an allegorical meaning, but is not dependent on it. According to Macaulay, the story comes from Hyginus.[4] Although the story is not in Ovid's *Metamorphoses*, it does occur in a version of Bersuire's commentary on that poem.[5] Bacchus, stranded with his army in the Lybian desert, prays to Jupiter. In the prayer, he alludes to the necessity of requesting specific temporal benefits from God:

> . . . and thanne Bachus preide
> To Jupiter, and thus he seide:
> 'O hihe fader, that sest al,
> To whom is reson that I schal
> Beseche and preie in every nede. . . .'   (VI.415–19)

The fact that in prayer the request is already known to God is alluded to in the phrase "that sest al." Bacchus envisions the satisfaction of his present thirst as a means of obtaining love, since without water they cannot return home to their ladies:

> Behold, mi fader, and tak hiede
> This wofull thurst that we ben inne
> To staunche, and grante ous forto winne,
> And sauf unto the contre fare,
> Wher that oure lusti loves are
> Waitende upon oure hom cominge.   (VI.420–25)

His prayer is immediately answered:

> And with the vois of his preiynge,
> Which herd was to the goddes hihe,
> He syh anon tofore his yhe
> A wether, which the ground hath sporned;
> And wher he hath it overtorned,
> Ther sprang a welle freissh and cler. . . .   (VI.426–31)

In Bersuire's commentary, the "wether" is glossed as Christ, who opens the fountain of baptism, the Holy Spirit, and grace to all men:

> *Liber pater* with his army signifies the blessed Peter with his army, that is, the band of the apostles and the other holy fathers. To them in their thirst and desire for the water of grace Jupiter appeared in the form of a ram, that is, the son of God in human nature, who

opened the fountain of baptism, the Holy Spirit, and grace to all men
and gave them the drink of virtues and gifts.[6]

In Gower's poem, the word *grace* is used to refer to the miracle granted by
Jupiter (VI.435). Genius then exhorts Amans to pray, putting a further
emphasis on grace:

> Forthi, mi Sone, after this chance
> It sit thee wel to taken hiede
> So forto preie upon thi nede,
> As Bachus preide for the welle;
> And thenk, as thou hast herd me telle,
> How *grace* he gradde and *grace* he hadde.   (VI.440–45;
>   my italics)

The possibility that grace refers also to success in love is not excluded, but
here its principal meaning is a favor granted by a god. There follows an
endorsement of prayer as speech, seemingly in reference to love:

> He was no fol that ferst so radde,
> For selden get a domb man lond:
> Tak that proverbe, and understond
> That wordes ben of vertu grete.
> Forthi to speke thou ne lete,
> And axe and prei erli and late
> Thi thurst to quenche, and thenk algate,
> The boteler which berth the keie
> Is blind, as thou hast herd me seie. . . .   (VI.446–54)

Now, however, the sweet tun will bring about sobriety, a clear contradiction
of what Genius said in lines 365–69:

> And if it mihte so betyde,
> That he upon the blinde side
> Per cas the swete tonne arauhte,
> Than schalt thou have a lusti drauhte
> And waxe of lovedrunke *sobre*
> And thus I rede thou *assobre*
> Thin herte in hope of such a grace. . . .   (VI.455–61;
>   my italics)

This final change of emphasis is unmistakable, although it has been hinted at
throughout the section. The emphasis on sobriety imparts to the word *grace* a
theological direction, which is accelerated by a final condemnation of all
love-drunkenness:

> For drunkeschipe in every place,
> To whether side that it torne,

> Doth harm and makth a man to sporne
> And ofte falle in such a wise,
> Wher he per cas mai noght arise.   (VI.462–66)

It is urgent that Amans speak out, but the cumulative meaning of grace, the emphasis on sobriety, and the condemnation of love-drunkenness —corroborated by an allusion to the most nefarious of all love potions, that of Tristan and Isolt (VI.471–75)—direct his speech to the Christian God. The value of the story of Bacchus consists in the tentative resolution of the ambiguous similarity between prayer and amorous persuasion in favor of prayer. Gower's technique in this part of the poem is still implication. Furthermore, in contrast to the treatment of prayer under Pride and Wrath, this section shows an increasing sensuousness, a development paralleled by the pattern of the Seven Deadly Sins, which exhibits a movement from interior, more spiritual sins to those that are exterior and more physical.

Book IV of the *Confessio Amantis* presents the greatest range of possible relationships between prayer and amorous persuasion in the shortest span. Of the six subspecies of Sloth that constitute the book's internal divisions, only two, Negligence and Idleness, do not mention the importance of speaking out. Once again, Book IV tends on the whole to reject amorous persuasion, although one of the two explicit references to Christian prayer reinforces and dignifies its amorous counterpart.

An atmosphere of despondency marks the confessional conversation about the first species of Sloth, Procrastination, and foreshadows the final mood of Book IV. After describing Lachesce, or Procrastination, Genius asks Amans about the extent of his guilt. Amans sadly admits that he has failed to speak at the proper time:

> . . . whanne I thoghte mi poursuite
> To make, and therto sette a day
> To speke unto the swete May,
> Lachesce bad abide yit,
> And bar on hond it was no wit
> Ne time forto speke as tho.   (IV.28–33)

The intimacy and effectiveness, as well as the psychological difficulty, of speech are suggested by the strategy Lachesce uses to propose a less direct confrontation between Amans and the lady:

> He seide, 'An other time is bettre;
> Thou schalt mowe senden hire a lettre,
> And per cas wryte more plein
> Than thou be Mowthe durstest sein.'   (IV.37–40)

He is undermined by his very anxiety for effective communication, and he defends himself by stressing his accomplishment in a mode of address that is totally ineffectual in the context of human love:

> For thogh my tunge is slowh to crave
> At alle time, as I have bede,
> Min herte stant evere in o stede
> And axeth besiliche grace. . . .   (IV.54–57)

It is evident that this kind of silent concentration is quite effective in prayer but completely ludicrous in the present context, although there is no explicit statement to that effect. The irony here, of course, is that in prayer to the Christian God such inner devotion would suffice.[7] The precise form of his procrastination is a subtle endorsement of Christian prayer. When the stories of Aeneas and Dido, Ulysses and Penelope, Grosseteste, and the Foolish Virgins have been told to clarify procrastination (IV.77–260), we learn that Amans's reluctance to speak has its basis in the lady's continuing refusal to listen:

> Bot yit hire liketh noght alyhte
> Upon no lure which I caste;
> For ay the more I crie faste,
> The lasse hire liketh forto hiere.   (IV.284–87)

While this is evidence that further attempts at amorous persuasion by Amans can end only in frustration, a similar perseverance in prayer would have more satisfying results.

Pygmaleon and Iphis, the protagonists in the two exempla illustrating the next species of Sloth, Pusillanimity, play out their roles in success stories. Prayer and amorous persuasion tend to be identified, although the deities involved in the exempla are Venus and Cupid respectively. The sensuous quality of this section is particularly marked, and the two exempla present a striking transition from the unnatural to the natural. The lovers in each story are prevented from reaching fulfillment by a major natural obstacle: in the case of Pygamaleon, the object of his love is, of course, a statue; in the second story, the girl Iphis loves another girl. The point made by each story is essentially the same. Prayer, literally to Venus and Cupid, can overcome nature in order to effect a more justly natural love. In the Pygmaleon story, amorous pleading is accepted as prayer to Venus; in the next story, the simple desire for natural sexual love (reminiscent of the silent concentration of Amans mentioned in regard to procrastination) qualifies as prayer to Cupid. Part of the muted edification is that Pygmaleon and Iphis, by the miracle of prayer, become remarkable examples of manliness, which is the virtue opposed to pusillanimity. This is fittingly corroborated by the fact that this section contains perhaps the most emphatic endorsement of the power of the spoken word in the whole poem.

The verses that introduce the section point out that a man rarely achieves the *Munus Amicicie* by silence, *ore muto*. Words must be used with moderation, but no love favors him who is sparing in his words:

> Est modus in verbis, sed ei qui parcit amori,
> Verba referre sua non favet ullus amor.

Pusillanimity recalls the lack of self-knowledge and esteem that militates against the virtue of truth. A conviction of his own theologically derived dignity would remove the lover's fear of speaking about himself. The pusillanimous are without this sense of "trouthe":

> . . . whan best were
> To speke of love, and riht for fere
> Thei wexen doumb and dare noght telle
> Withoute soun, as doth the belle,
> Which hath no claper forto chyme;
> And riht so thei as for the tyme
> Ben herteles withoute speche
> Of love, and dar nothing beseche. . . .   (IV.343–50)

Amans sadly admits his failure:

> Min herte is yit and evere was,
> As thogh the world scholde al tobreke,
> So ferful, that I dar noght speke
> Of what pourpos that I have nome,
> What I toward mi ladi come. . . .   (IV.358–62)

In the story itself, the theme of prayer becomes explicit and the emotional volume is raised several decibels. Fortune, Genius observes, favors him who "makth continuance/ To preie love and to beseche . . ." (IV.368–69). It is impossible to distinguish the prayer of Pygmaleon, in the sense of amorous pleading to his statue, from the prayer that is accepted by Venus. Since Christian prayer is never absent from the allusiveness when Gower presents such diction in its appropriate situation, Pygmaleon becomes, in fact, a daring example of devotional fervor. The surface equivalence of erotic and theological momentarily frees the reader from the obligation to distinguish between human and divine love:

> With all the herte of his corage
> His love upon this faire ymage
> He sette, and hire of love preide;
> Bot sche no word ayeinward seide.   (IV.391–94)

He takes the statue to bed, "And ofte he reuneth in hire Ere. . . ."

> And ofte his arm now hier now there
> He leide, as he hir wolde embrace,
> And evere among he axeth grace,
> As thogh sche wiste what he mente. . . .   (IV.408–11)

Pygmaleon perseveres in his service to love. Although he makes no clearly direct request of Venus, his unceasing amorous persuasion is accounted as prayer:

> He made such continuance
> Fro dai to nyht, and preith so longe,
> That his preiere is underfonge,
> Which Venus of hire grace herde;
> Be nyhte and whan that he worst ferde,
> And it lay in his nakede arm,
> The colde ymage he fieleth warm
> Of fleissh and bon, and full of lif.   (IV.416–23)

The statue is changed miraculously into a real woman. Just as Christian prayer must involve the whole person, physically as well as spiritually, so clearly does prayer as amorous persuasion. In the *Song of Songs*, passages just as erotic occur, and, as a matter of historical record, the exegetical tradition has not absolutely spiritualized the literal level. My point here is simply that although the story contains elements of an irony that becomes more marked as Book IV progresses, there is a temporary suspension of precise moral judgment that proposes a fusion of the erotic and the devotional. The passage from the unnatural to the natural has connotations of edification that further this synthesis without, however, making it explicit.

The reason for the miracle, in Genius's application, is that the lover gave his desire a verbal manifestation:

> Lo, thus he wan a lusti wif,
> Which obeissant was at his wille;
> And if he wolde have holde him stille
> And nothing spoke, he scholde have failed:
> Bot for he hath his word travailed
> And dorste speke, his love he spedde,
> And hadde al that he wolde abedde.   (IV.424–30)

As if this were not clear enough, Genius restates the application and makes the importance of speech even more emphatic. The power of both amorous persuasion and prayer is expressed in a way that recalls the natural power and theological efficacy of human speech:

> Be this ensample thou miht finde
> *That word mai worche above kinde.*
> Forthi, my Sone, if that thou spare
> To speke, lost is al thi fare. . . .   (IV.437–40; my italics)

The allusion to the principle that speech can change nature is a preternatural analogue from natural magic of the power of prayer to advance man to a supernatural level.

Prayer as a means of converting the unnatural to the natural continues to motivate the elements of the next example of pusillanimity, but in the pattern of silent, perhaps even unconscious, longing, which Amans had previously advanced as an excuse for his procrastination.[8] An infant daughter is born to Thelacuse, but Ligdus, her husband, has sworn to kill any but a male child. The goddess Isis advises her to disguise the child and raise it as if it were a boy. When Iphis, the child, is ten years old, she is married to Iante, a duke's daughter. The two gradually become very fond of each other, but nature prohibits physical expression of their love. The god Cupid changes the "pusillanimity" of Iphis to "manliness":

> Forthi Cupide hath so besett
> His grace upon this aventure,
> That he accordant to nature,
> Whan that he syh the time best,
> That ech of hem hath other kest,
> Transformeth Iphe into a man,
> Wherof the *kinde* love he wan
> Of lusti yonge Iante his wif. . . .   (IV.496–503; my italics)

The exchange between Genius and Amans following this story (IV.506–29) makes clear the fact that they are still discussing speech in love and prayer. The application Genius makes of the story is that the intention of the heart is effective as amorous persuasion and prayer to the god of love:

> It semeth love is welwillende
> To hem that ben continuende
> With besy herte to poursuie
> Thing which that is to love due.   (IV.507–10)

Amans reiterates generally his failure to speak on some occasions, but simultaneously claims fidelity in silent amorous prayer:

> I dar wel seie be mi trowthe,
> Als fer as I my witt can seche,
> Mi fader, as for lacke of speche,
> Bot so as I me schrof tofore,
> Ther is non other time lore,
> Wherof ther mihte ben obstacle
> To lette love of his miracle,
> *Which I beseche day and nyht.*   (IV.516–23; my italics)

In this instance, Amans's refuge in the silent prayer of erotic yearning meets no reprimand from his confessor. It is as though Genius were being particularly gentle with Amans's failure to speak here and assuring him with the story of Iphis that even without external speech some lovers have prospered. Once again, though, the example of Iphis finally undercuts the overt didactic purpose, since, in realistic terms, there can be no success in human love without some explicit overture. The technique here, as in Procrastination, actually serves to endorse Christian prayer, which alone is effective as silent longing. Venus, Cupid, "and swich rascaille" are players in the *game* while the *ernest* is yet to come.

The pattern in the next species of Sloth abandons indirection and condemns forgetfulness in amorous persuasion by the unmistakable criterion of evidently Christian prayer. Unlike the exploratory allusiveness of the first two species of Sloth, Procrastination and Pusillanimity (and indeed, church-robbery in Book V and love-drunkenness in Book VI), the reference to Christian prayer is manifest, but not at all prejudicial to amorous persuasion. The enlargement of the concept of prayer contributed by the physical implications of the two preceding sensuous illustrations is further enhanced by the ideal of complete remembrance opposed to the vice of forgetfulness (IV.539–866). This kind of sloth injures one's specifically human self-awareness and fragments the identity:

> For in the tellinge of his tale
> Nomore his herte thanne his male
> Hath remembrance of thilke forme,
> Wherof he scholde his wit enforme
> As thanne, and yit ne wot he why.
> Thus in his pourpos noght forthi
> Forlore of that he wolde bidde,
> And skarsly if he seith the thridde
> To love of that he hadde ment. . . .   (IV.545–53)

The deliberation and care implied in the imagery of the mind as a book in which Amans first anxiously writes his "lesson" renders his admission to failure more pathetic:

> And so recorde I mi lecoun
> And wryte in my memorial
> What I to hire telle schal,
> Riht al the matiere of mi tale:
> Bot al nys worth a note schale;
> For whanne I come ther sche is,
> I have it al foryete ywiss;
> Of that I thoghte forto telle
> I can noght thanne unethes spelle
> That I wende altherbest have rad,
> So sore I am of hire adrad.   (IV.562–72)

The letters have all been effaced from the book, and he is left in a state of isolation and virtual anonymity:

> That what as evere I thoghte have spoken,
> It is out fro myn herte stoken,
> And stonde, as who seith, doumb and def,
> That all nys worth an yvy lef,
> Of that I wende wel have seid.   (IV.583–87)

The fear characteristic of pusillanimity (which Genius mentions again in l. 707) also attacks his memory, producing a mood of self-contempt that recalls a similar experience in Book III:

> Wherof art thou so sore afered,
> That thou thi tunge soffrest frese,
> And wolt thi goode wordes lese,
> Whan thou hast founde time and space?
> How scholdest thou deserve grace,
> Whan thou thiself darst axe non. . . .   (IV.612–17)

His mood progressively changes and he displays another important cause of his forgetfulness. He seems almost to have become a mystic in love's religion; but not all such rapture is psychologically safe or theologically sound. The splendor of his lady as a celestial being induces an ecstasy of contemplation which seems to justify his speechlessness more than any previous excuse:

> For whan I se hir goodli face
> And thenke upon hire hihe pris
> As thogh I were in Paradis,
> I am so ravisht of the syhte,
> That speke unto hire I ne myhte
> As for the time, thogh I wolde:
> For I ne mai my wit unfolde
> To finde o word of that I mene,
> Bot al it is foryete clene;
> And thogh I stonde there a myle,
> Al is foryete for the while,
> A tunge I have and wordes none.
> And thus I stonde and thenke al one
> Of thing that helpeth ofte noght. . . .   (IV.680–93)

This assertion climaxes his other references to silent longing as a defense against the imputation of Lachesce and Pusillanimity, but the advice Genius gives, far from consoling him, launches a precise theological attack on his amorous insufficiency: even God, who knows man's needs completely, demands that an explicit request be made:

> For love his grace wol noght sende
> To that man which dar axe non.

> For this we knowen everichon,
> A mannes thoght withoute speche
> God wot, and yit that men beseche
> His will is; for withoute bedes
> He doth his grace in fewe stedes. . . .   (IV.712–18)

A particularly valid similarity between amorous persuasion and Christian prayer takes precedence, for the moment, over the many tentative investigations—both sensuous and psychological—of their relationship. Genius alludes to one of the classic objections against the validity of prayer for specific temporal benefits discussed in medieval theology: if God knows everything, making known one's needs is futile and absurd. The answer to the objection—that man prays in order to remember God, not that God may remember him—not only relates the memory to the immediate necessity for communication but reminds man of his contingency and dependence. Moreover, remembering to pray for specific temporal benefits (perhaps the most difficult element in the medieval doctrine of prayer, from a modern point of view) counters a tendency toward fatalism, which could be engendered by the belief in Divine foreknowledge. The point receives no great emphasis in Gower's text: the lines are almost thrown away. But no principle could be more applicable to the erotic quietism induced by Amans's tendency toward reverie, and nothing can restore the balance of Amans's affections so readily as the actual requirements of praying for specific temporal benefits, with its double focus on the transcendent and the immediate. In effect, Amans is urged to engage in an act of penetrating self-awareness that can only intensify the security of the human lover and prepare him equally for success or failure.

After Forgetfulness, there is no reference to amorous conversation and prayer until near the end of Book IV, in the final two subspecies of Somnolence and Despondency, where the love-conversation operates on a principle we have seen guiding the reader elsewhere in the *Confessio.* Just as the section on Forgetfulness repeats aspects of the preceding section on Pusillanimity, so the real significance of the Somnolence exempla comes in the treatment of Despondency that follows. The equal time allotted to the praise and blame of the analogy between Christian prayer and amorous persuasion finally gives way to a clear condemnation of the latter for Amans. Once again the figure of Mercury in the third illustration of Somnolence is the imaginative hinge.

The deeper level of self-awareness introduced by the reference to the memory with its relevance to a rapprochement between the transcendent and the practical continues in the first exemplum of Somnolence, which has to do with the truth of dreams, a kind of truth connected with the hidden ways of God's providence. The exchange between penitent and confessor is ironic. Amans tells of a dream in which he enjoys the bed of his lady and Genius counters with the tale of Ceix and Alcione, with its elements of drowning, suicide, and "halcyon" transformation. The two dreams are antithetical: Amans dreams of union; Genius tells of separation. We are tempted to look more deeply into the exemplum; perhaps the mythographical tradition has some relevance. The one point we can surely make is that the human love of Ceix and Alcione undergoes a death and metamorphosis, a transition which may hint at the necessity for withdrawal from human love on the part of Amans.

The sardonic humor of the next exemplum is less elusive. Amans has previously denied being guilty of somnolence and has described his reluctance to leave his lady at night. His efforts are met with failure. If he has gained permission to read to her about Troilus, he takes the opportunity to declare his love:

> So as I dar of mi desir
> I telle a part; bot whanne I preie,
> Anon sche bidt me go mi weie
> And seith it is ferr in the nyht. . . .   (IV.2800–2803)

Aware of his own verbal inadequacy, Amans makes a distinction between the answer he actually hears and the response his lady would make if she understood his condition. In fact, he puts a rather ridiculous semantic emphasis on what he considers the persuasiveness of his forlorn appearance. Her verbal denial is so vigorous that it merits identification with "daunger":

> And if sche thanne hiede toke,
> Hou pitousliche on hire I loke,
> Whan that I schal my leve take,
> Hire oghte of mercy forto slake
> Hire daunger, which seith evere nay.   (IV.2809–13)

The lack of self-knowledge revealed in this declaration is met by the humor of the second example of Somnolence, in which the requirement that prayer be truthful is violated. Cephalus (IV.3187–3275) prays, in a particularly effective aubade, for the night to be prolonged in order that he may achieve a heroic victory over Sloth in lovemaking. Even as it stands, the story is sure to draw a smile from the reader, but its irrelevance for Amans undercuts the value of prayer in the amorous sense and harmonizes with what we will say about Mercury and Argus. Since Amans's chances of winning the lady are minimal at best, the story of Cephalus is cruel and comical in its application. Even if Amans did get his lady to the verge of consummation, the prayer of Cephalus is still a vain exemplar, for, as the conclusion of the poem shows clearly (VIII.2408–32), old age has made Amans sexually impotent.

Even without these reflections, the kind of Sloth criticized by the story of Cephalus is indeed a rare vice, as Amans realizes:

> Mi fader, who that hath his love
> Abedde naked be his syde,
> And wolde thanne hise yhen hyde
> With Slep, I not what man is he:
> Bot certes as touchende of me,
> That fell me nevere yit er this.   (IV.3276–81)

The most Amans can hope for during the night is the possession of his lady in a dream. Rather irritably, he again points out the irrelevance of Cephalus's prayer to his own situation:

> So nedeth noght that I schal crave
> The Sonnes Carte forto tarie,
> Ne yit the Mone, that sche carie
> Hire cours along upon the hevene,
> For I am noght the more in evene
> Towardes love in no degree. . . .   (IV.3290–95)

The lack of "trouthe" in the misapplication of the story should caution Amans about the folly of certain prayers and urge him to interpret Genius's exhortations to pray only in the analogical sense of prayer to the Christian God.

An acceptance of contingency elicited by the memory, the tantalizing ambiguities of dreams, and the disillusionment of foolish prayer should have sharpened the penitent's appetite for a harsher and less speculative kind of truth than that presented in pusillanimity and prepared the way for the final rejection of amorous persuasion. The Mercury-Argus story, the third and last exemplum of Somnolence, is so closely followed in the poem itself by an acknowledged despair in amorous rhetoric and an expressed conviction of the superiority of Christian prayer that it confirms the mythographical connotations which I shall presently propose.

Juno had changed Io, one of Jove's mistresses, into a cow and handed her over to be guarded by Argus, a creature with a hundred eyes. Mercury, Jove's messenger, pipes and sings so well that he puts Argus to sleep, cuts his head off, and recovers Io. Preparatory to the action, we are told that Mercury

> . . . hadde a Pipe wel devised
> Upon the notes of Musiqe,
> Wherof he mihte hise Eres like.
> And over that he hadde affaited
> Hise lusti tales, and awaited
> His time; and thus into the field
> He cam, where Argus he behield
> With Yo, which beside him wente.   (IV.3334–41)

The persuasive techniques of the god of speech are mentioned once again when he begins his actual conquest of Argus:

> With that his Pype on honde he hente,
> And gan to pipe in his manere
> Thing which was slepi forto hiere;
> And in his pipinge evere among
> He tolde him such a lusti song,
> That he the fol hath broght aslepe.
> Ther was non yhe mihte kepe
> His hed, the which Mercurie of smot. . . .   (IV.3342–49)

Argus's mishap should indeed warn the penitent from somnolence, brought about as it is by the figure who embodies his preoccupation with verbal approaches to his amorous crisis. The danger of such a preoccupation is here presented in a narrative emblem, which the mythographical treatises explicate. Alexander Neckam, for example, in his commentary on this episode, indicts eloquence without wisdom:

> When anyone gives himself over completely to the exercise of worldly knowledge, eloquence, which is very harmful without wisdom, takes away his understanding (which is signified by Argus' head) and discretion, because his eyes (which signify intention) are given over to vain glory.[9]

More graphically and vigorously, Boccaccio extends this conventional interpretation of Mercury as eloquence to include the persuasions of carnal temptation:

> Man, when he is born, is committed to Argus for safekeeping, that is, the reason, which has always many lights indeed, to guard our safety. Mercury, that is, the craft of the coaxing flesh, by means of his staff, that is, the worst persuasions, leads the reason into sleep and destroys it; after it has been overcome and cast down, Juno, that is, the concupiscence of surpassing kingdoms and wealth, sends the gadfly to the cow, that is, the goad of acquisitive solicitude to human nature; then miserably we begin our course, we wander, and are driven and tossed about, seeking quiet in those things wherein there may be no quiet, but such unceasing labor, that it at last drives us uneasily into Egypt, the outer darkness, where there is weeping and gnashing of teeth; and unless we are extended help by the divine gift, we are forced to become Isis, the earth, for so Isis is interpreted, and we are trodden upon by all as a vile and dispossessed thing.[10]

The sleep of Argus, a token of failure in Gower's poem, is a moral disaster in the commentaries. The point is that in Alexander Neckam, Mercury represents speech by clear statement and in Boccaccio by implication. There are other commentaries to make this equation, however, and we must go on to the more important corollary. The tale of Mercury and Argus here is not a simple condemnation of amorous persuasion; it is rather a focus for the praise and blame of the analogy between prayer and amorous persuasion. For speech has other uses and contexts, which occurred, for example, to John of Garland:

> Mercury, the god of words, curing minds.
> The swiftness of speech is signified by the two-fold wing.
> The rod is power to put tyrants to sleep,
> and strengthen sick minds, it is said.[11]

The use of this myth enables Genius to caution Amans about the deep disservice which his concern for amorous rhetoric has performed and at the same time to suggest a mode of speech more profitable and salutary. In Arnulph of Orleans, for example, Io represents the soul, the eyes of Argus are the temptations of the world, and Mercury refers to "any eloquent man who by his persuasion destroys worldly concupiscence in her."[12] Bersuire goes furthest of all and casts Mercury in this episode as a figure most appropriate to the opposition in Gower's context between amorous rhetoric and prayer—the Word:

> . . . Argus is the devil, subtle and most hidden who holds captive Io, transformed into a cow, that is, sinful souls. But Mercury, that is, Christ . . . who was made man from God when the *Word was made flesh*, having taken up the shepherd's pipe of human nature, lulls the devil to sleep.[13] (My italics.)

The ruinous seduction of eloquence and the Incarnation of the Word are the two poles which, I submit, constitute the essential connotation of Gower's story; for, in the conversation which immediately follows in the *Confessio* and introduces the final story of Book IV, the two kinds of rhetoric are uppermost. Amans's trust in speech as a means of success in love is beginning to fail and lead him to despair:

> For be my trouthe I schal noght lie,
> Of pure sorwe, which I drye
> For that sche seith sche wol me noght,
> With drecchinge of myn oghne thoght
> In such a wanhope I am falle,
> That I ne can unethes calle,
> As forto speke of eny grace,
> My ladi merci to pourchace.
> Bot yit I seie noght for this
> That al in mi defalte it is;
> For I cam nevere yit in stede,
> When time was, that I my bede
> Ne seide, and as I dorste tolde:
> Bot nevere fond I that sche wolde,

> For oght sche knew of min entente,
> To speke a goodly word assente.   (IV.3473–88)

The futility of his perseverance in amorous speech, which recalls the sinister aspect of Mercury in the preceding story, reminds him, however, of a speech whose persuasiveness is unquestionable:

> And natheles this dar I seie,
> That if a sinful wolde preie
> To god of his foryivenesse
> With half so gret a besinesse
> As I have do to my ladi,
> In lacke of askinge of merci
> He scholde nevere come in Helle.   (IV.3489–95)

Amans has bitterly realized the inadequacy of his words to the lady; but the implied model of perfect expression has reminded him of prayer and evoked the presence of Mercury as the Word.

Finally, after the rich variety of similarities between amorous rhetoric and Christian prayer, this last reference to verbal persuasion in Book IV leaves no doubt concerning their difference and order of preference. The clear choice of Christian prayer over amorous persuasion is properly orthodox, and, I am sure, representative of Gower's sincere conviction; but the instances where the poem hesitates, as it were, between the two, showing that amorous persuasion as well requires promptness, courage, devotional fervor, and careful mental preparation, prevent a simple dismissal of the "prayer" of love.

Throughout this chapter we have seen various comparisons of prayer and amorous persuasion. The experiences of Albinus and Nebuchadnezzar have been treated as a continuum with the purpose of exhibiting prayer as the antidote of pride in speech. In the section on Cheste, on the other hand, prayer remedies a false humility on the part of the lover. These two culpable extremes of boastfulness and self-deprecation are precisely the vices to be avoided if Amans is to gain the equilibrium of the virtue of truth. The third section of the chapter highlighted the differences between the two kinds of speech. Paris was guilty of amorous persuasion in a place where he should have prayed, and the context of his story inveighed against the speech of human love in church. In the application of the story of Bacchus, Amans is urged to pray for success and happiness in love. Although the deity involved is ostensibly Jupiter, certain words and turns of phrase imply that the prayer is to the Christian God for grace to withdraw from human love.

The urgent necessity for the lover to declare his passion to the lady is the dominant theme of Book IV which we have discussed in the last section of this chapter. The heavy irony of Amans's own repeated comparisons between amorous persuasion and Christian prayer makes it obvious that Gower intends the reader to see the two speeches as radically opposed in some respects while at the same time psychologically similar. Both prayer and amorous persuasion gain by the frequent juxtapositions. By a pervasive synesthetic imagery, the whole person is involved in the act of prayer. In the story of Bacchus, prayer is associated with the sense of taste. The examples of Pygmaleon and Iphis associate prayer with the sexual act itself. The story of Paris and Helen, which cites a classic example of the disorder of war caused by a culpable displacement of prayer by amorous persuasion, gives a historical (in the medieval sense) and mythic dimension to the examination of speech. The most significant story of Book IV, as we have pointed out, is that of Mercury and Argus, which embodies the rejection of amorous persuasion, a judgment generally implied by the comparisons with Christian prayer. The fact that one figure, Mercury, stands both for harmful eloquence and also for the Verbum dramatically underlines the similarity between amorous persuasion and prayer.

The purpose of the urgency associated with amorous persuasion and prayer is to create a nervous, untenable ambivalence that demands resolution. The resolution which comes on the literal, contextual level of the Mercury-Argus story also provides an easy and logical transition to Christian prayer. The comparison with amorous persuasion has finally served only to produce a more bitter realization that the lover's words to the lady are inadequate; the implied model of perfect expression demands fulfillment in prayer and the Word.

4

The Lady's Speech

I

Gower's treatment of the lady's speech grows from a vast tradition of feminine figures, historical, figural, and allegorical. There are, for example, those homely illustrations of the *mulier fortis*—Rebecca, Judith, and Abigail —who so appall Chaucer's Merchant; Dante's Beatrice; the Pearl Maiden; Dame Prudence, the wife of Melibee; the Lady Philosophy of Boethius; the Philologia of Martianus Capella; and the feminine attributes of Sapientia in the Old Testament. The means by which the wisdom of these estimable ladies reaches their devotees is, of course, their conversation. The link by which the speech of the virtuous lady relates to the wisdom of God can be most suitably illustrated by the lover of Beatrice.

In the *Convivio*, III.vii, Dante discusses the theme of the various gradations by which creatural forms participate in the Divine Essence, using the commonplace example of light. In this familiar chain, there is no intermediate being between the lowest angel and the most perfect human soul, and between the most debased human soul and the highest animal:

> For these reasons we may therefore assume and firmly believe that there is some human being so noble and of such lofty condition that he can be hardly anything but an angel. . . . And such I affirm this lady to be, so that the divine virtue, in the same way as it descends into angels, descends into her.[1]

This literally angelic divine virtue is manifested in the specifically human way:

> I confirm this by the experience which may be had of her in those operations which are peculiar to the rational soul, into which the divine light radiates with less hindrance, I mean in speech and in the acts which are wont to be called behaviour and carriage.

> Wherefore it must be remembered that man alone among animals has the gift of speech, and has a behaviour and acts which are called rational, since he alone possesses reason in himself. And if any one contradicting us should wish to affirm that a certain bird speaks, as seems true of some birds, especially of the magpie and the parrot, and that certain beasts perform actions or behave themselves, as seems the case with the ape and some others, I reply that it is not true that they speak or behave themselves, because they do not possess reason from which such effects must needs flow.[2]

After attaching an almost equal importance to rational behavior, Dante puts a final emphasis on speech:

> For her speech, by reason of her loftiness and sweetness, engenders in the mind of the listener a thought of love, which I call a heavenly spirit because its origin is from above, and its message comes from above as has been told already.[3]

The Speech of God on the way down to the lover manifests itself in the speech of the lady. Since the lover perceives that she is somehow ineffable, that his love is correspondingly inexpressible, and that some kind of prayer must characterize his conversation with her, the lady's verbal responses in turn appropriately demonstrate reversibility, the descent of God's words to the lover.

But feminine speech is not always so edifying, and the speech of the Sirens is a deceptive parody of this descent. At the beginning of the *Confessio Amantis*, Genius warns Amans to guard his sense of hearing by a famous emblem of demonic feminine speech, the escape of Ulysses from the power of the sirens, whose ability to deceive mariners lies especially in the alluring quality of their voices:

> For whan the Schipmen leie an Ere
> Unto the vois, in here avys
> Thei wene it be a Paradys,
> Which after is to hem an helle.   (I.500–503)

Mistaking the speech of Hell for the speech of Heaven suggests the word of God as the proper cure for a sense of hearing weakened by sin, a remedy which we will presently describe. The importance of this episode and the related commentaries is that the whole erotic force of the sirens is concentrated in their voices. In the myth itself, apart from commentaries, the singing of the sirens, a form of vocal communication, is equated with their sexuality. Hugo Rahner has traced the symbolic peregrinations of these half-beautiful, half-monstrous creatures through the whole compass of ancient Greek culture.[4] Originally vampirelike things living on the blood of the dead, they came more and more to have an erotic connotation. Since the appeal to the ear remained a constant factor of their alluring nature, the bewitching power of their song was frequently used to describe human eloquence. Alcibiades tells of trying to escape the voice of Socrates "which lays bare the innermost depths of his soul, 'by force, if necessary, holding his ears as before the Sirens.' "[5] The Neoplatonic commentators on the *Cratylus* interpret the chthonic sirens as the pleasures of the world which fetter men "by sweet words."[6] Eventually the term *siren* was applied to anyone "who had great learning or even an easy flow of words."[7] In the *Confessio Amantis*, the sound produced by the Sirens has a semblance of goodness and truth:

> And overthis of such nature
> Thei ben, that with so swete a stevene
> Like to the melodie of hevene
> In wommanysshe vois thei singe,
> With notes of so gret likinge,
> Of such mesure, of such musike,
> Wherof the Schipes thei beswike
> That passen be the costes there.   (I.492–99)

The song of the sirens is a deliberate imitation of music associated with heaven: "the melodie of hevene," a similarity which Gower underlines by the marginal phrase "angelica voce." The meaning of the simile lies in the contrast of the falsity of the sirens' song with the truth of its religious opposite, the word of God. An interesting corroboration of this contrast is the inclusion of the story of the sirens in a section of the *Speculum Morale* entitled "De auditu" in which the word of God is recommended as the best guardian of the sense of hearing. The recommendation is as follows:

> Sixth, idle words; and this by hearing edifying words or being astounded by them, Proverbs.2 Let your ear hear wisdom. This is signified in 2 Kings.22. Bananias who is interpreted as the edification of the Lord, or response, or counsellor was the secretary of David, and signifies the word of God which ought to be the guardian of our ears.[8]

To return to the Sirens, the effect of their voices is the derangement of reason:

> For reson may noght with hem duelle,
> When thei tho grete lustes hiere;
> Thei conne noght here Schipes stiere,
> So besiliche upon the note
> Thei herkne, and in such wise assote,
> That thei here rihte cours and weie
> Foryete, and to here Ere obeie. . . .   (I.504–10)

The singing of the Sirens is equated by Boccaccio with the verbal persuasiveness of prostitutes:

> I remember reading this about them, in which one notices what the poets intended. . . . And Leontius asserts that according to the oldest report of the Etholians, the first prostitutes were among the Greeks and they were so effective with the enticement of eloquence, that they made almost all of Achaia their prey: and for this reason the fable of the origin of the sirens gained currency.[9]

The identification of their singing with persuasive speech is emphasized by the significance of their mother's name: "Because of the caressing eloquence of almost all of them, their mother was said to be Caliope, that is, pleasant sounding."[10] The interpretation of a person as a voice—Caliope as "bona sonoritas"—may also suggest the person of the Word as the ascetic and theological alternative.

The enticing power of the sirens' voices is at once a fairly clear reference to the power of the lady's voice and is also a traditional metaphor of falsehood in general. This general interpretation suggests a remedy in speech which is preeminently true, the spiritual counsel which Amans will hear from the confessor. In the section of the *Confessio Amantis* which we will discuss next, this counsel is specified to signify the word of God in the Gospel.

Although the section on Delicacy, a species of Gluttony, is discussed in terms of sight, hearing, and thought, the parable of Dives and Lazarus, with its inherent stress on attending to the word of God in due season, puts a greater emphasis on the sense of hearing.[11] Amans declares at length how he is fed by his lady's speech and the story of Dives and Lazarus is told to show the danger of delicacy. The profusion of oral imagery in the parable—the feast from which Lazarus receives only crumbs, the licking of his wounds by dogs, the request of Dives in Hell for a drop of water on his tongue—stimulated a series of interpretations revolving around the word of God. Even though one may not accept the application of these interpretations in all their detail to the use Gower makes of the parable, their general preoccupation with the word of God would make that theme relevant. With these interpretations in mind, the reader is invited to see, for example, the true nourishment of the word of God in Dives's feast in contrast to the banquet of the lady's speech; the sanative effects of the word in preaching and confession in the licking of the dogs; and the morally dangerous separation of speech and action in the interpretation of Dives's thirst in hell.

Amans confesses that the final feast of love is denied him, but that he fares as well as he can on the food provided by his eyes, ears, and thoughts. The part of his confession that pertains to the gratification of the sense of hearing illustrates the metaphorical possibilities of the spoken word as food. First there is the refreshment of what others say about his lady:

I hiere on seith that sche is wys,
An other seith that sche is good,
And som men sein, of worthi blod
That sche is come, and is also
So fair, that nawher is non so;
And som men preise hire goodli chiere:
Thus every thing that I mai hiere,
Which souneth to mi ladi goode,
Is to myn Ere a lusti foode.   (VI.838–46)

More exquisite still are the words which the lady herself speaks:

And ek min Ere hath over this
A deynte feste, whan so is
That I mai hiere hirselve speke;
For thanne anon mi faste I breke
On such wordes as sche seith,
That full of trouthe and full of feith
They ben, and of so good desport,
That to myn Ere gret confort
Thei don, as thei that ben delices.   (VI.847–55)

Her words have more sustenance and savor than any skillfully seasoned food prepared by the celebrated Lombard cooks:

For al the metes and the spices,
That eny Lombard couthe make,
Ne be so lusti forto take
Ne so forforth restauratif,
I seie as for myn oghne lif,
As ben the wordes of hire mouth. . . .   (VI.856–61)

The courtesy of her speech, like the gentle southern winds, has a curative effect on his heart:

For as the wyndes of the South
Ben most of alle debonaire,
So whan hir list to speke faire,
The vertu of hire goodly speche
I verraily myn hertes leche.   (VI.862–66)

Finally the ecstatic effect on him of her speech in song demands the analogy of paradise for its precise expression:

And if it so befalle among,
That sche carole upon a song,
What I it hiere I am so fedd,

> That I am fro miself so ledd,
> As though I were in paradis;
> For certes, as to myn avis,
> Whan I here of hir vois the stevene,
> Me thenkth it is a blisse of hevene.   (VI.867–74)

Another manner in which his ear is fed is through the reading of romances, the stories of those who loved before he was born:

> Fulofte time it falleth so,
> Min Ere with a good pitance
> Is fedd of redinge of romance
> Of Ydoine and of Amadas,
> That whilom weren in mi cas,
> And eke of othre many a score,
> That loveden longe er I was bore.   (VI.876–82)

The effect of this reading is to stimulate hope. He is reminded by these stories that sorrow does not endure forever and the hope of future success compensates to some extent for his present frustration:

> For whan I of here loves rede,
> Min Ere with the tale I fede;
> And with the lust of here histoire
> Somtime I drawe into memoire
> How sorwe mai noght evere laste;
> And so comth hope in ate laste,
> Whan I non other fode knowe.   (VI.883–89)

The sense that the satisfaction of the sense of hearing is inadequate to the more encompassing desire of the lover increases, and his erotic starvation makes him a kind of Lazarus at love's feast. The contrasting abundant sufficiency of the word of God as opposed to the words of the lady should be remembered in the following passage:

> And that endureth bot a throwe,
> Riht as it were a cherie feste;
> Bot forto compten ate leste,
> As for the while yit it eseth
> And somdel of myn herte appeseth:
> For what thing to myn Ere spreedeth,
> Which is plesant, somdel it feedeth
> With wordes suche as he mai gete
> Mi lust, in stede of other mete.   (VI.890–98)

After Amans describes how the cook, Thought, prepares the ingredients obtained by sight and hearing, Genius introduces the story of Dives and

Lazarus explicitly as the word of Christ. The importance attached to the original speaker of the exemplum, plus the semantic consciousness of Genius that by telling the story in English he is giving it a wider dissemination, inevitably contrast to the lesser significance of the lady's words:

> Of Cristes word, who wole it rede,
> How that this vice is forto drede
> In thevangile it telleth plein,
> Which mot algate be certein,
> For Crist himself it berth witnesse.
> And thogh the clerk and the clergesse
> In latin tunge it rede and singe,
> Yit for the more knoulechinge
> Of trouthe, which is good to wite,
> I schal declare as it is write
> In Engleissh, for thus it began.
> Crist seith. . . .   (VI.975–86)

Given the context of an erotic malnutrition, the starving condition of Lazarus is meant to parallel the hunger of Amans. At the feast of Dives,

> A povere lazre upon a tyde
> Cam to the gate and axed mete:
> Bot there mihte be nothing gete
> His dedly hunger forto stanche;
> For he, which hadde his fulle panche
> Of alle lustes ate bord,
> Ne deigneth noght to speke a word,
> Onliche a Crumme forto yive,
> Wherof the povere myhte live. . . .   (VI.996–1004)

An interpretation initiated by Gregory the Great makes the feast of Dives the divine law given to the Jews, and the scraps from the table the words of truth that came incidentally to the gentiles:

> But the wounded Lazarus wanted to be filled with the crumbs that fell from the table of the wealthy man and no one let him because that proud people despised allowing any gentile knowledge of the law. For they had the teaching of the law not towards charity, but towards elation, as if swelled up from the received abundance. And to him words flowed from knowledge, as if crumbs fell from the table.[12]

The dogs licking Lazarus's wounds soothe him in his starving condition:

> And as these holi bokes sein,
> The houndes comen fro the halle,

> Wher that this sike man was falle,
> And as he lay ther forto die,
> The woundes of his maladie
> Thei licken forto don him ese.   (VI.1010–15)

We should remember in the following interpretation by Gregory of the dogs as preachers and confessors that Amans's condition parallels that of Lazarus:

> But on the other hand dogs licked the wounds of the dying pauper. Sometimes preachers are indicated by dogs in the holy scripture. For the dog's tongue cures the wound when it licks it, and when the holy doctors instruct us in the confession of our sin, they, as it were, touch the wound of the mind with the tongue; and since they deliver us from sin by speaking, they lead us to salvation as if by touching our wounds.[13]

In Peter Riga's *Aurora*, a source which Gower knew, the same confessional interpretation is present:

> The poor man whose wounds the tongue of dogs healed signifies the gentiles whom confession cures.[14]

Amans is being summoned to the compensation proffered to Lazarus in the allegorical interpretation: the words of instruction from the confessor.

The theme of the word as pleasurable to the taste occurs also in a traditional allegorical interpretation of the epilogue in Hell. On the literal level of the parable, the parched tongue of Dives is a clear antithesis to and punishment of the pampered palate of his earthly existence. In a continuation of the passage quoted above from Gregory the Great, the abundant cuisine of Dives's former state is again interpreted as the words of the law:

> He is shown to burn more in his tongue, when he says: Send Lazarus that he may put the tip of finger in water to refresh my tongue, for I am tormented in this flame (Luke 16:24). A faithless people held in the mouth the words of the law which they despised performing in act. Therefore they burn more in that place where they show themselves aware of what they refuse to do. Wherefore it is well said through Solomon concerning the learned and negligent: all the labor of man is in his mouth, but his soul will not be filled (Eccles. 6:7), for whoever works only for this, to know what he ought to say, fasts with an empty mind from the very nourishment of his knowledge.[15]

In the latter part of the passage Gregory extends the application of the parable beyond an indictment of the Jews. Since the feast itself is the word of God, Amans is being cautioned not to misuse the spiritual nourishment available to him.

In the conclusion of the parable, Dives's request that Lazarus warn his

brothers against a life of Delicacy is refused on the grounds that man is
obliged to hear the word of God at the right time:

> Quod Habraham: "Nay sikerly;
> For if thei nou wol noght obeie
> To suche as techen hem the weie
> And alday preche and alday telle
> Hou that it stant of hevene and helle,
> Thei wol noght thanne taken hiede,
> Thogh it befelle so in dede
> That eny ded man were arered,
> To ben of him no betre lered
> Than of an other man alyve." (VI.1100–1109)

This final stress on hearing the word of God specifically opposes Amans's
delight in his lady's speech and the reading of romances. If delight in such
speech is a form of gluttony for Amans, the crumbs from the table of Dives
not only suggest an ascetical alternative but also refer him directly to the
word of God.

II

The acceptance of the counsel of a woman in the tale of Florent is placed
in such a context as to make unmistakable the parallel between the specific
counsel of Amans's lady and the "trowthe" of divine and human law. Speech
is the means by which this parallel is developed. The theme of speech as a
metaphor of the whole person is present in such a way as to make the whole
story an analogue of the operation of the Word in the soul.

The tale of Florent is told as an example of Murmur and Complaint, which
in turn are clearly related by Gower to the vice of Inobedience, a species of
Pride. The Latin verses which introduce the section of Inobedience state a
definite parallel between the effect of law and the courtly love concept of the
ennobling and ordering power of love:

> Quem neque lex hominum, neque lex divina valebit
>   Flectere, multociens corde reflectit amor.
> Quem non flectit amor, non est flectendus ab ullo,
>   Set rigor illius plus Elephante riget.
> Dedignatur amor poterit quos scire rebelles
>   Et rudibus sortem prestat habere rudem;
> Set qui sponte sui subicit se cordis amore,
>   Frangit in aduersis omnia fata pius.
>
> (Whom neither human nor divine law can
> bend, love will often change in his heart.

> Whom love cannot bend cannot be bent by anything.
> His inflexibility is greater than that of ivory tusks.
> Love scorns those whom he knows are rebellious
> and gives a harsh fortune to the uncouth.
> But he who subdues himself through the love of his heart
> is a match for any adverse fate through his piety.)

Genius begins by elaborating the preceding verses concerning the man who "toward his god ne boweth/ After the lawes of his heste" (I.1238–39). Genius wonders if even love can persuade such a person to an orderly existence:

> I not if love him myhte plie,
> For elles forto justefie
> His herte, I not what mihte availe.   (I.1249–51)

The phrase "justefie/ His herte" implies more than mere compliance to external law and connotes the total conversion of theological "justification." The interrogation of Amans focuses on his disobedience to his "ladi heste" (I.1269), and her command is principally that he stop importuning her and find love elsewhere. Amorous persuasion must give place to acceptance of his lady's words:

> Mi fader, this is on, that sche
> Commandeth me my mowth to close,
> And that I scholde hir noght oppose
> In love, of which I ofte preche,
> Bot plenerliche of such a speche
> Forbere, and soffren hire in pes.   (I.1274–79)

The use of "preche" reminds the reader of the context of the word in divine law and suggests the kind of speech Amans should be listening to. He describes his persistence in amorous persuasion, which is opposed to his lady's speech:

> Foe whanne I am ther as sche is,
> Though sche my tales noght alowe,
> Ayein hir will yit mot I bowe,
> To seche if that I myhte have grace:
> Bot that thing may I noght enbrace
> For ought that I can speke or do;
> And yit fulofte I speke so,
> That sche is wroth and seith, 'Be stille.'   (I.1282–89)

This command Amans should indeed obey in order to hear the speech of wisdom in his own soul. The continuing ineffectuality of his amorous persuasion harmonizes with the many references to the superiority of prayer. He cannot resolve the contradiction between the need of the lover to speak and the specific mandate of obedience:

> If I that heste schal fulfille
> And therto ben obedient,
> Thanne is my cause fully schent,
> For specheles may noman spede.
> So wot I noght what is to rede;
> Bot certes I may noght obeie,
> That I ne mot algate seie
> Somwhat of that I wolde mene;
> For evere it is aliche grene,
> The grete love which I have,
> Wherof I can noght bothe save
> My speche and this obedience:
> And thus fulofte my silence
> I breke. . . .   (I.1290–1303)

By enjoining obedience in this context, Genius is clearly arguing against amorous persuasion and in favor of listening to the lady's speech. The tale of Florent must be read in this context, as we hope to show.

The transition from Inobedience to the following section on Murmur and Complaint emphasizes the unity of the two categories. Amans introduced his description of the two commands of his lady that he could not obey as a cause of complaint:

> Bot other while I *grucche* sore
> Of some thinges that sche doth,
> Wherof that I woll telle soth:
> For of tuo pointz I am bethoght. . . .   (I.1264–67; my italics)

This passage occurs at the beginning of the treatment of Inobedience and anticipates by the word *grucche* the section on Murmur and Complaint. Then, at the beginning of the section on Murmur and Complaint, as we might expect, Amans uses some form of the word *gruchen* three times (I.1349, 1363, 1385); but also, to join this to the previous section on Inobedience, he uses "buxomnesse" (1355), "obeie," (1365), "unbuxomly" (1368), "desobeissant" (1392), "unbuxomnesse" (1394), "obedience" (1401). By anticipation and repetition, Gower implies that the two sections are integrally related; that is, that the tale of Florent illustrates Inobedience as much as it does Murmur and Complaint. This is further proven by the application at the end of the story (I.1856–71).

Proceeding to our analysis, we notice that just as the section on Inobedience was presented in terms of the lover's fear to abstain from the use of his own words, the tale of Florent continues this emphasis. The story opens with Florent in search of chivalric adventure. He is ambushed and, while defending himself, chances to kill a certain Branchus. The parents of the dead knight are afraid to kill Florent because of his reputation, "gentilesce," and family ties with the emperor. The "grantdame" of the slain Branchus devises a plan whereby the free agreement of Florent may be the cause of his own death:

> That sche schal him to dethe winne
> Al only of his oghne grant,
> Thurgh strengthe of verray covenant
> Withoute blame of eny wiht.   (I.1448–51)

Florent must obey the implications of his own verbal agreement. He must swear that if he cannot answer a certain question, he will accept the death penalty:

> And over this thou schalt ek swere
> That if thou of the sothe faile,
> Ther schal non other thing availe,
> That thou ne schalt thi deth receive.   (I.1462–65)

The frequent references to Florent's "trowthe" throughout the story hark back to this solemn verbal agreement and illustrate what can be considered his obedience to the old woman's proposal. The question, as everyone knows from Chaucer's Wife of Bath's tale, is: What do women most desire? Florent has no success in finding the answer, of course, and as the time comes for him to return, his "trowthe" requires him to keep his promise:

> This knyht hath levere forto dye
> Than breke his trowthe and forto lye
> In place ther as he was swore. . . .   (I.1511–13)

Riding through a forest, he comes upon a "lothly wommannysch figure." As if by an inversion of the convention that the lover reveal himself to his lady, the old hag gratuitously reveals her knowledge of Florent and his quest:

> 'Florent be thi name,
> Thou hast on honde such a game,
> That bot thou be the betre avised,
> Thi deth is schapen and devised,
> That al the world ne mai the save,
> Bot if that thou my conseil have.'   (I.1541–46)

We should recall that in the context of the story Amans is being urged to accept a lady's counsel. Another verbal agreement, like the one that began the quest, is struck, but the hag demands a repulsive reward:

> 'Thou schalt me leve such a wedd,
> That I wol have thi trowthe in honde
> That thou schalt be myn housebonde.'   (I.1558–60)

Just as Amans must abandon amorous persuasion, Florent must realize that his own verbal resourcefulness is profitless. The requirement that Florent accept the hag's words to save his life implies clearly that Amans too must accept his lady's advice. Florent agrees to marry the hag:

> 'If that non other chance
> Mai make my deliverance,
> Bot only thilke same speche
> Which, as thou seist, thou schalt me teche,
> Have hier myn hond, I schal thee wedde.'
> And thus his trowthe he leith to wedde.   (I.1583–88)

He is apprised that sovereignty over man's love is what women most desire. In a parallel to Amans's attachment to amorous persuasion, Florent is reluctant, when he confronts Branchus's grandmother, to use the hag's words instead of his own:

> Florent seith al that evere he couthe,
> Bot such word cam ther non to mowthe,
> That he for yifte or for beheste
> Mihte eny wise his deth areste.   (I.1641–44)

Understandably he puts off the hag's solution as long as he can, but he finally capitulates:

> And thanne he hath trewly supposed
> That he him may of nothing yelpe,
> Bot if so be tho wordes helpe,
> Whiche as the womman hath him tawht;
> Wherof he hath an hope cawht
> That he schal ben excused so,
> And tolde out plein his wille tho.   (I.1650–56)

His life is saved, but a new sorrow begins. He must go to the hag "or ben untrewe,/ To hire which his trowthe hadde" (I.166). Dreading to break his word, he goes "As he that was with trowthe affaited" (I.1671). The repetition of "trowthe" puts that concept in the context of obedience to a lady. The lengthy description of the hag's ugliness dramatizes the poignancy of Florent's situation. The cost of Florent's "trowthe" can be assessed by the hag's tiny, deep-set eyes, loose, hanging skin, and shrunken lips. "Trowthe" is again associated with deference or obedience to a woman:

> He wolde algate his trowthe holde,
> As every knyht therto is holde,
> What happ so evere him is befalle:
> Thogh sche be the fouleste of alle,
> Yet to thonour of wommanhiede
> Him thoghte he scholde taken hiede. . . .   (I.1715–20)

To demonstrate his "trowthe," Amans also must be obedient to his lady. The final relinquishing of his own words to the will of the mysterious hag occurs after they have retired to what promised to be a loathsome wedding night for Florent. The hag becomes a beautiful young girl who proposes another impossible choice to Florent. No longer disposed to murmur or complain, Florent, in a culminating act of obedience surely meant as hortatory to Amans, abandons his right to any further speech in the matter:

> 'O ye, my lyves hele,
> Sey what you list in my querele,
> I not what ansuere I schal yive:
> Bot evere whil that I may live,
> I wol that ye be my maistresse,
> For I can noght miselve gesse
> Which is the beste unto my chois.
> Thus grante I yow myn hole *vois.* . . .   (I.1821–28; my italics)

Since the sin of Murmur and Complaint is a verbal manifestation of Inobedience, it is rhetorically and morally appropriate that Florent—and, by application, Amans—should obey by surrendering his own words. The use of "vois" in the last quoted line as a synecdoche for his whole person is a clear summation of this verbal emphasis.

Paradoxically this verbal commitment releases the spell placed on his wife and rescues her beauty from the requirement of alternate phases. A similar obligation to his lady's command is placed on Amans:

> Forthi, my Sone, if thou do ryht,
> Thou schalt unto thi love obeie,
> And folwe hir will be alle weie.   (I.1862–64)

Furthermore, since "vois" represents the totality of Florent's submission and fits Amans's case so justly, we are tempted to point out the analogy of the absorption of human speech in the Verbum. The command of his lady anticipates his final dismissal from the court of Venus and contains the will of God for him. The frequent mention of "trowthe" in the tale must be read in the whole context of Inobedience, which involves human and divine law, a function of the Verbum. Florent's fidelity to the "trouthe" of his original verbal agreement leads logically to the final total surrender of his "vois." The courtly love principle, alluded to in the Latin verses introducing Inobedience, of the ennobling effect of human love suggests a hierarchical progression to a divine "trowthe" represented by a woman. With Florent, the implication is that henceforth the lady will speak for him; he will have no "vois" apart from hers. Their union is represented by this identification of speech. We may also suppose that the union of God which Amans achieves at the end of the poem is also a duly proportioned identification of his own "vois" with the Verbum; for, in fact, he does finally abandon amorous persuasion in favor of prayer. In the tale of Florent, the speech pattern opposes the acceptance of the hag's word to the inobedience of Murmur and Complaint. In regard to Amans, the lady's command that he silence his ineffectual and self-deluding love-talk occurs in the context of a promulgated divine law, a perfection of speech clearly pointing to the Word.

III

For the two principal suitors in Gower's tale of Constance, her speech, or even what she is reported to have said, is an inducement to love and persuasion to Christianity almost simultaneously. The sultan of Syria and the King of Northumbria fall in love and are converted principally through hearsay knowledge of Constance, or her good reputation.[16] Because of the virtual identification in the story between the reputation of Constance and the word of God, the sin of Detraction, which the story illustrates, takes on blasphemous overtones. Detraction, which is manifested in two incidents, the murder of Hermyngheld and the allegation of the monstrous birth, is countered not by any declaration of Constance herself but, in the first instance, by the testimony of a miraculous voice and, in the second, by the formal presentation of her son to her husband. The fact that the heroine does not speak on her own behalf and even refuses consistently to identify herself makes the discovery of her identity an important goal of the narrative. In fact, the function of reputation in the gradual unfolding of identity and the interplay between reputation and identity give direction to the various elements of the story. The effect of all this is to present the helplessness of an individual in the face of detraction and to focus attention on the difference between reputation and identity, which is an aspect of the larger difference between appearance and reality.

The penitent of the *Confessio Amantis* engages freely in the character assassination of his rivals, but does not readily admit this. Leading up to Amans's rather imperceptive defense of his own particular kind of detraction is a general description of the vice. The introductory Latin verses give a summary of characteristics and make an amorous application:

> Set generosus amor linguam conseruat, ut eius
>   Verbum quod loquitur nulla sinistra gerat.

> (But noble love preserves the tongue, that
>   the word it speaks bear nothing sinister.)

The cramped narrowness of detraction, a kind of negative anticipation of the generosity of Constance, is made vivid by a character from the *Romance of the Rose,*

> . . . Malebouche,
> Whos tunge neither pyl ne crouche

> Mai hyre, so that he pronounce
> A plein good word withoute frounce
> Awher behinde a mannes bak.   (II.389–93)

As the nettle burns, fades, and pales the fresh roses, and the "scharnebude" prefers animal feces to flowers, so the "janglere Envious" scants the virtues of a man and says the worst about the slightest fault.

The dubious motive Amans gives for his own detraction of rival lovers is the protection of his lady; but her shrewdness, the existence of which he admits, would seem to render this unnecessary:

> She lieveth noght al that sche hiereth,
> And thus fulofte hirself sche skiereth
> And is al war of 'hadde I wist'. . . .   (II.471–73)

He worries, however, that his lady's innocence is but a fragile defence, and he must inform her of the insincerity of his rivals:

> And evere I am adrad of guile,
> In aunter if with eny wyle
> Thei mihte hire innocence enchaunte.
> Forthi my wordes ofte I haunte
> Behynden hem, so as I dar,
> Wherof my ladi may be war. . . .   (II.479–84)

Failing to see the impossible nature of his own love, Amans tries to distort the perceptions of his lady. His sin of detraction is compounded by his obvious incompetence as a liar:

> I sai what evere comth to mowthe,
> And worse I wolde, if that I cowthe;
> For whanne I come unto hir speche,
> Al that I may enquere and seche,
> Of suche deceipte, I telle it al,
> And ay the werst in special.   (II.485–90)

Significantly, however, although Amans has begun his answer to Genius by defending his sin and excusing his detraction, he progresses to an almost brutal acknowledgment:

> Thus toward hem that wicke mene
> My wicked word was evere grene.
> And natheles, the soth to telle,
> In certain if it so befelle
> That althertrewest man ybore,
> To chese among a thousend score,
> Which were alfulli forto triste,
> Mi ladi lovede, and I it wiste,

> Yit rathere thanne he scholde spede,
> I wolde swiche tales sprede
> To mi ladi, if that I myhte,
> That I scholde al his love unrihte. . . .   (II.495–506)

He no longer pretends to be defending his lady or that the objects of his detraction are undeserving scoundrels. This movement from interior disguising to a harsh discernment of self, not unlike the shift in the Constance story from the appearances of reputation to the reality of identity, is intrinsic to the poem's framework and points to the final repentance of Amans.

Although the superiority of Chaucer's version of the story is a critical commonplace, the fact and significance of Gower's greater insistence on the reputation of Constance has not been pointed out. Among the additions to Nicholas Trivet that increase the religious quality of Chaucer's Man of Law's Tale, Edward A. Block cites the opinion of others concerning Constance.[17] The context of detraction makes Gower's more numerous instances of these opinions more appropriate; and, in fact, the recognitions of Constance at the end of the story depend for their deeper sense on the gradually escalated significance of this element.

Introducing this pattern at the beginning of the story is the heroine's reputation for devotion:

> And sche the god so wel apaide,
> That al the wide worldes fame
> Spak worschipe of hire goode name.   (II.594–96)

The persuasive speech of Constance on behalf of the Christian Faith generates the events of the story. She is so "full of feith" that when certain Barbary merchants come to Rome, her conversation takes a missionary turn:

> Sche hath hem with hire wordes wise
> Of Cristes feith so full enformed,
> That thei therto ben all conformed,
> So that baptesme thei receiven
> And alle here false goddes weyven.   (II.606–10)

After their return home, the merchants' honest praise of Constance, which is part of their reply to the sultan as to why they accepted Christianity, establishes her reputation against the subsequent detractions of the story and causes the sultan to fall in love with her:

> The matiere of here tale tolde
> With al the hole circumstance.
> And whan the Souldan of Constance
> Upon the point that thei ansuerde
> The beaute and the grace herde,
> As he which thanne was to wedde,

> In alle haste his cause spedde
> To sende for the mariage.   (II.618–25)

Falling in love through simply hearing about Constance initiates the sultan's conversion to Christianity—a sequence that makes her reputation a fusion of amorous and apostolic persuasion:

> And furthermor with good corage
> He seith, be so he mai hire have,
> That Crist, which cam this world to save,
> He woll believe. . . .   (II.626–29)

In Chaucer's version, the merchants are not converted and the sultan deliberates at some length before deciding to accept Christianity [II(B)171–231]. Gower's handling of the incident, although less plausible, makes its own point more surely, with unequivocal congruence between framework and tale. "Realism" of characterization gives place to precision of thematic emphasis: the charismatic reputation of Constance as the antithesis of detraction and an immediately effective instrument of grace.

The jealous reaction of the sultan's mother further externalizes this relationship between Constance's reputation and the Christian message, which, far from being irrelevantly didactic, forges the key to her final "identity." In pretending to praise her son's decision, the sultan's mother rightly attaches greater importance to Constance's religion than to her imperial dignity, but fails to understand her own emphasis:

> Mi Sone, I am be double weie
> With al myn herte glad and blithe,
> For that miself have ofte sithe
> Desired thou wolt, as men seith,
> Receive and take a newe feith,
> Which schal be forthringe of thi lif:
> And ek so worshipful a wif,
> The doughter of an Emperour,
> To wedde it schal be gret honour.   (II.656–64)

Her true response to Constance's reputation, latent in the irony of her statement, is a dramatic and horrible rejection of the word of God: at the wedding feast, she has her own son murdered, together with all those who embraced Christianity. The action of the sultan's mother dramatizes not only the incompleteness of Constance's reputation by itself, but also the potentially misleading aspects of the fusion of Christianity with imperial power. Knowing someone by reputation must give way to immediate and complete experience; conversion to the Faith must be deepened by true understanding.

In the subsequent incidents of the story, the reputation of Constance consists entirely of her Christianity, and only at the end of the story can her imperial dignity be revealed once more. Christianity must be shown most powerful in the helplessness of Constance before it can safely be joined to empire once again. Hence a reduplication of the plot is necessary, and in the remaining two journeys of Constance, no part of her reputation is known beforehand and she refuses to identify herself. Constance, having been put upon the sea in an open boat by the sultan's mother, is off on another missionary enterprise. Arriving safely in Northumbria and solaced by Elda and Hermyngheld, Constance is nevertheless completely unknown, that is, without fame or reputation, and, curiously, refuses to reveal her identity:

> Bot sche hire wolde noght confesse,
> Whan thei hire axen what sche was.   (II.738–39)

Mysteriously reticent about herself, Constance, who

> . . . no maner joie made,
> Bot sorweth sore of that sche fond
> No cristendom in thilke land. . . .   (II.744–46)

begins to preach the Faith. By replacing her personal history with the word of God, she sets the scene for a logomachy in which detraction will be vanquished by the cumulative effect of her preaching and finally by a divine voice. The conversion pattern of the merchants and the sultan of Syria is repeated, but with a substantially greater externalization of the supernatural power surrounding the heroine. Her explanation of the Faith to Hermyng-held, the wife of the king's chamberlain, prepares for a public profession of belief, which in turn causes a miracle:

> Dame Hermyngheld, which was the wif
> Of Elda, lich her oghne lif
> Constance loveth; and fell so,
> Spekende alday betwen hem two,
> Thurgh grace of goddes pourveance
> This maiden tawhte the creance
> Unto this wif so parfitly,
> Upon a dai that faste by
> In presence of hire housebonde,
> Wher thei go walkende on the Stronde,
> A blind man, which cam there lad,
> Unto this wif criende he bad,
> With bothe hise hondes up and preide
> To hire, and in this wise he seide:
> 'O Hermyngeld, which Cristes feith,
> Enformed as Constance seith
> Received hast, yif me my sihte.'   (II.749–65)

Listening to Constance has born fruit, for Hermyngheld publicly acknowledges Christianity (a kind of "confession" which is by no means irrelevant to the sacrament of penance):

> '. . . In trust of Cristes lawe,
> which don was on the crois and slawe,
> Thou bysne man, behold and se.'   (II.769–71)

The blind man sees and the event makes its impression:

> Wherof thei merveile everychon,
> Bot Elda wondreth most of alle:
> *This open thing* which is befalle
> Concludeth him be such a weie,
> That he the feith mot nede obeie.   (II.774–78; my italics)

The meaning of Constance's influence is manifest to Elda here, but in Chaucer's version, Elda doesn't understand and asks for an explanation [II(B)568–74]. The way the two poets handle the next episode, the murder of Hermyngheld and its attribution to Constance, explains the difference. Since in Gower's story the narration of the murder is framed by Elda's deliberate journey to Alla, king of Northumbria, for the expressed purpose of describing Constance as a possible wife, his certainty of the miracle's significance reinforces the apostolic nature of Constance's reputation:

> This Elda forth unto the king
> A morwe tok his weie and rod,
> And Hermyngeld at home abod
> Forth with Constance wel at ese.
> Elda, which thoghte his king to plese,
> As he that thanne unwedded was,
> Of Constance al the pleine cas
> Als goodliche as he cowthe tolde.
> The king was glad and seide he wolde
> Come thider upon such a wise
> That he him mihte of hire avise,
> The time appointed forth withal.   (II.780–91)

The reputation of Constance begins, as in the case of the sultan, to function as amorous persuasion. In Chaucer, this pattern is absent and we are told that after the murder Elda came and Alla was with him [II(B)603–4]. Reputation is not the same as identity, however, and before the king can meet Constance, she refuses the dishonorable advances of a young knight, who, in revenge, murders Hermyngheld and accuses her. Elda, having himself discovered the body of his wife upon his return, challenges this attack on the reputation of Constance by demanding an oath upon a book—of gospels, but even its identity is concealed—which exposes the detraction. The young knight is struck down miraculously for his lie, and forced to confess:

> A vois was herd, whan that they felle,
> Which seide, 'O dampned man to helle,
> Lo, thus hath god the sclaundre wroke
> That thou ayein Constance hast spoke:
> Beknow the sothe er that thou dye.'
> And he told out his felonie,
> And starf forth with his tale anon.   (II.879–85)

Significantly, it is not a question here of Constance defending herself, but of a divine voice, the apotheosis of her reputation, taking up her cause and forcing the guilty to confess—an effect which calls attention to the framework dialogue between Genius and Amans. The divine voice, by virtue of its miraculous authenticity, removes the distance between reputation and identity in Constance and makes them one, for the moment at least. We are not finished with reputation in the story by any means, however. In regard to this incident the most important difference between the two versions of Chaucer and Gower lies in the fact that Gower's Alla was not present during this testimony. He must depend once more on hearsay knowledge, which, in keeping with the pattern exemplified by the sultan, converts him to Christianity and love of Constance:

> For the seconde day a morwe
> The king cam, as thei were acorded;
> And whan it was to him recorded
> What god hath wroght upon this chaunce,
> He tok it into remembrance
> And thoghte more than he seide
> For al his hole herte he leide
> Upon Constance, and seide he scholde
> For love of hire, if that sche wolde,
> Baptesme take and Cristes feith
> Believe, and over that he seith
> He wol hire wedde, and upon this
> Asseured ech til other is.   (II.890–902)

As Chaucer's Alla witnesses the whole scene [II(B)659–86], there is not the same dynamism of mystery and discovery that we find in Gower's version, where Alla's wife will not reveal her complete identity:

> Bot for no lust ne for no rage
> Sche tolde hem nevere what sche was. . . .   (II.910–11)

There is no mention in Chaucer that Alla is even concerned with this point.

While Chaucer lingers with tasteful realism over the wedding night [II(B)708–14], Gower goes immediately to the event which occasions the next detraction, Constance's pregnancy:

> The hihe makere of nature
> Hire hath visited in a throwe,
> That it was openliche knowe
> Sche was with childe be the king. . . .   (II.916–19)

The causal hierarchy of Gower's statement of the event, in remarkable contrast to Chaucer's more humanized rendering ("On hire he gat a knave child anon," II[B]715), is not simply pious, but by contrast anticipates and answers the detraction of the unnatural birth. In both versions, Alla is absent when the child is born, and the second hostile mother-in-law of the story, Domilde, intercepts and changes the message of the birth sent to the king. She writes that Constance is "of fairie" and has delivered a monstrous child. The aptness of this second detraction of the story to the identity of Constance should not be overlooked. Constance has been intimately associated with two supernatural events (not to mention her mysterious arrival from the sea), the healing of the blind man and the testimony of the divine voice. The question raised by the alteration of the letters is, What is the source of Constance's power? Is she a human saint and an emissary of a benevolent God, or is she an alien creature of malicious intent? Is the allegedly monstrous child evidence of amorous and religious deception? It is the accumulated contextual force of detraction which in Gower's version makes this exchange of letters so crucial to the reputation and identity of Constance. In Chaucer's story, the actions of Domilde represent simply wickedness.

Alla's return letter calls for close observation of Constance, but Domilde intercepts once more and forges an order for Constance and the child to be put once more upon the sea. Although Chaucer has Constance refer to the detraction before the voyage, his obvious interest, as evidenced by the number of lines devoted to the pathetic situation of the child (II[B]834–61), is elsewhere. In Chaucer, furthermore, the direct prayer of Constance is an acceptance of Providence: "Lord, ay welcome be thy sonde" (II[B]826). In Gower, on the other hand, her prayer appeals unequivocally to the divine truth, the ultimate defense against detraction, and complements the previous intervention of the divine voice:

> And thanne hire handes to the hevene
> Sche strawhte, and with a milde stevene
> Knelende upon hire bare kne
> Sche seide, 'O hihe mageste,
> *Which sest the point of every trowthe,*
> Tak of thi wofull womman rowthe
> And of this child that I schal kepe.'   (II.1055–61; my italics)

The final adversity suffered by Constance before the reversal of her fortune continues to show the difference in purpose between Chaucer and Gower. After a period on the sea, Constance and her child come to rest by a castle wall in a heathen land. A renegade knight attempts to ravish Constance. In Chaucer's version, during the course of a struggle, through the help of the Virgin Mary, as the narrator observes, the attacker falls overboard (II[B]918–24). In Nicholas Trivet and in Gower, Constance, pretending consent initially, urges the knight to look around first—in Trivet, for a suitable place on land; in Gower, to make sure they are alone. Trivet's Constance, more enterprising than her two sisters, goes up behind the felon and pushes him overboard.[18] Ludicrously and least plausibly in one sense, but with sure consistency of tone and theme, Gower's Constance

> . . . . preide god, and he hire herde,
> And sodeinliche he was out throwe
> And dreynt. . . .   (II.1120–22)

In Chaucer and Gower, the scene embodies the apogee of helplessness in the story, rendered by the fact that Constance is completely unknown in a situation where telling who she is would accomplish nothing. Completely without reputation, she retains her identity as a Christian through a miraculously answered prayer—a necessary and timely correlative of the efficacious preaching for which she has heretofore been known. Chaucer's realism eschews this pattern, and Trivet's handling of the event completely lacks the solitary pathos.[19]

Three years later her boat drifts in among the vessels of a large fleet, and the movement of her reintegration into the society of her origin begins in the encounter with the Roman senator sent to punish the sultan's mother. When asked to identify herself, Constance gives a few brief facts and the Anglo-Saxon form of her name:

> 'Mi name is Couste,' sche him seide:
> Bot forthermor for noght he preide
> Of hire astat to knowe plein,
> Sche wolde him nothing elles sein
> Bot of hir name, which sche feigneth
> Alle othre thinges sche restreigneth,
> That a word more sche ne tolde.   (II.1163–69)

Constance learns the nature of the senator's mission to Syria and discovers that his wife is her aunt. Her refusal to reveal herself completely, for the second time in the story, is a lucid dramatization of the difference between simple identity and the symbolic complexity that has accrued to the character of Constance. Constance is finished with proselytizing, but she once more replaces her personal history, not with overt preaching, but with silent and saintly conduct. The most striking aspect of this second concealment of her identity is that her new protectors, Sallust and her aunt Helen, know her Roman and Syrian histories but do not recognize her. For twelve years, Constance lives the humble self-effacement of this disguise. The fact that Sallust and his wife know Constance and are directly involved in her life but do not recognize her has the artistic purpose of emphasizing once again the subordination of human reputation to authentic identity, which for Constance lies in her Christianity.

It is appropriate to the framework of the *Confessio Amantis* that Alla of Northumbria initiates the final narrative movement of the story by a desire to confess his sins. It is the third confession scene in the story, for in addition to the acknowledgment of Hermyngheld's murderer, the wicked mother-in-law, Domilde, eventually admits the detraction of the monstrous birth and her role in the exile of Constance. The mother-in-law in Chaucer has no such spiritual release; in fact, Chaucer's Alla comes to Rome to confess the murder of his mother. In Gower, Domilde is executed, but this is represented as a just penalty for her crimes. The fact, then, that, in Gower, Alla comes to confess more out of devotion than grim necessity contributes significantly to the tone of the final discovery of Constance. Chaucer is once more "humanizing" and "realistic," whereas Gower joins pilgrimage and confession to a deepening in the faith to which Alla was converted by Constance:

> Whan he hise werres hadde achieved,
> And thoghte he wolde be relieved
> Of Soule hele upon the feith
> Which he hath take, thanne he seith
> That he to Rome in pelrinage
> Wol go, wher Pope was Pelage,
> To take his absolucioun.   (II.1311–17)

Since Sallust is requested to aid in Alla's accommodations while at Rome, Constance hears of the imminent arrival of her husband and swoons in joyous anticipation. After Alla confesses to the pope, he decides to mark the occasion with a feast. The household of Sallust is invited, and Constance instructs her son Morris to catch the eye of Alla as often as he can:

> Moris tofore the kinges yhe
> Upon the morwe, wher he sat,
> Fulofte stod, and upon that
> The king his chiere upon him caste,
> And in his face him thoghte als faste
> He sih his oghne wif Constance;
> For nature as in resemblance
> Of face hem liketh so to clothe,
> That thei were of a suite bothe. ·
> The king was moeved in his thoght
> Of that he seth, and knoweth it noght;

> This child he loveth kindely,
> And yit he wot no cause why.   (II.1370–82)

This first stage in the discovery of Constance is clearly related to the detraction of the monstrous birth, but the point to remember is that Alla has only *heard* that the child was normal and Constance is ignorant even of this stage of his knowledge. This dependence of Alla on hearsay knowledge gives way to a visual recognition of his wife's lineaments in his son. The normality of the child, together with the long self-effacement of Constance, demonstrates the beneficence of the supernatural power manifested in her, and meaningfully parallels the miraculous voice which overturned the other detraction of the story. These two means by which detraction has been overcome complementarily represent the incarnational union of the supernatural power of Christianity with ordinary humanity.

Just as the reputation of Constance effected a fusion of Christianity and human love, the progressive discovery of her identity validates and deepens both. Having been informed that the name of the child's mother is "Couste" (meaningless to Sallust, for "Couste in Saxoun is to sein/ Constance upon the word Romein," II.1405–6), Alla is so overcome with emotion that

> . . . contenance for a throwe
> He loste, til he mihte knowe
> The sothe: bot in his memoire
> The man which lith in purgatoire
> Desireth noght the hevene more,
> That he ne longeth al so sore
> To wite what him schal betide.   (II.1419–25)

The simile of purgatory and heaven further refines the theological connotation of the discovery scene with a lightly eschatological allusion. Constance does not represent the Beatific Vision, but Alla's final union with his wife would have been impossible without his desire for a deepening of faith through sacramental confession. The discovery of Constance coincides with and even results from this spiritual purpose.

Husband and wife are united at last, and we begin to see that the stages in the discovery of Constance's identity constitute the reintegration of a self: the union of her miracle-working, proselytizing, and alluring femininity with her ordinary human role as mother and wife. Her identity is still incomplete, however, and we are told of Alla,

> Bot so yit cowthe he nevere plese
> His wif, that sche him wolde sein
> Of hire astat the trowthe plein,
> Of what contre that sche was bore,
> Ne what sche was, and yit therfore
> With al his wit he hath don sieke.   (II.1450–55)

Having perceived the combination of the supernatural and the ordinary in Constance, Alla still does not know she is a princess. The son Morris is sent to the emperor, as he was to Alla, to invite him to a feast. Constance then rides out to meet him and reveals herself. There is great joy, and Morris is designated as the emperor's heir. Alla's final discovery of the identity of Constance as a princess, by which fact his son becomes heir to the Roman Empire, adds a social and political note to the personal and theological consummation of the story. Not only is Constance once more united to her husband and her father, but England becomes heir to the power and prestige of Rome. Alla's belief in the good reputation of Constance and his conversion to Christianity receive their material reward, which can be seen as an objectification of the spiritual kingdom dramatized by the humility associated with the concealment of her identity. Constance has gone from being the cynosure of Roman society, to being totally isolated during the attempted assault in the boat, and back again to union with the society of her husband and father, and finally to union with the whole of the Roman Empire through her son. Her remarkable odyssey dramatizes the spiritual and temporal triumph of good reputation, bolstered by authentic Christian identity, over the evil of detraction. The divine voice that counters the detraction of Constance indicts Amans's carelessness with his rivals' reputations, and the difference between reputation and identity enacted in her life exhorts him to spiritual self-discovery.

IV

In Book VII, under Truth, the first point of Policy, the story of Alcestis illustrates the speech of a woman in prayer. The motivation of Alcestis in her prayer is to seek the truth about her husband's cure. Her prayer is answered by the audible speech of the pagan goddess of wisdom, Minerva, who was often interpreted as Wisdom in the biblical sense. This juxtaposition of "trowthe," woman, and God, in Gower's particular phrasing, suggests a common characteristic in the three elements of the alignment. "Trowthe," at the beginning of the section, means truth as a quality of speech, but in the story of Alcestis its meaning is extended to fidelity and generous love. Discussing "trowthe" as fidelity in the context of truth as a quality of speech puts the whole section in the context of amorous conversation. Love of her husband motivates Alcestis's speech of prayer.

Truth, as the first point of policy, regulates man in his relations with God and other men:

> Among the vertus on is chief,
> And that is trouthe, which is lief
> To god and ek to man also. . . .   (VII.1723–25)

The encompassing nature of this virtue is indicated by making it the principal moral excellence, but its particular relationship to speech is clear from Aristotle's injunction to Alexander that he love truth with his whole heart:

> So that his word be trewe and plein,
> Toward the world and so certein
> That in him be no double speche:
>
> . . . .
>
> The word is tokne of that withinne,
> Ther schal a worthi king beginne
> To kepe his tunge and to be trewe,
> So schal his pris ben evere newe.   (VII.1731–40)

After further praise of this virtue, Genius tells the story of Alcestis within a narrative adapted from the Third Book of Esdras. Daires the Persian calls together three counselors and asks them which is the most powerful: wine, woman, or the king. Arphages, giving the first answer, chooses the power of the king; Manachaz describes the superior power of wine; and Zorobabel asserts that the strength and influence of woman surpass the claims of king and wine. The biblical story then comes to the point that justifies its inclusion under "trouthe." After illustrating the power of women, Zorobabel delivers a discourse on truth as the most powerful force of all. His exaltation of this quality emphasizes the contrast of evil human action:

> Wine is evil, the king is evil, women are evil, all the sons of men are evil, and all their works are evil, and there is no truth in them, and they will perish in their evil, and truth remains and grows strong forever and lives and holds strong for all ages.[20]

Genius's way of telling Zorobabel's answer departs significantly from the source. First, he embellishes Zorobabel's illustration of woman's power with a courtly statement about woman as an incentive to virtue:

> Among the men is no solas,
> If that ther be no womman there;
> For bot if that the wommen were,
> This worldes joie were aweie:
> *Thurgh hem men finden out the weie*
> *To knighthode and to worldes fame;*
> *Thei make a man to drede schame,*
> *And honour forto be desired:*
> Thurgh the beaute of hem is fyred
> The Dart of which Cupide throweth,
> Wherof the jolif peine groweth,
> Which al the world hath under fote.   (VII.1900–1911;
>   my italics)

Genius, in contrast to Zorobabel, posits a causal relationship between woman and virtue, or the pursuit of knighthood and honor, which is one of the meanings of "trouthe" in this section. This relationship foreshadows the conclusion of the section. Before Genius comes to the real climax of Zorobabel's answer, that truth is most powerful, he tells the story of Alcestis. It is important to recognize the fact that the power of "trouthe" and the character of woman are united in the person of Alcestis to such an extent that she becomes a synecdoche for "trouthe." The tale begins with her husband Admetus in a condition of mortal illness. Significantly, speech as prayer plays an important role in the story:

> Alceste his wif goth forto preie,
> As sche which wolde thonk deserve,
> With Sacrifice unto Minerve,
> To wite ansuere of the goddesse
> Hou that hir lord of his seknesse,
> Wherof he was so wo besein,
> Recovere myhte his hele ayein.
> Lo, thus sche cride and thus sche preide,
> Til ate laste a vois hir seide,
> That if sche wolde for his sake
> The maladie soffre and take,
> And deie hirself, he scholde live.
> Of this ansuere Alceste hath yive
> Unto Minerve gret thonkinge,
> So that hir deth and his livinge
> Sche ches with al hire hole entente. . . .   (VII.1920–35)

Since the prayer is on behalf of her husband, and since it is a prayer rather than another kind of speech, both the amorous and religious motifs are suggested. Moreover, "trouthe" in speech is best illustrated by prayer, since, as we have indicated earlier, "trouthe" is the goal and reward of prayer. "Trouthe" in speech is also obviously present in a miraculous divine voice answering the prayer of a woman who loves faithfully or in "trouthe." She actively accepts and assimilates the message as a remedially truthful directive. We should also note that the answer to her prayer involves a permanent withdrawal from the pleasure of human love, an effect which harmonizes with what is required of Amans. Here again we may suggest, because of the divine voice and the context of "trouthe," the analogy of the operation of the Word in the soul.

The comment on Alcestis's generosity in giving her life for her husband's recovery clarifies Gower's purpose in intermeshing the classical with the biblical story:

> So mai a man be reson taste,
> Hou next after the god above

> The trouthe of wommen and the love,
> In whom that alle grace is founde,
> Is myhtiest upon this grounde
> And most behovely manyfold.   (VII.1944–49)

Opposed to the theme of "iniquae mulieres" of Zorobabel, Genius's statement virtually identifies woman and "trouthe," because, as suggested by the adjectives, "myhtiest" and "behovely," they share an almost identical function as executors of God's power and providence. The next speech of Genius adheres more closely to the biblical narrative:

> Lo, thus Zorobabel hath told
> The tale of his opinion:
> Bot for final conclusion
> What strengest is of erthli thinges,
> The wyn, the wommen or the kinges,
> He seith that trouthe above hem alle
> Is myhtiest, hou evere it falle.   (VII.1950–56)

This praise of truth's supremacy, which continues for almost thirty lines, raises the problem of a seeming inconsistency. In the last two passages quoted above, Genius says first that the "trouthe" of woman is most powerful and secondly that "trouthe," whether found in a woman or not, is in itself most powerful. The solution to the problem is that woman and truth are identified by a synecdochal relationship. The relationship in this section among the members of the series, speech, woman, truth, and God is simply juxtapositive or paratactic, but the following connection is clearly implied: Speech is incomplete without "trouthe," which derives from and leads ultimately to God, and is best exemplified in a virtuous woman. Because of her synecdochal participation in this process, woman is figurally identified with "trouthe."

Since this portion of the poem, Book VII, has a didactic centrality, we are justified in reading this treatment of the Alcestis story as a culmination of Gower's "legend of good women." Constance, the hag in the story of Florent, Peronelle in the Three Questions, Thaise, the daughter of Apollonius, whose story comes late in Book VIII, and the Blessed Virgin, present symbolically in stories with the Annunciation theme, are instruments of divine truth in their manner of speaking in reference to human love. The conversations these women have with their lovers are atypical of the conventional amorous exchange, which has been sufficiently indicated, however, by the emblem of the Sirens at the beginning of the poem and by the treatment of the lady's speech in the section on Delicacy.

From the examples discussed in this chapter, we can generalize briefly to some notion of Gower's view of human love. The conversation of human love can be an analogue of God's conversation with the soul as experienced in hearing the word of God. The command of Amans's lady that he stop his amorous pleading, a surrender of speech illustrated by the tale of Florent, is God's word for Amans. The amorously persuasive preaching of Constance is a hint to Amans about where he can find a more satisfying love than that which impels him to a rhetorical use of the sin of detraction. The nourishment of the word of God, a theme contained allegorically in the biblical story of Lazarus and Dives, is opposed to his gluttonous appetite for his lady's words. The conversation between Alcestis and Minerva, goddess of wisdom, consisting of a prayer and the answer of a divine voice, is a climactic illustration of truth in speech and the role of woman in sexual love considered in a Christian context. Human love is unsuitable for Amans as an individual. Its attraction for him is a siren's song that occasions gluttony and detraction, but Gower's basic view stresses the deeply religious potentialities of amorous experience.

5

Dialogue and Recognition

The primary narrative structure of Gower's poem is, of course, a confessional dialogue between Amans and Genius, preceded and followed by a prayer-conversation with Venus. Our whole concern in reading the poem has been the dialogue stories, but even within this perspective there are examples which more closely mirror the overall framework of the poem. More precisely, the roles of Venus and Genius as counselors are most explicit, and, although the element of counsel is never completely absent from the dialogue stories, a number of them share the expressed emphasis of the framework paradigm. The function of a counselor is to inform and reveal, in accordance with true friendship, avoiding the excessive praise of flattery and the meaningless blame of contentiousness. Essential to the sacramental dialogue of confession is the acknowledgment of sin, and to this end the counsel of confession is directed. Analogous to this confessional requirement is a primary element of plot which Aristotle calls the anagnorisis, or recognition scene.[1] The last complete story in Gower's poem, as I hope to show, gives us a blend of the two: The recognition scene of the romance of Appollonius of Tyre is tied in with the necessity for Amans to acknowledge his sin, not simply in its specific relation to a misguided sexuality, but in relation to a whole moral order that issues from Providence through the promulgation of the Word into the various laws of fortune and society.[2] The recognition scenes of the other stories we will look at are similarly parallel to the confessional acknowledgment and are initiated by the speech of a counselor, usually the word of God in some form.

This chapter is divided into five sections, the first of which deals with the relation of the Word to confession and counsel. After discussing the initial conversation between Venus and Amans which precedes the confession proper, we proceed to the story of Perseus and Medusa. The sword of Mercury, upon which this story centers, contains in a single image the twofold obligation of listening to and declaring the "trouthe." The allusion to Mercury has the additional very important effect of introducing the theology of the Verbum to the confessional situation. The fulfillment of the lover's desire for verbal completeness and persuasiveness is also suggested by the allusion.

The second section begins with another story involving Mercury, from whose conversations Lycurgus receives a sense of justice and the ability to use his powers of verbal persuasion to found a legal system. Complementing this with a Christian variation on the same pattern, the story of Constantine shows the progression from the counsel of natural law to the Word as embodied in the gospel and establishing the basis of social order.

In the third section of this chapter, the theme of counsel to a king continues with the implication that every man has a moral realm to govern. All the stories in this section are taken from the discussion of Flattery in Book VII and display an emphasis on tactless candor as the appropriate remedy. The criteria of the virtues of truth and friendship are applied to counsel throughout the section, and in the final story, flattery is countered by an ironic use of the word of God.

The fourth section examines the story of Apollonius of Tyre, which constitutes an important transition from the use of exempla in the poem to the final confession of Amans. The theme of the story concerns the unfathomable workings of fortune's interference in human love. The acknowledgment of fortune as an instrument of God's providence, with which the story of Apollonius concludes, is the model which Amans must follow in his final confession and recognition.

The fifth and last section of this chapter concerns the conclusion of the poem, where the two dialogues of confession and prayer are so closely related as to preclude separate treatment. The possession of truth made possible by confession enables the poet to make a final request for love, no longer considered as the union of the lover with his lady, but the emotional and intellectual union of man with God which results in charity toward all men.

I

The introductory dialogues that Amans engages in, first with Venus and then with Genius, are followed by three brief prefatory exempla relating to the senses of hearing and sight, the most important of which, for our purposes, is the emblematic story of Medusa and Perseus. The ideal resplendence of sexuality, the Venus Celestis,[3] has eluded Amans; his response has not been to sexual beauty in its existential relation to all that is creative and unitive, but in its capacity to numb and confuse. The Venus of the poem is this ideal conception of sexuality, who by demanding that Amans search out his "trouthe" in confession, relates the ideal to the acknowledgment of a total world order. Medusa, a demonic antitype of Venus, represents Amans's distorted experience of sexuality, and the sword of Mercury, by which she is destroyed, points the way toward an authentic sexuality through the speech of confession. Hence the emphasis on sickness that runs through Amans's first conversation with Venus is heightened and specified by the immediately following reference to Medusa, and the urgent importance of plain speech, brought out in Amans's initial conversation with Genius, is embodied in the sword of Mercury.

The first framework dialogue begins with Amans at the point of death, praying to Venus for grace, whereupon she appears and bids him say his "trouthe." The fact that Amans is puzzled by this requirement indicates the necessity of counsel in the poem, for obviously he fails to understand the nature of his guilt:

> O Venus, queene of loves cure,
> Thou lif, thou lust, thou mannes hele,
> Behold my cause and my querele,
> And yif me som part of thi grace,
> So that I may finde in this place
> If thou be gracious or non.   (I.132–37)

From Amans's point of view, the poem begins and ends with a prayer. When Venus appears, Amans declares his lovesickness and asks whether he shall live or die. Her immediate response is an exhortation to confession. She stresses the dependence of the cure on his revelation of the malady and the importance of "trowthe" to the whole process. When Amans identifies himself as a servant of hers who has long attended her and deserves some reward for his pains, Venus becomes suspicious. Her assertion assumes the opposition between frequently false amorous speech and the truth demanded by confession:

> And sche began to loure tho,
> And seide, 'Ther is manye of yow
> Faitours, and so may be that thow
> Art riht such on, and be feintise
> Seist that thou hast me do servise.'   (I.172–76)

If the conventional Venus of medieval love poetry favors lying, this one does not. To the dismay of Amans, she wants some assurance of his "trowthe":

> And natheles sche wiste wel,
> Mi world stod on an other whiel
> Withouten eny faiterie:
> Bot algate of my maladie
> Sche bad me telle and seie hir trowthe.   (I.177–81)

Amans's feeling about the injustice of Venus's suspicion is important. He considers his "trowthe" unimpeachable because he sincerely loves his lady, but by "trowthe" Venus means his total physical and moral capacity for love.

His sexual impotence, which is clearly stated at the end of the poem (VIII.2412–39), is an external counterpart of his spiritual weakness and makes all his protestations of sincerity ludicrously ineffectual.

The next few exchanges between Venus and Amans suggest some reluctance on his part to confess. He protests his willingness too much; Venus, on her part, must order him to begin several times:

> 'Ma dame, if ye wolde have rowthe,'
> Quod I, 'than wolde I telle yow.'
> 'Sey forth,' quod sche, 'and tell me how;
> Schew me thi seknesse everydiel.'   (I.182–85)

Amans balks at the self-probing involved in confession by insisting on his sickness:

> 'Ma dame, that can I do wel,
> Be so my lif therto wol laste.'
> With that hir lok on me sche caste,
> And seide: 'In aunter if thou live,
> Mi will is ferst that thou be schrive. . . .'   (I.186–90)

Both the necessity and the difficulty of verbal declaration in the poem are clearly established by this mild altercation. The withdrawal of the rather awesome goddess and the arrival of the confessor alleviate the difficulty somewhat, and further help will be found in the grace of the Word, indicated by the conventional meanings of the god Mercury, which we will shortly examine.

The confessor Genius begins the second framework dialogue, and in his opening words we see another contrast between confession and the speech of love. After the opening "Benedicite" he emphasizes plainness of speech, which, as we have seen, is not the common technique of lovers:

> What thou er this for loves sake
> Hast felt, let nothing be forsake,
> Tell pleinliche as it is befalle.   (I.209–11)

The requirement of "trouthe" in confession constitutes an uninterrupted comment on the many stories of deceitful lovers told throughout the poem. Whereas the lady inhibits the lover's communication, the confessor, by counsel and sympathetic interrogation, will respond to his troubled appeal:

> I prai the let me noght mistime
> Mi schrifte, for I am destourbed
> In al myn herte, and so contourbed,
> That I ne may my wittes gete,
> So schal I moche thing foryete:
> Bot if thou wolt my schrifte oppose

> Fro point to point, thanne I suppose,
> Ther schal nothing be left behinde.
> Bot now my wittes ben so blinde,
> That I ne can miselven teche.   (I.220–29)

The confessional dialogue, by intimate and orderly analysis in the service of memory, will integrate his scattered wits. Genius, by his use of the verb *preche* in his reply to Amans, acknowledges his correlative duty to convey the word of God:

> Tho he began anon to preche,
> And with his wordes debonaire
> He seide tome softe and faire. . . .   (I.230–32)

An atmosphere of friendship is suggested by his affable manner. Genius promises to expound the vices clearly and state their relevance to love, for he knows that the completeness of the confession depends largely upon his part in the dialogue. Clarity and plainness of speech are necessary to both penitent and confessor:

> For what a man schal axe or sein
> Touchende of schrifte, it mot be plein,
> It nedeth noght to make it queinte,
> For trowthe his wordes wol noght peinte:
> That I wole axe of the forthi,
> My Sone, it schal be so pleinly,
> That thou schalt knowe and understonde
> The pointz of schrifte how that thei stonde.   (I.281–88)

Appropriate to our emphasis on the relationship between framework and contained dialogues is the second of three brief stories told by Genius to demonstrate the temptations of sight and hearing. The story of Perseus and Medusa contains a suggestion of how to overcome the evils of "Mislook" in that Perseus is victorious through his use of the shield of Pallas and the sword of Mercury. The likelihood that this presage of moral victory at the beginning of the poem should contain some hint of the part played by speech is validated by the use Perseus makes of Mercury's sword. This sword, as we shall see, suggests many of the uses of speech that we have described: the speech of the penitent, which requires considerable moral courage; the difficulty of the speech of the lover to the lady; and the confessor's speech to the penitent.

The snaky locks of Medusa change those who gaze on her, and are guilty of "mislook," into stone. Perseus, by using the shield of Pallas and the sword of Mercury, overcomes her power and destroys her:

> Bot Perseus that worthi knyht,
> Whom Pallas of hir grete myht

> Halp, and tok him a Schield therto,
> And ek the god Mercurie also
> Lente him a swerd. . . .   (I.419–23)

The significance of the story is as follows: Amans can be cured of his sickness, admittedly an effect of gazing on Medusa, by learning from the example of Perseus—that is, by using the shield of Pallas, which is an obvious metaphor of self-knowledge, and the sword of Mercury, which I interpret, on the evidence of the mythographical commentaries, as a metaphor of speech. That is, Amans must carefully examine his conscience and give explicit verbal form to what he discovers. Moreover, the sword itself, as we will show later, represents not only Amans's confession but also the counsel of the confessor.

That Medusa is a metaphor of excessive love is indicated by the context of the *Confessio Amantis*. When Genius asks Amans if his eyes are guilty of Mislook, he replies:

> I have hem cast upon Meduse,
> Therof I may me noght excuse:
> Min herte is growen into Ston
> So that my lady therupon
> Hath such a priente of love grave,
> That I can noght miselve save.   (I.551–56)

The rather startling fact that Amans admits the figure of Medusa as a symbolic substitute for his lady in some sense indicates the ambiguity of his own response to love. Even in the terms of the context exclusively, Medusa represents destructive sexuality and the cause of his sickness. The association of excessive love, or lust, with Medusa has some foundation in Ovid, who explains her ugliness as the result of an unchaste action—her rape by Neptune in the temple of Athena:

> Medusa was once renowned for her loveliness, and roused jealous hopes in the hearts of many suitors. Of all the beauties she possessed, none was more striking than her lovely hair. I have met someone who claimed to have seen her in those days. But, so they say, the lord of the sea robbed her of her virginity in the temple of Minerva. Jove's daughter turned her back, hiding her modest face behind her aegis: and to punish the Gorgon for her deed, she changed her hair into revolting snakes. To this day, in order to terrify her enemies and numb them with fear, the goddess wears as a breastplate the snakes that were her own creation.[4]

That the goddess whose temple was violated lends her shield for the final destruction of Medusa is noteworthy. Although it would seem that Neptune is the guilty party, Medusa's original innocence is an unchivalric irrelevance not uncommon in mythology. The quality of hers which was most beautiful, her hair, becomes most ugly. We see here a pattern, frequent in myth and mythographical commentaries, of a kind of poetic justice, suggesting, in a Christian context, the possible misuse of any reality—here the potentially destructive aspects of creatural beauty. Boccaccio's interpretation of the change is not far from making this point. To him the power of Medusa has sexual overtones, although subtly perceived. The transformation of the beholders into stone is the effect of extraordinary physical beauty:

> That the onlookers were turned into stone is a fiction that means, in my opinion, that the greatness of their beauty astounded the viewers who became mute and immobile not otherwise than if they had become stones.[5]

We should note particularly in this passage the word *mute*, which fits into the convention of the difficulty the lover has speaking to his lady.

The commentary of Bersuire definitely implies lust and the resulting debility of reason, a theme that occurs frequently in the *Confessio:*

> These snakelike monsters can signify evil and beautiful women who have a snakelike, that is, malicious, nature. . . . They change those who look at them into stone: for from viewing and beholding women, men become stones: that is, they are made insensible and because of the stupor and temptation they conceive, they are deprived of the sense of proper discretion.[6]

It seems quite obvious, then, in view of the connection between Medusa and lust, that when Amans admits to having gazed on her, he is designating excessive love or lust as the cause of his present sickness. Immoderate love, as the subject of the whole poem, is mentioned early in Book I, where Gower states his subject matter:

> And that is love, of which I mene
> To trete, as after schal be sene.
> In which ther can noman him reule,
> For loves lawe is out of reule,
> That of *tomoche or of tolite*
> Welnyh is every man to wyte. . . .   (I.15–20; my italics)

Gower's emphasis here is Aristotelian, suggesting that the ideal is a mean between excess and defect. The first Latin marginal note of Book One emphasizes excess: "Et quia nonnulli amantes ultra quam expedit desiderii passionibus crebro stimulantur, materia libri per totum super hiis specialius diffunditur." (And because several lovers are incited beyond what is expedient to the passions of desire, the matter of this book is especially concerned with these things throughout.)[7]

Just as Perseus used the sword of Mercury to render the power of Medusa inefficacious, so Amans must confess by word of mouth to remove the effects of lust from his soul. The obligation of verbal declaration with an emphasis on "trowthe" is clearly a part of Gower's poetic machinery. The probability that the sword of Mercury would remind the reader of the role of speech in confession rests on a number of mythographical commentaries. Explaining the classical story, Giovanni del Virgilio interprets the sword as the word: "The virtuous man, therefore, wishes to kill her [Medusa] and takes up the shield of wisdom and the sword of virtue, which is the *word (eloquium)* and overcomes her" (my italics).[8] The combination of wisdom and strength (the Latin *virtus* has this additional connotation) is explicitly referred to in the text, where Perseus,

> which *wisdom* and *prouesse*
> Hadde of the god and the godesse,
> The Schield of Pallas gan enbrace,
> With which he covereth sauf his face,
> Mercuries Swerd and out he drowh,
> And so he bar him that he slowh
> These dredful Monstres alle thre.   (I.429–35; my italics)

Since Gower discusses the sacrament of confession in the *Mirour de l'omme* as part of the virtue of Prouesce,[9] the use of the term here in conjunction with the sword of Mercury suggests an allusion to the sacrament.

The curved or two-directional quality of Mercury's sword suggests to Bersuire the reciprocity of hearing the word of God and responding by prayer: "a curved sword, that is, the word of God and prayer. . . ."[10] John of Garland makes Perseus virtue and the sword eloquence: "Perseus is virtue and by the sickle-shaped sword is meant eloquence."[11] A gloss quoted by Ghisalberti confirms the sword as an instrument of eloquence: ". . . by the sickle-shaped sword of Mercury, that is, by the fluent counsel of the most eloquent men. . . ."[12] The role of counsel in confession is suggested here.

Further evidence of the identification of the sword of Mercury with the word is found in the interpretations of other exploits of Perseus. In his fight to save his future bride, Andromeda, from a sea monster, Perseus again uses the sword of Mercury, which Giovanni del Virgilio identifies as a moral eloquence: "But by Perseus understand virtue, which receives the rational mind as a wife and delivers her from the devil with beautiful words."[13] These words could refer to the speech of a preacher or the words the individual addresses to himself, in the internal colloquy described by Bernard of Clairvaux.[14] In a versified treatment of the same incident, Giovanni del Virgilio repeats his interpretation of the sword as sacred word: Perseus overcomes the monster "with the sword of the sacred word."[15] When Phineus attempts with his followers to rob Perseus of the fruits of his victory, the famous sword serves him in good stead once more. Phineus and his band are the "crimina" which rise up to destroy virtue, but "virtue cuts them down with the word."[16] Again *word* could conceivably refer to prayer or moral persuasion. The curved quality of the sword suggests to Arnulph of Orleans an eloquence tempered by humility: "For *arpis* is a sword curved backwards and signifies the eloquence of a virtuous man which in the way it curves back upon itself never rises to the arrogance of boasting."[17] This interpretation is almost a definition of the Thomist-Aristotelian virtue of truth, which enjoins effective speech without the extreme of *iactantia*.[18]

Boccaccio's discussion of the relation between Mercury and speech, in terms of the physiological means of producing articulate sounds and of the urgency of the attempt to communicate, illustrates the power of the myth to span the whole physical and spiritual experience. Just as Amans is made physically infirm by his love, the cure of confession demands physical exertion. The planetary cause of the relationship between Mercury and speech in the following passage is overshadowed by the appreciation of speech as the means of delivering man from the isolation of his "secreta":

> I believe then that the ancients wanted some Mercury or other to be the god of eloquence because the mathematicians assert that every sound-producing organ looks to the planet Mercury or that it provides a pipe in our bodies, and hence many believe him designated the messenger and interpreter of the gods, because through the organs ordered by him our innermost hearts are laid open, which can be called the secrets of the gods, since unless they are expressed by speech or a nod, no one but God knows them, and thus is he the interpreter of such secrets, for words, which are organized by organs, are by him [Mercury] disposed, interpreted, and disclosed, for they cannot be sufficiently understood by a nod only.[19]

The convention of the lover's difficulty in speaking is interpreted in at least one instance as a result of lust; Rémi of Auxerre, in the course of explaining the "picture" of Cupid, makes such a connection:

> A boy is depicted because base love is puerile and so speech often fails in lovers as in boys. Hence Virgil: "She began to speak, and stopped in mid voice" [*Aeneid* IV. 76].[20]

The reference is, of course, to Dido, who is made speechless by Aeneas. Servius, commenting on this passage in the *Aeneid*, refers to a similar speechlessness recorded by Horace in an amorous situation.[21] In Book IV of his *Carmina*, the first song, beginning "Intermissa, Venus, diu/ Rursus bella moves," has the following stanza:

> My Ligurinus, why
> Should the reluctant-flowing tears surprise these dry
>   Cheeks, and my fluent tongue
> Stumble in unbecoming silences among
>   Syllables?[22]

The figure of Mercury, because of the identification with speech and words, came to be interpreted in the Christian tradition as the Word par excellence, the Second Person of the Trinity. In the Greek philosophical tradition, the Neoplatonic Logos was identified with the god Hermes (the Latin Mercury); the Christian apologist Justin took the next logical step and drew a parallel between the Hermes-Logos and the Jesus-Logos. "In this we are at one with you," he says, "in that we both regard the Logos, whom you call Hermes, as the messenger of God."[23] Hippolytus also affirms the identity of Hermes and the Logos and a passage in the Pseudo-Clementine *Recognitiones* states that "Mercury by tradition is the *Word*."[24] Augustine seems to refer to this tradition in a criticism of Varro in the *De Civitate Dei*.[25] When Genius, the confessor, urges the imitation of Perseus, who relied on the aid of Mercury, there is the implication that Amans should invoke the assistance of the Word for his own words. Amans, or the Christian, can speak only what is spoken to him. Augustine describes this dependence of the just man on the Word:

> *I became deaf, and I was brought low, and I was silent of the good.* Ps. 38:3. Whence was I to say good things, unless indeed I heard them? *For you will give my hearing exultation and joy.* And the friend of the spouse stands and hears him, and greatly rejoices because of the voice, not his own, but of the spouse. In order to say the truth, he hears what he should say. For the man who speaks a lie, speaks on his own.[26]

In these last two sentences, we have again the notion that the truth of man's speech depends on the degree to which he listens to the Word in his soul. A less closely reasoned comparison between the spoken word and the Second Person of the Trinity than that developed by Augustine in the *De Trinitate* appears in the *De Naturis Rerum* of Alexander Neckam. It is significant that Neckam does not equate Mercury himself with the Word; he devotes attention simply to Mercury's rod, only an aspect of the god's accoutrement. It is clear from the passage, however, that the physical and psychological aspects of speech, the iconography of Mercury, and the Verbum are linked in a more or less inevitable association :

> Although I do not indeed believe that the voice is air, yet without the help of air it can be neither produced nor heard. The voice then is heard by many without any loss of itself, so that by a certain generosity of nature, it grants the use of itself to many without envy or diminution. Whence also the word of the Father is enough for the whole world, gives itself entirely to the whole church, a common solace and a common salvation. The word of the Father is wisdom. Wisdom is a noble treasure, because without any detriment to itself, it offers itself to all and suffices all. The voice indeed sets forth the passions of the soul, so that the living voice literally prints on the

minds of the listeners the character of thought more efficaciously than dead marks. I don't know what kind of latent energy, or internal working, the living voice has within itself. The voice, even when its production has already stopped, still seems to speak internally in the soul of the hearer. For words are sharp arrows, drawing a kind of fervent blood from the inmost heart. Words enter deep within the soul, so that at times the soul is pierced by the sting of pain, at times joyfully depicts for itself images of delight. Is the painting of the rod of Mercury pointless, that represents one part as life-giving, and another part as deadly? Are not life and death in the power of the tongue?[27]

The relaxed, associative development of this passage is modally similar to the use of speech in the *Confessio Amantis* itself and contains the main elements of our overall interpretation. The excellence and power of the spoken word derive from the more than metaphorical relationship between it and the "verbum patris," the Second Person of the Trinity. The spoken word is also a sign of the person of the speaker, for just as the "verbum patris" is the summation of the Father's knowledge, the spoken word of a man "sets forth the passions of the soul, so that it seems to be a kind of letter of the internal will." The importance attached to the psychological power of the spoken word recalls the almost magical virtue attributed to speech during the Middle Ages. The relation of all this to Mercury is markedly synecdochic: by being a consistent element in this recurrent sequence of meanings, he stands for them all.

A quotation from a commentary on the *De Nuptiis Mercurii et Philologiae* will conclude our discussion of the association of Mercury with the Verbum. The commentary is unpublished and tentatively attributed to Alexander Neckam. Philologia is interpreted as a man who, led by reason, seeks his *principium* or origin. Since Mercury, as the Verbum, is this origin, we have once again the pattern described by Augustine: "So the likeness of the created image approaches as much as possible the likeness of the begotten image. . . ." The passage treats the paradox within the *De Nuptiis* that speech is considered more noble than reason. The solution is that the speech referred to is the Word:

> The fact that the dignity of Mercury is everywhere preferred to that of Philologia is evident here. Mercury is understood as the Word, that is, the son of God. Otherwise it would make no sense, since the discourse of the mind is nobler than the speech of the mouth. To this, that is, to the son of God, is Philologia wedded, that is, the man, who with reason as his guide, tends to his origin [principium]. What then should be understood through Mercury and Philologia if not husband and wife, that is, Christ and the church. . . .[28]

The referential extensiveness of the sword of Mercury in terms of the meanings outlined above permeates the whole *Confessio Amantis*. Perseus's use of the sword to decapitate Medusa represents the confessional dialogue and foreshadows all the situations in the exempla in which the word of God enters the action and provokes a recognition scene.

II

The presence of Mercury as the counselor who most effectively initiates an acknowledgment of an embracing moral order figures prominently and appropriately in the discussion of Justice in Book VII. The analogue to the counsel of confession here is the promulgation of law, which Mercury gives to Lycurgus and which Lycurgus in turn gives to the Athenians. In the *Gesta Romanorum*, Gower's source for the story, Lycurgus receives the laws from Apollo.[29] By departing from the source and substituting Mercury, the embodiment of pagan eloquence, the speech of Jove, and, by virtue of a long tradition, the Verbum, Gower reinforces the theme of counsel within a precise framework of the speech *topos*. Furthermore the role of the Verbum in the promulgation of the eternal law exactly parallels the function of Mercury in Gower's adaptation of the Lycurgus story. According to Aquinas, who is here highly traditional, the promulgation of the Eternal Law is by the Verbum: ". . . Promulgation takes place by word and writing, and in each way does the eternal law have promulgation on the part of God, who promulgates, because the divine Word is eternal and the writing of the book of life is eternal."[30] The acknowledgment or confirmation of the eternal law in time was accomplished first of all by the prophets and by Jesus Christ, the Word Incarnate. To quote one of Gower's sources: "The divine law is from nature; and nevertheless it was put into writing and confirmed first by the prophets, and that is the Old Testament. Then there was the New Testament, and it was confirmed by Jesus Christ and his disciples."[31] Eloquence as the cause of an acknowledgment of order manifested in the submission to law is not an uncommon theme in other mythographical configurations. Orpheus's ability to affect the stones by his music is interpreted as the power of eloquence to persuade men to virtue.[32] Mercury plays a similar role in the story of Amphyon, who by the power of his harp makes stones assume the shape of walls, which in turn make possible the Theban state. The harp, given to him by Mercury, is interpreted as eloquence.[33]

Paralleling the acknowledgment made by the penitent are, first, Lycurgus's admission that the source of his laws is divine and, second, the acceptance by the Athenians of the virtual permanence of these laws.

Genius begins the story with an idyllic description of how Lycurgus

> the lawe in every cas,
> Wherof he scholde his poeple reule,

> Hath set upon so good a reule,
> In al this world that cite non
> Of lawe was so wel begon
> Forth with the trouthe of governance.   (VII.2920–25)

"Trouthe of governance" means a correspondence between justice and the administration of the laws; the phrase suggests the similarity between human and eternal law. The result of Lycurgus's rule was that the common good was preferred to the singular, and love and peace existed without envy. The basis of the order is the correspondence between the system of Lycurgus, who is described as one who "for evere wolde plese/ The hihe god" (VII.2940–41), and the divine mind. In a parliament summoned to further ensure the preservation of law, he formally recognizes and acknowledges Mercury as the source of his legal inspiration:

> Bot of o thing I am *beknowe*,
> The which mi will is that ye knowe:
> The lawe which I tok on honde,
> Was altogedre of goddes sonde
> And nothing of myn oghne wit. . . .
> The god Mercurius and no man
> He hath me tawht al that I can
> Of suche lawes as I made,
> Wherof that ye ben alle glade;
> It was the god and nothing I. . . .   (VII.2959–71; my italics)

This part of Lycurgus's statement is primarily an acknowledgment, but it is also the beginning of an attempt to counsel the Athenians to an enduring acceptance of the order he has brought. Mercury, he declares, has summoned him to an island for further instruction in governance:

> He hath comanded of his grace
> That I schal come into a place
> Which is forein out in an yle,
> Wher I mot tarie for a while,
> With him to speke, as he hath bede.
> For as he seith, in thilke stede
> He schal me suche thinges telle,
> That evere, whyl the world schal duelle,
> Athenis schal the betre fare.   (VII.2973–81)

Having made public this divine message, Lycurgus must obtain some kind of ratification. He eloquently urges the Athenians to swear, to make a solemn verbal agreement, that they will keep the laws he has given them, while he is away conversing with the god:

> Bot ferst, er that I thider fare,
> For that I wolde that mi lawe

> Amonges you ne be withdrawe
> Ther whyles that I schal ben oute,
> Forthi to setten out of doute
> Bothe you and me, this wol I preie,
> That ye me wolde assure and seie
> With such an oth as I wol take,
> That ech of you schal undertake
> Mi lawes forto kepe and holde.   (VII.2982–91)

What the Athenians are presented with is, in effect, a hieratic example of a ruler in prayer—more specifically, in a dialogue with the Verbum. His proposal is accepted:

> Thei seiden alle that thei wolde,
> And therupon thei swore here oth,
> That fro the time that he goth,
> Til he to hem be come ayein,
> Thei scholde hise lawes wel and plein
> In every point kepe and fulfille.   (VII.2992–97)

The acceptance of this pact has indeed involved the Athenians in an anagnorisis, a movement from ignorance to knowledge in regard to the divine authority of their ruler. The proof of this lies in their suspension of dissent and almost millennial confidence that he will in some fashion return.

The companion piece to the Lycurgus story in the context of promulgation and acceptance of law is that of Constantine and Silvester. In Canto XXVII of Dante's *Inferno*, Guido of Montefeltro, in recounting the act that brought him from conversion once more to sin, contrasts with bitter irony his own conduct with that of Silvester, whose preaching of Christianity to Constantine is the subject of Gower's story. Suffering in the *bolgia* of the evil counselors and appropriately enveloped in a tongue of flame, Guido alludes to a piece of advice which became archetypal for the Middle Ages and which he should have emulated instead of aiding Boniface VIII, whom both Dante and Gower excoriate:

> But as Constantine sought out Sylvester in Soracte to cure his leprosy, so this man sought me out as his physician to cure the fever of his pride.[34]

The counsel that Silvester brings to completion in Constantine is initiated in the mind of the ruler and involves a recognition and rejection of sin, an offense against what is very clearly the natural law.

The development of the action originates in some particularly cruel counsel. Constantine has contracted leprosy, and the "grete clerkes" he summons advise him to bathe in the blood of children under seven years of age:

> So longe thei togedre dele,
> That thei upon this medicine
> Apointen hem, and determine
> That in the maner as it stod
> Thei wolde him bathe in childes blod
> Withinne sevene wynter age. . . .   (II.3202–7)

After he has gathered the children, however, other voices occasion another kind of counsel:

> The Modres wepe in here degre,
> And manye of hem aswoune falle,
> The yonge babes criden alle:
> This noyse aros, the lord it herde,
> And loked out, and how it ferde
> He sih, and as who seith abreide
> Out of his slep. . . .   (II.3236–42)

The wailing of the mothers and children, an inarticulate but powerful form of complaint, stresses the nonhuman level to which they have been reduced, but, paradoxically, it is more effective than the more sophisticated persuasion of the great clerks. This display of genuine grief promulgates a law of the human condition and is matched by an unspectacular recognition on the part of Constantine. He acknowledges in the privacy of his soul that all men, subjects and rulers alike, are governed by what "kinde hath in hire lawe set. . . ." The leveling power of fortune begets in Constantine a sense of pity and responsibility. Just as Lycurgus converses with Mercury, the Word as lawgiver, Constantine progresses in his interior monologue to a remembrance of the divine author of the law of nature:

> And ek he tok a remembrance
> How he that made lawe of kinde
> Wolde every man to lawe binde,
> And bad a man, such as he wolde
> Toward himself, riht such he scholde
> Toward an other don also.   (II.3274–79)

We must remember here that the promulgation of this law, a temporal manifestation of Eternal Law, was thought to be a special function of the Verbum.

Rejecting the counsel of his doctors, Constantine dismisses the children and uses money from his own treasury to send them home with their mothers. The counsel implicit in the promulgation of law continues to spark the development of the plot. Constantine is visited by Saints Peter and Paul, who advise him to find Pope Silvester for the cure of his body and soul; thus, as a reward for his pity, Constantine is given the opportunity for a deeper,

supernatural acknowledgment. Although Constantine has hitherto opposed
the law of Christ, he has merited, by acknowledging the natural law of pity,
to hear the new law of the gospel. The apostles tell Constantine that Silvester
lives on a mountain

> For drede of thee, which many day
> Hast ben a fo to *Cristes lay,*
> And hast destruid to mochel schame
> The prechours of his holy name.
> Bot now thou hast somdiel appesed
> Thi god, and with good dede plesed,
> That thou thi pite hast bewared
> Upon the blod which thou hast spared
> Forthi to thi salvacion
> Thou schalt have enformacioun,
> Such as Silvestre schal the teche:
> Thee nedeth of non other leche.   (II.3353–64; my italics)

As the last four lines of the quotation indicate, the counsel, or the
"enformacioun" of the word of God, will cure his leprosy. Through the clarity
of his preaching, Silvester promulgates the new law of the word of God:

> The ground of al the *newe lawe*
> With gret devocion he precheth,
> Fro point to point and pleinly techeth. . . .   (II.3432–34;
> my italics)

The words which are an essential part of the sacrament of baptism also have a
healing power. As Constantine is standing naked, up to his neck in water, in
the vessel originally intended for the blood of the children, the words of the
sacrament cause the scales of leprosy to fall off:

> And evere among the *holi tales*
> Lich as thei weren fisshes skales
> Ther fellen from him now and eft,
> Til that ther was nothing beleft
> Of al his grete maladie.   (II.3455–59; my italics)

The choice of the phrase *holi tales* suggests an at least symbolic inclusion of
the redemptive events of Christianity, a "telling" and a recapitulation of the
"new law" in the words of baptism.

Gower concludes his story with a conventional derogatory allusion to the
donation of Constantine,[35] who, out of gratitude to Silvester, gives to the
Church "possessioun/ Of lordschipe and of worldes good" (II.3480–81). With
the word "lordschipe," we come once again to the theme of law. In Brunetto
Latini's summary of famous lawgivers, most of whom Gower mentions in
Book VII, the name of Constantine constitutes a climax. After referring to

Moses, Mercury—most important for our discussion—Lycurgus, and other administrators of justice during the period of the Old Law, Latini records the achievement of Constantine: "Mais li empereres Constantins recommenca a fere noviele loi. . . ."[36] Constantine's greatness consisted in his unification of two manifestations of the Eternal Law: He gave the "new law" of Christianity an enduring civil form.

But Gower's attitude is like that of Walther von der Vogelweide[37] in an earlier generation and like that of Dante, who applauded the conversion of Constantine by Silvester but lamented the presumed endowment of the Church with temporal power:

> Ah, Constantine, to how much evil gave birth, not thy conversion, but that dower the first rich Father had from thee![38]

In Gower's story, as soon as Constantine made this donation of power and wealth to the Church,

> A vois was herd on hih the lifte,
> Of which al Rome was adrad,
> And seith: 'Today is venym schad
> In holi cherche of temporal,
> Which medleth with the spirital.'   (II.3488–92)

This awesomely prophetic voice of obviously divine origin not only adds an important qualification to the relationship of divine and civil law, but also completes a pattern of authoritative proclamation which begins in the story immediately preceding that of Constantine and Silvester, the relevance of which requires brief mention here. Motivated by temporal greed, the ecclesiastic who was to become Pope Boniface VIII has a young clerk hide in the closet of Pope Celestine and in the middle of the night blow a trumpet,

> Fro hevene as thogh a vois it were,
> To soune of such prolacioun
> That he his meditacioun
> Therof mai take and understonde,
> As thogh it were of goddes sonde.   (II.2874–78)

The clerk also conveys to Celestine in this flamboyant manner how to go about resigning the papacy, an action which he does perform. Boniface himself then becomes pope and thenceforth a symbol, to Dante as well as to Gower, of the criminal confusion in the church of the temporal with the spiritual (II.2988–89). An allusion to Joachim of Flora's prediction of the commercialization of the church (II.3056–65) reminds us how traumatic the abdication of Pope Celestine was for thirteenth-century Christendom. A genuine idealism as well as a voting deadlock was the impetus behind the election of this unlettered monk, Peter Murrone, to the papacy, but his holiness was unfortunately not complemented by administrative ability. His voluntary resignation, the source of much controversy, was followed by the election of Boniface, an ambitious and worldly prelate whose bull *Unam Sanctam* was the most assertive claim to temporal power ever made by a pope.[39] Gower's story is factually wrong, but structurally appropriate. The voice from heaven prophesying the trouble which will follow the mingling of the temporal and spiritual in the "donation of Constantine" is historically consummated in Boniface VIII, who reverses the order of promulgation and acceptance of divine authority by arrogating to himself the divine voice.

III

The treatment of Flattery in Book VII (ll. 2187–2694), a section of the poem that is in effect devoted exclusively to the speech of blame, demands our special attention. The illumination of Lycurgus by Mercury is direct and meets no resistance; and Constantine's conversion, although a fairly lengthy process, takes place in a willing subject. Recognition seldom comes so easily, however. In the stories of both Lycurgus and Constantine, the emphasis is on their acceptance of the counsel of the word of God and the resulting action taken. In the five stories of this section, however, only one ruler, Caesar, responds to his interlocutor, and Caesar alone in the stories is the object of direct flattery. The silence following the delivery of the reprimands emphasizes the courage of those who will not flatter. The first three of the five stories illustrate a kind of speech that closely approximates contentiousness, the opposite extreme of flattery, with the result that a particularly free speech is advocated. The fact that in the last story the principal counselor is an Old Testament prophet makes a connection between advice to the king and the word of God. We should recall that the discussion of Cheste in Book III developed into an assertion of the lover's right to candid speech to his lady, derived from his right to frankness in prayer.

The flatterer, says Gower, paraphrasing the spurious letter of Aristotle to Alexander, offends God, the king, and society. Flattery is defined as a lie about what pertains to a person intimately:

> Whan thei be sleihte and be fallas
> Of feigned wordes make him wene
> That blak is whyt and blew is grene
> Touchende of his condicion. . . .   (VII.2186–89)

The irony of the virtue of friendship is that the truth often looks like the extreme of defect, or contentiousness; but "correptio amici," in the medieval tradition, is a sign of true friendship. A flatterer will not endanger his own position with the king by this kind of truth:

> For whanne he doth extorcion
> With manye an other vice mo,

> Men schal noght finden on of tho
> To groucche or speke therayein,
> Bot holden up his oil and sein
> That al is wel, what evere he doth;
> And thus of fals thei maken soth. . . .　　　(VII.2190–96)

The first story told in this section is that of Diogenes and Aristippus. After studying philosophy at Athens, they both return to Carthage, where Diogenes continues his intellectual pursuits. Aristippus however goes to the court,

> Wher many a wyle and many a wente
> With flaterie and wordes softe
> He caste, and hath compassed ofte
> How he his Prince myhte plese. . . .　　　(VII.2250–53)

One day Aristippus comes upon Diogenes picking and washing herbs. He chides Diogenes with the remark that if he knew how to please his king, he would not have to pick herbs. Diogenes answers that if Aristippus knew how to pick herbs, he would not have to live by flattery. Aristippus in the episode is guilty of contemptuous speech, which represents the logical swing of the pendulum from his profession of flattery. The reply of Diogenes, in addition to its content of unflattering truth, is wittily phrased. It highlights the value of what is most worthless to Aristippus and declares the superiority of truth to a life of comfort.

We are reminded, in a passage which introduces the next example, that flattery surpasses even money and political advancement in winning affection:

> Bot flaterie passeth alle
> In chambre, whom the court avanceth;
> For upon thilke lot it chanceth
> To be beloved nou aday.　　　(VII.2324–27)

The value of tactlessly truthful speech as an antidote to flattery is stressed. The insistence on candor is driven home in the following passage by the balancing of the twofold repetition of "pleine" and the reflexive irony of "pleigne":

> Bot wher the pleine trouthe is noted,
> Ther may a Prince wel conceive,
> That he schal noght himself deceive,
> Of that he hiereth wordes *pleine;*
> For him thar noght be reson *pleigne,*
> That warned is er him be wo.　　　(VII.2340–45; my italics)

The prince cannot justly "pleigne," that is, indulge in complaint or verbal fault-finding if his advisers have previously been honestly critical and "pleine." The proof is from Roman history:

> And that was fully proeved tho,
> Whan Rome was the worldes chief,
> The Sothseiere tho was lief,
> Which wolde noght the trouthe spare,
> Bot with hise wordes pleine and bare
> To Themperour hise sothes tolde. . . .   (VII.2346–51)

Genius proceeds to a description of the role played by a "Ribald" in the Roman Triumph. To oppose the flattering effect of the chariot drawn by four white horses, the victor's prisoners marching on either side, and the nobles riding in front, the Ribald sat in the chariot audibly recollecting the defects of the emperor's character and life:

> With these wordes and with mo
> This Ribald, which sat with him tho,
> To Themperour his tale tolde:
> And overmor what evere he wolde,
> Or were it evel or were it good,
> So pleinly as the trouthe stod,
> He spareth noght, bot spekth it oute. . . .   (VII.2397–2403)

Not only the Ribald but the total citizenry had the same privilege of virtually contentious speech on this solemn occasion:

> And so myhte every man aboute
> The day of that solempnete
> His tale telle als wel as he
> To Themperour al openly.
> And al was this the cause why;
> That whil he stod in that noblesse,
> He scholde his vanite represse
> With suche wordes as he herde.   (VII.2404–11)

The next example has the same quality of tactless candor. The setting is the coronation day of an emperor. In the middle of the celebration, when "every Disour hadde seid/ What most was plesant to his Ere," in come the masons who inquire with macabre naïveté

> Wher that he wolde be begrave,
> And of what Ston his sepulture
> Thei scholden make, and what sculpture
> He wolde ordeine therupon.   (VII.2428–31)

This example stimulates Gower to a lengthy praise of time past when good counsel prevailed over flattery:

> Tho was ther flaterie non
> The worthi princes to bejape;

> The thing was other wise schape
> With good conseil; and otherwise
> Thei were hemselven thanne wise,
> And understoden wel and knewen.
> Whan suche softe wyndes blewen
> Of flaterie into here Ere,
> Thei setten noght here hertes there;
> Bot whan thei herden wordes feigned,
> The pleine trouthe it hath desdeigned
> Of hem that weren so discrete.
> So tok the flatour no beyete
> Of him that was his prince tho. . . .   (VII.2432–45)

The story of Caesar's answer adds a touch of subtlety to the dominant motif of painful frankness. The structure of the story resembles that of Diogenes and Aristippus in Caesar's inversion of the flatterer's speech. As Caesar is sitting on his throne, a man approaches, falls on his knees, and does him reverence befitting a god. He then arises and sits beside Caesar as a peer. He glosses his conduct as inclusive of the two possibilities that Caesar is either divine or human. If divine, he has given worship; if human, he has acted properly toward a being of the same nature. Caesar exposes the absurdity of the man by observing that he has acted either irreverently by sitting next to a god or foolishly by worshiping a man.

The significance of the device employed by the flatterer lies in its subtlety. On the face of it, it is hard to convict the man of flattery, since his second act is a bold dispraisal of Caesar's rank. Caesar's response is exemplary in its perception of the subtlety of the danger confronting him. Appropriately this example follows the two most extreme examples of candid speech: the role of the Ribald in the Roman triumph and the naïveté of the masons who interrogate the emperor about his taste in funerary monuments on the day of his coronation.

The fifth and last example in this series, the story of Ahab and Micaiah, involves a condemnation of flattery by the speech of God Himself. The effectiveness of the story derives mainly from the fact that it embodies a studied, habitual refusal of recognition on the part of Ahab, which is capped by the representation of God as reversing His own role of bringer of truth to that of a king who at his leisure and with much deliberation plans to deceive. Ahab's preference for flattery, a categorical refusal of the harshness of truth, evokes a reversal of roles in God Himself. The biblical story has a fine boldness to it, which Gower, as we have seen, has heightened by prefacing it with an ample selection of empirical and secular instances of the speech of blame.

The setting of the action in the kingdom of Israel is described in terms of what kind of speech prevails:

> Bot who that couthe glose softe
> And flatre, suche he [Ahab] sette alofte
> In gret astat and made hem riche;
> Bot thei that spieken wordes liche
> To trouthe and wolde it noght forbere,
> For hem was non astat to bere,
> The court of such tok non hiede.   (VII.2531–37)

When Ahab tries to persuade King Josaphat to help him take Ramoth Galaath back from the king of Syria,

> This Josaphat seith to the king,
> Hou that he wolde gladly hiere
> Som trew prophete in this matiere,
> That he his conseil myhte yive
> To what point that it schal be drive.   (VII.2558–62)

The desire of Josaphat coincides exactly with the theme of counsel that pervades the *Confessio Amantis*. Ahab calls on his chief prophet, Sedechie, who foretells victory in the attack against Ramoth Galaath, and the other prophets concur in his prediction. Ahab's perversion of prophecy into flattery does not guarantee divine approbation for his actions but rather demonstrates the independent vitality of the word of God. Indeed, Josaphat is still doubtful and asks if there is any other prophet in the land. It becomes clear that Ahab has no interest in the truth and rewards only flatterers:

> Quod Achab thanne, 'Ther is on,
> A brothell, which Micheas hihte;
> Bot he ne comth noght in my sihte,
> For he hath longe in prison lein.
> Him liketh nevere yit to sein
> A goodly word to mi plesance. . . .'   (VII.2594–99)

This is the only declaration Ahab is permitted in Gower's story, and it constitutes a confession without recognition. He indicts himself without realizing it. This irony is heightened by the fact that those who release Micaiah from prison beg him not to contradict what Sedechie has prophesied:

> Micheas upon trouthe tho
> His herte sette, and to hem seith,
> Al that belongeth to his feith
> And of non other feigned thing,
> That wol he telle unto his king,
> Als fer as god hath yove him grace.   (VII.2618–23)

Micaiah's interior resources, fidelity to truth, and hope of divine inspiration set him off vividly from Ahab and result in a highly effective statement. The validity of his present prophecy derives from the actual voice of God:

> I was tofor the throne on hih,
> Wher al the world me thoghte stod,
> And there I herde and understod
> The vois of god with wordes cliere
> Axende, and seide in this manere. . . .   (VII.2640–44)

The question God asks is not, How can I finally shock Ahab into a realization of the truth? Rather, it is the opposite: He queries His attendant spirits as to how He may best deceive Ahab. One of them replies that Ahab should be deceived in his hearing,

> With flaterende prophecie
> In suche mouthes as he lieveth.   (VII.2652–53)

The inaccessibility of truth for a man who prefers flattery to candid advice is dramatized by rendering even the word of God inefficacious, for the word of God itself becomes a lie—not objectively, of course, but through the subjective malice of a man who consistently refuses the truth from this source. In the sharpest contrast to the illumination by the word granted to Lycurgus and Constantine, the false prophets have in their flattering lies ironically enunciated the word of God for Ahab. There is a mocking contempt in the story which is itself most effective as an antidote to flattery.

This whole section in dispraise of flattery should prepare Amans for the harsh speech of Venus at the end of the poem. As a king in regard to the dominion of his moral life, the individual Christian requires the unflattering counsel of the Confessor and the word of God.

Further reflection on the relationship between this section and the sacrament of confession suggests a twofold application to Amans. By approving those who speak without flattery to kings, he must therefore applaud similar speech directed toward himself. Secondly, if the penitent has the courage ultimately to face the truth about himself, he can presumably speak ingenuously to others. In other words, the proper speech of the courtier, a result of the virtues of friendship and truth, is reinforced by the speech of the confessional.

IV

The recognition scene in a romance takes various forms: it can be a discovery of literal identity on the part of the *Dümmling* or unsophisticated youth (Perceval, Lancelot, Li Biaus Descouneus, for example) who finally learns who his parents are; or, as Larry D. Benson has shown in *Gawain and the Green Knight*, the recognition scene may be directed toward some moral or psychological realization.[40] *Apollonius of Tyre*, virtually the last story in the poem, involves a literal recognition as a self-contained story, but as an exemplum finding its complete significance in a confessional context, it is an attempt to force Amans to the recognition of self-knowledge. Again, the tokens of recognition are manifold: scars, flame issuing from the mouth, rings, weapons, articles of clothing, to mention just a few.[41] The means of effecting the recognition in *Apollonius*, however, though not unique, is unusual in romance and folklore:[42] The hero is recognized by his lost wife as he publicly narrates the details of his fortune by the order of God in the temple of Diana. Gower could not have chosen a more appropriate form for the last exemplum of his confessional poem, and the originally less sophisticated autobiographical public oration finds more justification in Gower's context than anywhere else.[43]

Leading up to this fusion of exemplum and framework are four principal sections, in which the radical of speech generates the action: (1) courageously unflattering speech to a ruler, occasioning the solution of the riddle and inviting the persecution of Antiochus; (2) the amorous dialogue consisting of Apollonius singing and the letter written by the princess who becomes his wife; (3) the adventures of his daughter, illustrating the speech of woman as wisdom; (4) affable speech as the unrecognized sign of the father-daughter relationship.

In the framework of the *Confessio Amantis*, the story is told to illustrate incest; the dispersion of the family of Apollonius, a characteristic of the Greco-Byzantine romance, seem offered as a balance to this destructive proximity.

Bereft of his beautiful wife, Antiochus (after whom the city of Antioch was named) forces his unnatural attentions on his daughter, the fame of whose beauty has attracted many suitors. To keep his daughter for himself, he devises a riddle, which, if answered incorrectly by a suitor, results in execution. Since the riddle is actually a concealed confession of incest, the suitor is required, in effect, to manifest the guilt of Antiochus. The situation at once touches indirectly on the confessional theme, and offers an example of truthful, courageous speech to a flattering counselor or a timorous lover. Apollonius, though conscious of the many unsuccessful suitors who went before him, is not deterred from making the verbal declaration necessary to win the lady. An ideal courtier, he possesses the virtues of wisdom and eloquence:

> Of every naturel science,
> Which eny clerk him couthe teche,
> He couthe ynowh, and in his speche
> Of wordes he was eloquent. . . .   (VIII.390–93)

Macaulay finds the riddle unintelligible in its details, as it surely is, although incest is clearly the subject. The general nature of Apollonius's answer indicates his knowledge of the shameful deed concealed by the riddle:

> The question which thou hast spoke,
> If thou wolt that it be unloke,

> It toucheth al the privete
> Betwen thin oghne child and thee,
> And stant al hol upon you tuo.   (VIII.423–27)

Hoping to prevent the revelation of his crime, Antiochus pretends that the answer is wrong, but stays the execution for thirty days. Apollonius, who "understod wel what it mente" (VIII.442) and knows that "he the king his sothe tolde" (VIII.448), goes home, provisions a ship, and, to the distress of his subjects, leaves Tyre and begins his wanderings. Antiochus does in fact send an assassin, whose discovery that Apollonius has fled eventually causes the incestuous king to abandon the pursuit. Apollonius in the meanwhile lands in Tharsis, where he wins the gratitude of the people by relieving a famine with the stores of grain he has brought along. A subject of his from Tyre happens to meet him and discloses the plot laid by Antiochus. Unaware of his persecutor's present indifference, Apollonius sails from Tharsis.

With this mistakenly motivated action, and the comment on fortune that follows, begins the pattern upon which the anagnorisis or recognition scene of the romance focuses. As in the tale of Constance, we see the workings of what to the modern mind is a ludicrously inexorable fortune. The genre, however, is akin to tragedy, in which the recognition scene involves seeing how a series of painful incidents was caused by a tragic flaw, or hamartia. The hamartia in this genre is not in one character (although Antiochus is indeed villainous) but in the apparent malevolence and incomprehensibility of chance. The final anagnorisis is essentially an acceptance of the same law that is at work in the stories of Lycurgus and Constantine. The fault of Amans is the refusal or failure to recognize, as Apollonius does, the will of God in fortune.

Genius makes an explicit allusion to fortune after the departure of Apollonius from Tharsis:

> Fortune hath evere be muable
> And mai no while stonde stable:
> For now it hiheth, now it loweth,
> Now stant upriht, now overthroweth,
> Now full of blisse and now of bale,
> As in the tellinge of mi tale
> Hierafterward a man mai liere. . . .   (VIII.585–91)

Apollonius's ship is destroyed in a storm, but he is saved and the presence of God in fortune is pointed out:

> Bot he that alle thing mai kepe
> Unto this lord was merciable,
> And broghte him sauf upon a table,
> Which to the lond him hath upbore. . . .   (VIII.628–31)

After enduring the consequences of unflattering speech to a ruler, which was the sole condition of winning the lady, Apollonius begins his next adventure in love. He goes to Pentapolis, wins an athletic contest, and is invited to the palace for supper. His sadness attracts the attention of the king, who sends his daughter to cheer him. The daughter experiences no particular attraction to Apollonius until her sense of hearing is ravished by his musical skill, especially his voice:

> He takth the Harpe and in his wise
> He tempreth, and of such assise
> Singende he harpeth forth withal,
> That as a vois celestial
> Hem thoghte it souneth in here Ere,
> As thogh that he an Angel were.   (VIII.777–82)

Since the "vois celestial" probably has the same hierarchical context as the passage in Dante's *Convivio* quoted earlier, and since a voice from heaven in a literal sense unites Apollonius with his wife later in the story, "vois celestial" here suggests the providential presence of God in speech. The voice of Apollonius has its greatest effect on the king's daughter:

> Thei gladen of his melodie,
> Bot most of all the compainie
> The kinges doghter, which it herde,
> And thoghte ek hou that he ansuerde,
> Whan that he was of hire opposed,
> Withinne hir herte hath wel supposed
> Than he is of gret gentilesse.   (VIII.783–99)

Through his singing voice and his manner of answering, Apollonius has made the girl fall in love with him. The theme of the difficulty of speech for someone in love is present in the delicacy that keeps the girl from expressing her love by word of mouth. Instead of speaking, she writes her father a note:

> The schame which is in a Maide
> With speche dar noght ben unloke,
> Bot in writinge it mai be spoke;
> So wryte I you, fader, thus:
> Bot if I have Appolinus,
> Of al this world, what so betyde,
> I wol non other man abide.   (VIII.894–900)

A more desirable family relationship than that between Antiochus and his daughter is presented and foreshadows the ideal paternal love of Apollonius for his daughter. Apollonius marries the princess and subsequently a ship from Tyre accidentally—or, we should say, providentially, in keeping with the pattern of the story—puts into port with the news that Antiochus has paid for his crimes in a rather spectacular death by thunder and lightning. Apollonius and his young wife, who is now pregnant, set sail for Tyre. Fortune again intervenes when his wife appears to die in childbirth. Thinking that his wife is truly dead, he bewails his condition:

> Ha, wif,
> Mi lust, mi joie, my desir,
> Mi welthe and my recoverir,
> Why schal I live, and thou schalt dye?
> Ha, thou fortune, I thee deffie,
> Nou hast thou do to me thi werste.   (VIII.1062–67)

The remaining incidents of the story continue to actualize and amplify the ruinous possibilities of fortune. His wife, after being sealed in a casket and thrown into the sea at the insistence of the superstitious sailors, reaches land and is revived by a great physician. Thinking that her husband and child are victims of the sea, she consecrates her life to the service of Diana, the goddess of chastity and fortune. Unaware that his wife is alive, Apollonius arrives in Tharsis once again and leaves his infant daughter, Thaise, to be educated, while he returns to Tyre to take up the duties of government.

Thaise, however, suffers her own misfortunes. When she reaches maturity, her jealous guardians try to have her killed, but she is saved by pirates who sell her to a brothel, further emphasizing the theme of demonic sexuality. The grace of God makes her chaste reluctance such a deterrent that none of the customers can bring himself to violate her. Thinking that her virginity is the main obstacle, the brothel keeper sends his servant to ravish her, but the eloquence of her tearful complaining reduces him to sorrow for her condition. Just as the eloquence of Constance is exercised on behalf of the Christian faith, Thaise persuades her owner, improbably enough, to change the brothel to a school for young ladies, where she will be the principal instructor:

> And thus sche kepte hirself fro schame,
> And kneleth doun to therthe and preide
> Unto this man, and thus sche seide:
> 'If so be that thi maister wolde
> That I his gold encresce scholde,
> It mai noght falle be this weie:
> Bot soffre me to go mi weie
> Out of this hous wher I am inne,
> And I schal make him forto winne
> In som place elles of the toun,
> Be so it be religioun,
> Wher that honeste wommen duelle.'   (VIII.1446–57)

As Thaise improves her fortunes, Apollonius, who is unaware of all this, goes to Tharsis with the intention of bringing her back to Tyre, only to encounter further bad news. When her guardians, Strangulio and Dionisis, falsely narrate the sudden death of his daughter and show him her tomb, he once again laments his fortune, but is eventually reconciled to the will of God:

> He curseth and seith al the worste
> Unto fortune, as to the blinde,
> Which can no seker weie finde;
> For sche him neweth evere among,
> And medleth sorwe with his song.
> Bot sithe it mai no betre be,
>> He thonketh god and forth goth he. . . .

(VIII.1584–90;
indentation in
Macaulay)

His bad fortune has run its full course, but it is chance which once again drives his vessel from its course; and he arrives in Mitelene, where his daughter has gained a reputation for wisdom and womanly grace. The scene that ensues, the first of the two "recognitions" of the story, proceeds at a pace sufficiently gradual to highlight significant elements. First, it is the turning point of the action in that the romance hero begins the recovery of what is rightfully his. Moreover, it is the third father-daughter confrontation. We can now see that the purpose of Apollonius's separation from his daughter is to enable them to meet later as strangers and adults. The fact that father and daughter confront each other simply as man and woman gives poignancy to their conversation, alludes to the incest theme, and ends by dramatizing an ideal familial love.

The townspeople, celebrating the feast of Neptune, wonder who this sad king is. They send for Thaise, who, after failing to cheer him up with her harp, has more success with words:

> And whan sche sih that he so ferde,
> Sche falleth with him into wordes,
> And telleth him of sondri bordes,
> And axeth him demandes strange,
> Wherof sche made his herte change,
> And to hire speche his Ere he leide
> And hath merveile of that sche seide.

(VIII.1674–80)

Although the gracious conversation of Thaise captivates Apollonius momentarily, he relapses into his taciturn grief. When she touches him as a further indication of sympathy, Apollonius, in an uncharacteristic act of rudeness, strikes her. Melodramatic though it is, the incident serves to demonstrate her verbal resourcefulness. In accordance with the virtue of friendship, she calmly rebukes the stranger and hints at her real identity:

> . . . and thus whan sche him fond
> Desesed, courtaisly sche saide,

> 'Avoi, mi lord, I am a Maide;
> And if ye wiste what I am,
> And out of what lignage I cam,
> Ye wolde noght be so salvage.'   (VIII.1694–99)

We are compelled here to see the response of Thaise as an answer to the helpless attitude of the daughter of the incestuous Antiochus, who was more gravely wronged by her father but "dorste him nothing withseie" (VIII.347). The recognition proper then begins, with a convergence of the elements of truthful, loving speech and Providence. Thaise's rebuke awakens Apollonius to his accustomed civility. An unexplainable impulse to love the young girl precedes a divinely ordered, reciprocal self-disclosure:

> And yit the fader ate laste
> His herte upon this maide caste,
> That he hire loveth kindely,
> And yit he wiste nevere why.
> Bot al was knowe er that thei wente;
> *For god, which wot here hol entente,*
> *Here hertes bothe anon descloseth.*   (VIII.1705–11; my italics)

He questions her and she finds it easy to respond. Like Constance, she has kept silent about her unhappy experiences, but the natural relationship to Apollonius, of which she is still unaware, makes concealment impossible:

> Fro point to point al sche him tolde,
> That sche hath longe in herte holde,
> And nevere dorste make hir mone
> Bot only to this lord al one,
> To whom hire herte can noght hele,
> Torne it to wo, torne it to wele,
> Torne it to good, torne it to harm.   (VIII.1725–31)

The affability of Apollonius is the means by which the providence of God effects the recognition.

The second scene, which provides the transition to the recognition inherent in the lover's confessional acknowledgment, begins after Thaise is promised in marriage to the king of Mitelene and they all set out for Tharsis to punish those who injured Thaise. Once more, however, a course of action different from Apollonius's plan unfolds, as God, who has been guiding his fortune, intervenes:

> . . . he that wot what schal betide,
> The hihe god, which wolde him kepe,
> Whan that this king was faste aslepe,
> Be nyhtes time he hath him bede
> To seile into an other stede. . . .   (VIII.1788–92)

The scene is being set for the recognition of Apollonius by his long-lost wife, but with this are fused the self-revelation of a lover, prayer, and an allusion to the sacrament of confession:

> To Ephesim he bad him drawe,
> And as it was that time lawe,
> He schal do there his sacrifise;
> And ek he bad in alle wise
> That in the temple amonges alle
> His fortune, as it is befalle,
> Touchende his doghter and his wife
> He schal beknowe upon his life.   (VII.1793–1800)

God's command in the dream that Apollonius "beknowe" (a word from which the connotation of confession cannot be excluded) his fortune in the temple of Diana—appropriately the goddess of fortune and chastity—obviously involves an acknowledgment of providence. The manner in which this mysterious injunction is carried out suggests its relevance to prayer, confession, preaching the word of God, and the speech of love:

> The dore is up, and he in wente,
> Wher as with gret devocioun
> Of holi contemplacioun
> Withinne his herte he made his schrifte;
> And after that a riche yifte
> He offreth with gret reverence,
> And there in open Audience
> Of hem that stoden thanne aboute,
> He tolde hem and declareth oute
> His hap, such as him is befalle,
> Ther was nothing foryete of alle.   (VIII.1836–46)

His awareness of the religious nature of his action is shown by his devout manner. He very literally confesses within his heart, an action which would here involve a rethinking of his whole life, to effect a more complete self-revelation. His declaration is the self-revelation of a lover—not, certainly, in the sense which has obsessed Amans, but in a ritualized, almost iconographical way, wherein the lack of complication gives the act a simple and direct power. His wife recognizes him not only by the voice and appearance, but presumably by the incidents of his tale, in which she has acted a part:

> His wif, as it was goddes grace,
> Which was professed in the place,
> As sche that was Abbesse there,
> Unto his tale hath leid hire Ere:
> Sche knew the vois and the visage. . . .   (VIII.1847–51)

The long-separated married lovers are finally united and the story ends after the punishment of Thaise's betrayers.

The emphasis on providential fortune in the tale, which receives its final significance in the autobiographical declaration of Apollonius, passes into the application made by the confessor:

> Fortune, thogh sche be noght stable,
> Yit at some time is favorable
> To hem that ben of love trewe. (VIII.2013–15)

The ensuing response of Amans makes this application less conventional than it seems. Missing the point of providential vocation and identity, Amans replies:

> I not what ye fortune acompte,
> Bot what thing danger mai amonte
> I wot wel, for I have assaied. . . . (VIII.2041–43)

What in the story of Apollonius was fortune and acknowledgment of providence becomes, in the reaction of Amans, *danger* and amorous persuasion. In rejecting the emphasis Genius puts on fortune, Amans also ignores its providential meaning and the exhortation to acknowledge or "confess" an identity analogous to that of Apollonius. Opposed to the public, confessional verbal acknowledgment of providence in fortune made by Apollonius is the immediate emphasis Amans puts on his perseverance in amorous persuasion:

> For whan myn herte is best arraied
> An I have al my wit thurghsoght
> Of love to beseche hire oght,
> For al that evere I skile may,
> I am concluded with a nay:
> That o sillable hath overthrowe
> A thousend wordes on a rowe
> Of suche as I best speke can. . . . (VII.2044–51)

Though the whole poem does not become in one stroke an allegory of foolish man in love with fortune, the meaning of Amans's speech must not be overlooked. The goddess Fortuna is an intractable female indeed and will not yield her favors to amorous persuasion; but fortune is *danger* in the metaphor of the soul's courtship of truth—an endless series of potentially misleading appearances, which, however, are the only route to the ultimate divine reality. Making *danger* a correlative of fortune places the microcosm of Amans's failure in love in the larger universe of theological wisdom. The aloofness of his lady is made to exemplify the elusive paradoxes of evil in a world controlled by a beneficent God. Amans must acknowledge providential fortune and abandon his attempts at amorous persuasion. The speech

appropriate to the sacrament of confession must finally replace the lover's
rhetoric.

V

Keeping in mind the examples of speech not only from the Apollonius story
but from the section of Flattery in Book VII and the discussions of Mercury as
the Word in the beginning of this chapter, we can proceed with understanding to the concluding parts of the poem. Amans remains unreceptive to
counsel, but an atmosphere of courtesy still characterizes his conversations
with Genius and Venus. As we have pointed out, however, reprimands are an
essential part of the speech of friendship. The examples of candid speech
throughout this chapter, in addition to the command of Venus at the
beginning of the poem that Amans declare his "trouthe," should have
persuaded him to look honestly at himself. His refusal to do so necessitates
Venus's cruelly frank statement that old age has made him sexually impotent.
This harshly truthful piece of counsel casts him into a deep sleep in which his
dream recapitulates some of the exempla of the poem. His denial of human
love, upon awakening and being shown a mirror, is his final confessional
declaration. There follows a prayer for charity, which is the theological
transformation of the amorous persuasion so copiously illustrated throughout
the poem.

After missing the point of the Apollonius story, Amans ironically asks
Genius for counsel and is exhorted to turn to the "trouthe":

> Mi Sone, unto the trouthe wende
> Now wol I for the love of thee,
> And lete alle othre truffles be.   (VIII.2060–62)

The elliptical "Now wol I" implies that Genius has not been dealing with the
truth. Although he speaks more openly here than previously, there have been
abundant foreshadowings of his true nature. The reply of Genius to Amans's
final request for counsel contains the familiar medieval ascetical view of
human love as transitory and unreasonable (VIII.2084–2105). An important
part of this speech, in terms of the unity of the whole poem, is the statement
that every man is a king in need of counsel:

> Forthi, bot if it so befalle
> With good conseil that he be lad,
> Him oghte forto ben adrad.
> For conseil passeth alle thing
> To him which thenkth to ben a king;
> And every man for his partie
> A kingdom hath to justefie,

> That is to sein his oghne dom.
> If he misreule that kingdom,
> He lest himself, and that is more
> Than if he loste Schip and Ore
> And al the worldes good withal. . . .   (VIII.2106–17)

The theme of speech in love is thus united to the speech of the confessional
and the need of the king for counsel. Amans's answer is contentious:

> Mi fader, so as I have herd
> Your tale, bot it were ansuered,
> I were mochel forto blame.   (VIII.2149–51)

He looks upon himself as an opponent in a debate instead of a penitent
humbly seeking wisdom. Genius, he asserts, is ignorant of the experience of
love; but since the former is a priest of Venus, this seems a curious accusation.
We have an example of Amans's rhetorical clumsiness in his attempt to flatter
Genius into speaking to Venus on his behalf:

> Bot, fader, if ye wolde thus
> Unto Cupide and to Venus
> Be frendlich toward mi querele,
> So that myn herte were in hele
> Of love which is in mi briest,
> I wot wel thanne a betre Prest
> Was nevere mad to my behove.   (VII.2171–77)

Still conscious of prayer in the wrong sense, Amans proposes to write a
"Supplicacion/ With pleine wordes and expresse" (VII.2184–85) to Venus.
The "Supplicacion" is a twelve-stanza poem containing conventional remarks
about nature, reason, and fortune, and concludes with a request for success in
love or, alternatively, death. The attitude of Venus when she appears is
slightly mocking, but on the whole gracious. Her first denial of Amans's
request is kindly and indirect. Her opinion concerning the relationship of
nature to her own court shows that she can hardly represent lust simply:

> For Nature is under the Mone
> Maistresse of every lives kinde,
> Bot if so be that sche mai finde
> Som holy man that wol withdrawe
> His kindly lust ayein hir lawe. . . .   (VIII.2330–34)

Such an opinion indicates at least the participation of this Venus in a
Christian universe. Her endorsement of the law of Nature introduces the
reason why Amans is to be dismissed from her court. The sins which Venus
condemns plausibly include violations of law in Nature as perceived by
reason and hence any unreasonable love:

> Bot of these othre ynowe be,
> Whiche of here oghne nycete
> Ayein Nature and hire office
> Deliten hem in sondri vice,
> Wherof that sche fulofte hath pleigned,
> And ek my Court it hath desdeigned
> And evere schal; for it receiveth
> Non such that kinde so deceiveth. (VIII.2337–44)

The transition from this principle to the first dismissal of Amans from her court is a good example of affable courtesy and tact:

> For al onliche of gentil love
> Mi court stant alle courtz above
> And takth noght into retenue
> Bot thing which is to kinde due,
> For elles it schal be refused.
> Wherof I holde thee excused,
> For it is manye daies gon,
> That thou amonges hem were on
> Which of my court hast ben withholde. . . . (VIII.2345–53)

The actual refusal is subordinated and deemphasized by the "wherof" and "excused." Amans's love opposes an aspect of Nature that he should know well, his own old age. He refuses this hint and persists in the conventional imputations of injustice to Venus. She is "withoute lawe" (VIII.2377); "The trewe man fulofte aweie/ Sche put. . ." (VIII.2382–83). The partial truth contained in these reflections is nullified by Amans's failure to realize his own condition. Since graciousness has failed, Venus, avoiding flattery in the true spirit of friendship and love, and "halvynge of scorn," resorts to harsher methods. The statement concerning old age clearly implies sexual impotence. Amans, she says is among those

> That outward feignen youthe so
> And ben withinne of pore assay.
> *Min herte wolde and I ne may*
> Is noght beloved nou adayes;
> Er thou make eny such assaies
> To love, *and faile upon the fet,*
> Betre is to make a beau retret. (VIII.2410–16; my italics)

He is not, she continues "sufficant/ To holde love his convenant" (VIII. 2419–20). His will is good,

> Bot more behoveth to the plowh,
> Wherof the lacketh, as I trowe. . . . (VIII.2426–27)

The Latin verses that immediately precede line 2376 anticipate the theme of sexual impotence. That the "trouthe" of which Amans is unaware should be based on this fundamental fact makes his previous lack of self-knowledge pungently ludicrous. Venus finally exhorts him to acknowledge his condition, an act which is his primary obligation in the sacrament of penance:

> So sitte it wel that thou beknowe
> Thi fieble astat, er thou beginne
> Thing wher thou miht non ende winne.
> What bargain scholde a man assaie,
> Whan that him lacketh forto paie?
>
> . . .
>
> Forthi mi conseil is that thou
> Remembre wel hou thou art old.   (VIII.2428–39)

Just as the speech of his lady has affected Amans deeply, this last speech of Venus causes him to sleep and dream of the young and old companies of lovers (VIII.2440–2725). In the majority of these examples of lovers, love has manifested character defects or has resulted in some misfortune, a characteristic that emphasizes the adverse effects of love. The list of youthful lovers is concluded by a reference to four women whose stories have been told in the poem and who are famous for their marital fidelity: Penelope, Lucrece, Alcestis, and Ceix. The company of old lovers is much smaller and, with the exception of Samson, consists of men famous for intellectual or artistic achievement: Salomon, Aristotle, Ovid, and Virgil. The theme of prayer occurs once more as the old lovers unanimously pray to Venus for some solution to Amans's plight. Some of the young join in the prayer in the spirit "of gentilesse and pure trouthe" (VIII.2741). As Venus turns to Cupid for assistance, a debat ensues among the lovers as to the degree of Amans's guilt. Some of them berate the folly of love in such an old man (VIII.2765–70). Finally Cupid withdraws the "fyri Lancegay" from Amans's heart and he awakes. Showing him a mirror in which he beholds his unattractive, elderly features, Venus asks him jokingly what love is. Significantly, in view of his earlier arrogant claim to surpassing amorous knowledge, he can talk of it no longer. The embarrassment of his denial of love is an acknowledgment, or confession, of his folly:

> And I for schame
> Ne wiste what I scholde ansuere;
> And natheles I gan to swere
> That be my trouthe I knew him noght;
> So ferr it was out of mi thoght,
> Riht as it hadde nevere be.   (VIII.2872–77)

As the mild oath indicates, human love is no longer part of Amans's "trouthe," a self-knowledge which was the purpose of the confession.

The prayer that follows Amans's realization that human love is not for him is the fulfillment of the allusions to Christian prayer throughout the poem and the confirmation of the change in Amans. The separation of lovers from the community and their preoccupation with selfish ends have afforded prominent examples of "divisioun" in the poem. One function served by the dream was to give Amans a realization of a natural community bound together by human love. The old lovers and some of the young, "of gentilesse and pure trouthe" (VIII.2741), we will recall, had prayed to Venus for him. Amans inverts and improves the concern of this community for him by his final prayer for the whole Christian community.

This final prayer is a summary of the uses of the theme of speech in the poem. The selflessness of his concern for the whole community implies a new character possessed of "trouthe," neither boastful nor deprecatory. Significantly, the poet now adopts his own name in place of "Amans." His confession has been essential in helping him achieve this virtue. His prayer, which is also thinly disguised counsel to the king and every estate, is an act of true friendship and love in that it is neither flattering nor insulting. The prayer begins with an acknowledgment of God's omnipotence and man's dignity in being made in God's image:

> He which withinne daies sevene
> This large world forth with the hevene
> Of his eternal providence
> Hath mad, and thilke intelligence
> In mannys soule resonable
> Hath schape to be perdurable,
> Wherof the man of his feture
> Above alle erthli creature
> Aftir the soule is immortal. . . .   (VIII.2971–79)

We should recall the relation of such a statement to the virtue of truth and its opposition to the diffidence or boasting of the lover. The statement of the ideals which the various estates should achieve is a form of praise, and these ideals describe the controlled dignity of truth for them. Accordingly, to the clergy especially belongs the duty of prayer. Just as amorous speech throughout the poem has love as its object, the principal object of the clergy's prayer is to secure charity for the whole community:

> Ferst forto loke the Clergie
> Hem outhte wel to justefie
> Thing which belongith to here cure,
> As forto praie and to procure
> Our pes toward the hevene above,
> And ek to sette reste and love
> Among ous on this erthe hiere.

> For if they wroughte in this manere
> Aftir the reule of charite,
> I hope that men schuldyn see
> This lond amende.　　(VIII.2995–3005)

A balance is struck between praise and blame of the knightly class:

> And ovyr this,
> To seche and loke how that it is
> Touchende of the chevalerie,
> Which forto loke, in some partie
> Is worthi forto be comendid,
> And in som part to ben amendid. . . .　　(VIII.3005–10)

Instead of resorting to extortion and robbery to support their large retinues, they should defend the common good and the freedom of the church. Gower then takes up the complaint of the people about the unjust administration of the laws (VIII.3029–35). The merchants are chided for pursuing "singuler profit" (VIII.3039) when working for the common good can bring prosperity to the whole land. Finally, the power and duties of the king are described with an emphasis on his obligation to conform to the justice of the heavenly king (VIII.3054–3105), an admonition which reminds us of the Mercury allusion in the Lycurgus story. Then, in the course of repeating the purpose of his poem, and probably forbidding an overly serious consideration of its ambiguities by placing it "between ernest and game" (VIII.3109), Gower recapitulates the theme of the two loves, human and divine. Human love he disparages on Aristotelian grounds "that it hath evere som travers/ Or of to moche or of to lite. . ." (VIII.3158–59). That is, human love is never a mean between two extremes. The final request for charity is preceded by a statement of its wholesomeness for body and soul:

> Such love is goodly forto have,
> Such love mai the bodi save,
> Such love mai the soule amende,
> The hyhe god such love ous sende
> Forthwith the remenant of grace;
> So that above in thilke place
> Wher resteth love and alle pes,
> Oure joie mai ben endeles.　　(VIII.3165–72)

The solipsistic pleas of the lover are thus transformed, through the penitent's verbal acknowledgment guided by the confessor's counsel, into a prayer for charity which will result in spiritual, social, economic, and political justice.

Amans has been brought to this solution of his dilemma through the demand of Venus that he confess his "trouthe," a correspondence not only between his mind, speech, and action, but also a realization of the existence of natural and divine law, executed by providence. While it is true that every story in the poem is an example of counsel, the stories we have chosen to analyze in this chapter exhibit a more explicit relationship. The stories involving Mercury as the Word indicate the theological beginning and end of counsel. In the section on Flattery, a more empirical analysis of "trouthe" in counsel was given, again with a final emphasis on the speech of God in the story of Ahab and Micaiah. The story of Apollonius, which concerns the hardships of even rightly ordered human love, is meant to help Amans make a transition to divine love. His failure to see the theme of providential fortune in the story is a rejection of "trouthe" in counsel. This persistent insensitivity to spiritual values necessitates the final harsh "trouthe" of his old age and impotence bluntly stated by Venus. The prayerful and almost charitable concern of the young and old lovers softens the bitter realization of this "trouthe" and foreshadows the culmination of the theme of speech in the poem. With Cupid's arrow removed and in possession of the "trouthe" of self-knowledge, Amans makes his final amorous plea—this time in a wholly theological sense—a prayer for universal charity. His awareness that human words are inadequate has traversed the way up to the Word and come back again by applying prayer to the temporal concerns of society.

6

Praise and Blame

I

It might at first seem specious to discuss the *Confessio Amantis* as belonging to the autobiographical or "confessional" form of narrrative, among whose most eminent practitioners are Augustine, Dante, Rousseau, and Joyce.[1] Such autobiographies or "confessions," however, usually embody a condemnatory break with a past mode of conduct, which is the mark of the medieval sacrament of confession; and the fiction of Gower's poem is at least conventionally autobiographical. Moreover, as we have pointed out, a mental confession introduces the final autobiographical speech of Apollonius of Tyre, whose history is the last exemplum brought to bear on the penitent, Amans, by his confessor. The distinguishing mark of the genre, akin to that of the Saint's Life, is the "discovery of true vocation," the perception of an integrated pattern which may be theological, artistic, or characterized by almost any quality that gives the author a unique role in his society. The motive for promulgating this discovery is the belief that the personal experience has universal relevance. Such an intention is stated at the beginning of the *Confessio Amantis:*

> . . . therfore I
> Woll wryte and schewe al openly
> How love and I togedre mette,
> Wherof the world ensample fette
> Mai after this, whan I am go,
> Of thilke unsely jolif wo. . . .   (I.83–88)

Although the presentation of the erotic autobiography of Amans in terms of the Seven Deadly Sins is largely conventional, his moral reintegration is unique in its progress from a concern with amorous persuasion to prayer by means of "trouthe" in sacramental confession. Most important, it is the fact that Venus herself enjoins Amans to pray, appropriately giving him beads

145

"por reposer" and sending him where "vertu moral duelleth" (VIII.2925), that particularizes the exemplary quality of this lover's *vita*. The vocation of prayer, then, develops in some way out of Amans's experience of sexuality. In his autobiographical *Confessions,* Augustine centers his conversion in large part on answers to questions that encompass the whole of reality: the nature of God, good and evil, creation, time, memory. Amans's conversion to a vocation of prayer does not rise from so broad a base, but sexual love, summed up and personified by the Venus who enjoins him to prayer, is placed in a highly individualized context of universal order.

In Book VII of the *Confessio Amantis,* an encyclopedic account of the world is given by Genius, the priest of Venus, with a candid emphasis on those qualities which contribute to peaceful sexual love, for the "moral Gower" is no prude. Encyclopedic poetry, a kind of ambitious synthesis still possible in Gower's time, attempts what Angus Fletcher calls a "microcosmic reduction of the symbolic center."[2] Rehearsing the cosmos in miniature makes it less formidable and allows one to gain control of it. This is even more true when such a summary of universal knowledge is further reduced by a single point of view, that of peace in love, a goal most important to the definition which we must finally give to Venus.

The lore taught to Alexander (who reminds us of the Annunciation allusion at the end of Book VI) by Aristotle—Theoric, Rhetoric, and Practic—parallels the thought-word-deed formula of the moral handbooks and of the Verbum tradition. The sustaining principle of the world order to which sexuality as realized by Amans belongs is, of course, God Himself, who holds first place in a sequence of causes. Aristotle

> . . . clepeth god the ferste cause,
> Which of himself is thilke good,
> Withoute whom nothing is good,
> Of which that every creature
> Hath his beinge and his nature.   (VII.86–90)

Although virtue in sexual love is the principal theme in this encyclopedic summary, a detailed exposition of the four elements that underlie the four complexions is necessary to place sexuality within a pattern of causes:

> For upon hem [the elements] that I have seid
> The creatour hath set and leid
> The kinde and the complexion
> Of alle mennes nacion.   (VII.381–84)

A motif of sexual inadequacy, related to moral imperfection, characterizes his summary of complexional physiology. As regards the melancholy man,

> . . . unto loves werk on nyht
> Him lacketh bothe will and myht:

> No wonder is, in lusty place
> Of love though he lese grace.   (VII.405–8)

A particular susceptibility of this complexion to fear and wrath lays it open to neurasthenic agitation:

> What man hath that complexion,
> Full of ymaginacion
> Of dredes and of wrathful thoghtes,
> He fret himselven al to noghtes.   (VII.409–12)

The affliction of the phlegmatic man nullifies physical ability by lack of desire, for he

> . . . is of kinde sufficant
> To holde love his covenant,
> Bot that him lacketh appetit,
> Which longeth unto such delit.   (VII.417–20)

The ability to make love is not as widespread as one might have thought. The choleric man, as we might now expect, is similarly unsuccessful:

> Of contek and folhastifnesse
> He hath a riht gret besinesse,
> To thenke of love and litel may:
> Though he behote wel a day,
> On nyht whan that he wole assaie,
> He may ful evele his dette paie.   (VII.435–40)

The total impression of the inadequacies of the complexions suggests a norm between precipitance and lethargy. The sanguine man is the only successful lover:

> Of alle ther is non so good,
> For he hath bothe will and myht
> To plese and paie love his riht. . . .   (VII.424–26)

Whatever meanings and functions we may attach to the Venus of the poem must take these passages into consideration. Absence of wrath, fear, sloth, contentiousness, and haste is a state of soul radically dependent on the elements of the physical world through the four complexions and necessary to sexual consummation, itself therefore a sign of order achieved. The four elements of earth, air, fire, and water, reach their highest ontological expression in the complexions of man as a microcosm, the virtuous ordering of which is essential to the complete service of Venus.

Venus has commanded Amans to pray: What does this mean conceptually? When Venus declares her approving adherence to the law of Nature, we know that she is more than a personification of a blind desire.[3] Her deference to order adds an additional quality to her description of herself as seeking only her own pleasure. More explicitly, the sexual appetite, as we have seen, depends in Gower's context on moral achievement for its fulfillment. Therefore, the command of Venus to pray is at least an impetus toward universal order which derives from the sexual instinct viewed teleologically, as part of a universe which has God as First Cause, and as dependent on the moral control of the complexions. These characteristics constitute a variation of the medieval commonplace that makes love the fundamental bond of universal order. They bring the goddess of the poem into alignment with the Venus Celestis, the personification of an attitude toward sexuality which occurs in Plato and becomes a *topos* in medieval and Renaissance culture. The peace that John Gower prays for at the end of the poem is an extension to society at large of his own newly found solution to a moral conflict. This larger peace, a civil and religious order which Venus has explicitly commanded him to pray for, has its instinctual counterpart and symbol in sexual consummation, which, as we have seen, is an integral part of the poem's conclusion and is itself a principle of order. Prayer for peace and charity is a necessary consequence, for Gower, of an examination of sexual love in its cosmic setting, an imperative of the fully human and virtuous experience of sexuality. This is what Amans has discovered through confession, and although old age and impotence exclude the complete experience from his autobiography, its exemplary relevance is crucial to all who would find peace in love.

As an autobiographical discovery, the significance of prayer to the universe is further clarified by the encyclopedic description of the planets and their effects. The section on Astronomy, also a part of Theoric, repeats the usual commonplaces about the influence of the heavenly bodies on success and failure in love as well as every other human action, but Genius immediately adds that the holy man can overcome these influences by prayer (VII.662–63). Reinforcing the power of speech in prayer as a means of mitigating the influence of the planets is speech in "Magique natural" (VII.1301) which concludes the whole section on Theoric. Here, notably, it is not the teaching of Aristotle to Alexander, but that of Nectanabus:

> Among the whiche forth withal
> Nectanabus in special,
> Which was an Astronomien
> And ek a gret Magicien,
> And undertake hath thilke emprise
> To Alisandre in his aprise
> As of Magique naturel
> To knowe, enformeth him somdel
> Of certein sterres what thei mene. . . .   (VII.1295–1303)

The important point for our perspective is this: We are reminded of

Nectanabus, whose seduction of Olimpia was accomplished by natural magic in what we have called an Annunciation context, and we are finally told that the order imposed on the influence of the stars (especially concerning love) by natural magic is an effect principally of the spoken word. The transition from the discussion of Theoric to Rhetoric makes this evident. The enumeration of the stars with their cooperant herbs and stones, a catalogue which takes up about one hundred and fifty lines (VII.1280–1438) leads into and is climaxed by the Latin verses which introduce the discussion of Rhetoric:

> Compositi pulchra sermonis verba placere
>> Principio poterunt, veraque fine placent.
> Herba, lapis, sermo, tria sunt virtute repleta,
>> Vis tamen ex verbi pondere plura facit.

> (The lovely words of a careful speech can please
>> at the start and please by a true conclusion.
> Herb, stone, speech, the three are full of power,
>> but the force of the strength of the word does more.)

The power of herb and stone, surpassed by that of speech, here obviously alludes to natural magic; this superiority of the word is paraphrased in English several lines later:

> In Ston and gras vertu ther is,
> Bot yit the bokes tellen this,
> That *word* above alle erthli thinges
> Is vertuous in his doinges,
> Wher so it be to evele or goode.   (VII.1545–49; my italics)

This efficacy of human speech, both as an instrument of natural magic and rhetorical persuasion, was evil in the use made of it by Nectanabus, but association with the Annunciation points to the Verbum as the fulfillment and goal of this efficacy. The section on Rhetoric is immediately followed by the first point of Practic, which is Truth, the moral perfection of the faculty of speech. To sum up, the order suggested by the priority of virtue to sexual consummation and threatened by the adverse influences of fortune can be confirmed by prayer, the power of speech in natural magic, rhetoric, and finally by the moral power of speaking the "Truth," the first point of Practic. The relevance of all knowledge to the faculty of human speech confirms the vocation of prayer to which Venus has ordered Amans.

II

In the confession or autobiography, conversion is achieved and pattern discovered by a number of techniques. The new way of life is praised and the old way blamed. The personal habits, the people and places, the institutions that kept the writer from a recognition of the role he was to play in society are often vehemently excoriated. This is certainly true in the case of Augustine, whose *Confessions* are filled with reproach—the denunciation of sin in himself and others, his criticism of Faustus, the Manichees, sophistry in the teaching of rhetoric, unruliness in schoolboys. Dante's confession in the *Purgatorio* is intensely autobiographical in its implications and is preceded by the uniquely uncompromising judgments of the *Inferno*.

The blame distributed by Amans is principally in the nature of a lover's complaint, although Genius, on the other hand, by virtue of his role of priest in confession, denounces sin in his penitent and in society at large. There are just reprimands that belong to the tradition of true friendship and the sacrament of confession delivered to Amans by Genius throughout the poem, and the final reprimand of Venus. Further examples of legitimate complaint in the poem are found under Flattery in Book VII, in the unmasking of the pagan gods in Book V, and in numerous passages in the poem which bear a tonal reference to the denunciation of vice, for the mere presentation of vice is a form of blame. Amans's complaints as a lover are often just, particularly in the treatment of Cheste in Book II, but most of his objections to the arguments of Genius and the complaint in his final supplication to the court of Venus are parts of his sin, his foolish clinging to a love that is impossible for him.

The final exorcism of this unjust complaint in Amans has an important relevance to "complaint" as the ground swell of satire. Complaint in the sense of straightforward, morally certain condemnation of vice is judged by John Peter as inartistic.[4] John Fisher, however, although rather uncritically accepting Peter's criteria, maintains that Gower's moral sense contributed to a philosophical underpinning for Chaucer's more adept, concrete, stylistically varied satirical tone.[5] John Peter's distaste for religious literature, his tendentious review of complaint, and his rather dated use of irony as a criterion of literary excellence hide the merits of straightforward complaint discussed by such critics as Northrop Frye and Robert C. Elliott.[6] The direct, straightforward speech of blame has its own kind of excellence, for as Frye wryly observes: "It is an established datum of literature that we like hearing people cursed and are bored with hearing them praised, and almost any denunciation, if vigorous enough, is followed by a reader with the kind of pleasure that soon breaks into a smile."[7]

Larger generic questions of this kind suggest the possibility of variations in the handling of complaint which I believe are exhibited in the *Confessio Amantis*. Compared to the *Vox Clamantis*, however, and the *Mirour de l'omme*, there is in Gower's English poem certainly not less concern with the eradication of vice, but a change of mode, a softening of the harshness and earnestness of complaint, which is at least rhetorically autobiographical. The relationship between John Gower and the Amans of the poem will not, I hope, become as complicated as the discussion concerning Chaucer as man and fictional persona. But the author of the *Confessio Amantis* tells us that he has been sick, and we know that he was getting old. After a lengthy complaint against society's ills in the Prologue to the *Confessio Amantis*, he begins Book I with the following admission:

> I may noght strecche up to the hevene
> Min hand, ne setten al in evene
> This world, which evere is in balance:
> It stant noght in my sufficance
> So grete thinges to compasse,
> Bot I mot lete it overpasse
> And treten upon othre thinges.
> Forthi the Stile of my writinges
> Fro this day forth I thenke change
> And speke of thing is noght so strange.   (I.1–10)

There is certainly an element of convention in this, but at the very beginning of the poem is another passage that states a change in literary intention:

> Bot for men sein, and soth it is,
> That who that al of wisdom writ
> It dulleth ofte a mannes wit
> To him that schal it aldai rede,
> For thilke cause, if that ye rede,
> I wolde go the middel weie
> And wryte a bok betwen the tweie
> Somwhat of lust, somwhat of lore.   (Prol. 12–19)

In his own person, then, Gower tells us at the beginning that he has undergone a change. What actual incidents in his life this statement reflects, or whether it is truly autobiographical at all, I do not intend to inquire. Gower's famous association with Richard II and Henry IV, together with his enormous literary output with its keen sense of social and moral obligation, certainly point to a conviction of a unique vocation. The question that intrigues the reader of the *Confessio Amantis*, however, is whether this English poem marks a substantial change in his conception of just what this role was. What is important is that the tone of the *Confessio Amantis* is greatly different from that of either the *Vox Clamantis* or the *Mirour de l'omme*. Having the narrator of the *Confessio Amantis* throw up his hands at the beginning of the poem and say that he is incapable of righting the enormities of society is a rhetorically effective gesture. By being less denunciatory, he becomes more persuasive, going the middle way between earnest and game. In the *Cronica Tripertita*, a piece of unabashed but sincere Lancastrian propaganda, he returns to earnest with a vengeance.[8] In the

Confessio Amantis, however, he at least pretends for rhetorical purposes to have undergone an important change.

Complementing the vocation of prayer, then, which is the apotheosis of the speech of praise, is a renunciation of complaint, a mood of letting go. This attitude pervades the confession of an old lover, but it is particularly evident in Book V, where complaint is seen as ungrateful and hence avaricious. Moreover, the natural order, to which virtuous sexuality belongs and which is especially graced by man in prayer, also has a particular relationship to the speech of unjust complaint and finally even to legitimate blame. The word *unkindeschipe,* which in Book V of the *Confessio Amantis* refers specifically to ungratefulness (V.4885–5504), allows the punning significance of "unnaturalness" to unify a series of concepts and illustrations.[9] The overriding theme here, of course, is that Avarice violates nature, but the proposition that I want particularly to trace through Book V is that complaint, as a form of avarice, is unnatural. Opposed to this is an attitude of gratefulness to the generosity of nature.

The first subdivision of Book V concludes with an illustration of unjust complaint as a manifestation of jealousy, which is itself related to Avarice, the subject vice of Book V. The jealous man chooses a most inopportune moment to accuse his wife:

> And whanne it draweth to the nyht,
> If sche thanne is withoute lyht,
> Anon is al the game schent;
> For thanne he set his parlement
> To speke it whan he comth to bedde,
> And seith, 'If I were now to wedde,
> I wolde neveremore have wif.'
> And so he torneth into strif
> The lust of loves duete
> And al upon diversete.   (V.481–90)

This inability of the jealous man to enjoy love anticipates the causal connection between lack of virtue and sexual failure developed in Book VII (ll. 405–26) which we have already discussed. He is attended, as we might expect, by the "janglere" (V.517–26), the character type who in medieval literature virtually personifies foolish accusation and who here sums up in his person sins of speech previously treated at length in the poem (Cheste, III. 417ff.; grucchinge, I.1264, 1349, see above pp. 53–56, 87–91).

> Bot as a man to love *unkinde*
> He cast his staf, as doth the blinde,
> And fint defaulte where is non;
> As who so dremeth on a Ston
> Hou he is leid, and groneth ofte,

Whan he lith on his pilwes softe.
So is ther noght both strif and *cheste;*
Whan love scholde make his feste,
It is gret thing if he hir kisse:
Thus hath sche lost the nyhtes blisse,
For at such time he *gruccheth* evere
And berth on hond ther is a levere,
And that sche wolde an other were
In stede of him abedde there;
And with tho wordes and with mo
Of Jelousie, he torneth fro
And lith upon his other side,
And sche with that drawth hire aside,
And ther sche wepeth al the nyht.   (V.535–53; my italics)

It is the unnatural avarice of complaint, signaled by the word *unkinde*, which, because of a desire to extract more than is natural or "kind" in the modern sense of the term, gives the scene an effective poignancy.

Fortune, an important part of the natural order, is seen as the real object of complaint as this theme continues in Book V. Certain courtiers complain among themselves that their merit is not rewarded as it should be. The king, upon hearing their grumbling, fills two coffers, one with treasure and the other with straw and stones. The courtiers are given their choice and they pick the stones. Here, complaint, motivated by greed, is exorcized by a realization that some grievances are beyond human redress. The courtiers forsake complaining speech in favor of prayer for mercy:

Thus was this wise king excused,
And thei lefte of here evele speche
And mercy of here king beseche.   (V.2388–90)

The story immediately following (V.2391–2441) is a close variation of the same plot except that fortune is placed more explicitly in the control of God. One beggar asserts that wealth is in the gift of the king; the other asserts that wealth is God's gift. The emperor Frederick prepares two pasties, one with a capon and the other with florins inside. As in the case of the two coffers in the previous story, the persons involved are allowed their own choice. Although it is no surprise that the devout beggar's choice results in affluence, the Boethian point is nevertheless effective. Of the one who made the wrong choice, it is said:

Of that he hath richesse soght,
His infortune it wolde noght.   (V.2433–4)

An amorous application is made also:

Riht so fulofte it stant be love:

> Thogh thou coveite it everemore,
> Thou schalt noght have o diel the more,
> Bot only that which thee is schape,
> The remenant is bot a jape.   (V.2448–52)

Complaint continues to be a disservice and a form of avarice in the illustration of parsimony, or "Skarsnesse." The introductory Latin lines foreshadow the verbal correlative of stinginess:

> Pro verbis verba, munus pro munere reddi
> Convenit, ut pondus equa statera gerat.
>
> (It is fitting to exchange words for words,
>   gift for gift, for an equal balance to bear the weight.)

Parsimony as a refusal to give presents to the lady is accompanied by a diminution of one's word hoard. Conversely, largeness of spirit manifests itself not only in material generosity but in gracious conversation. Croceus, endowed with this virtuous combination, attracts the admiration of the lady:

> Sche sih him large of his despence,
> And amorous and glad of chiere,
> So that hir liketh wel to hiere
> The goodly wordes whiche he seide;
> And therupon of love he preide. . . .   (V.4838–42)

As in the case of the two coffers, the habit of complaining puts up a barrier against the gifts of fortune a man might receive, so that Babio, the rival of Croceus, loses out:

> Of Babio sche wol no more,
> For he was grucchende everemore,
> Ther was with him non other fare
> Bot forto prinche and forto spare. . . .   (V.4851–54)

The most effective valediction to complaint as a form of avarice concludes the second of two stories where the violation of man's own nature takes the form of infidelity to a spoken promise, an "unkindeschipe" which is also an act of ingratitude. The story which clearly defines this relationship is that of Adrian and Bardus (V.4937–5162). The "nature" of Adrian, who has fallen into a pit, is shown in the ability to make a verbal covenant. This is conveyed by the fact that Bardus is drawn to the pit by the sound of a human voice, which promises a great reward in return for help. To Bardus's great alarm at a possible "jape of fairie," an ape emerges from the pit by means of a rope which he has lowered. Again a human voice calls out, and again, instead of a human being, a serpent comes out. For the third time, the human voice pleads with Bardus, and finally Adrian is drawn up. The function of this part of the episode is to drive home the fact that the faculty of speech is a sign of human nature, because Adrian breaks his markedly verbal promise concerning the reward and hence proves to be "unkinde"—unfaithful, ungrateful, and unnatural. The ape and the serpent, on the other hand, transcend their nature by helping the impecunious Bardus gather wood and obtain wealth. The relationship between the power of speech, nature, and gratitude is summed up in the following lines:

> . . . the worm and ek the beste,
> Althogh thei maden no beheste,
> His travail hadden wel aquit;
> Bot he which hadde a mannes wit,
> And made his covenant be mouthe
> And swor therto al that he couthe
> To parte and yiven half his good,
> Hath nou foryete hou that it stod,
> As he which wol no trouthe holde.   (V.5131–39)

Gower leads up to this defining exemplum by several associations of the unnatural with sins of speech. The false witness of his goddess-mother Thetis brings it about that Achilles, unnaturally disguised as a woman, becomes the bedfellow of Deidamia, whom he eventually deflowers, for "kinde wole himselve rihte" (V.3058). Medea, the victim of Jason's perjury and "untrouthe" (V.4210ff), goes above nature, as it were, when she rejuvenates his father, and against nature when she kills her own and his sons. Ariadne, whose betrayal by Theseus is told as an explicit illustration of "unkindeschipe," exclaims that

> It is gret wonder hou he mihte
> Towardes me nou ben unkinde,
> And so to lete out of his mynde
> Thing which he seide his oghne mouth.   (V.5452–55)

As is frequently the case in the *Confessio Amantis*, the section immediately following "Unkindeschipe" continues the theme of infidelity with unnaturalness. The complaint treated in the story of Tereus, Procne, and Philomene, although completely just in itself, has, from the point of view of Gower's consistently providential attitude toward fortune, a touch of the avarice seen elsewhere in Book V. This complaint is finally absorbed and overwhelmed by the generosity of nature and finally takes the form of a highly traditional image which can serve as an emblem of the tone that I think pervades the whole *Confessio Amantis*.

The story itself is filled with injustices, and ample grounds for complaint. Procne sends her husband Tereus to bring her sister Philomene for a visit. Ignoring his married state, he rapes her. Her wholly justified complaint is vehement and topographically universal. She will tell all the world what he has done: the stones, the woods, the birds:

> For I so loude it schal reherce,
> That my vois schal the hevene perce,
> That it schal soune in goddes Ere.   (V.5673–75)

He compounds his infidelity ("untrewe," V.5681; "untrouthe," V.5682) by cutting off her tongue, and his conduct begins a chain reaction of unnatural acts. Procne, upon discovering the cruel infidelity, considers him "the most untrewe and most unkinde" (a juxtaposition that reminds the reader of the composite meaning of "unkindeschipe" in the previous subdivision of Book V); but forgetting her own motherhood, she kills and prepares her own son in a stew,

> With which the fader at his mete
> Was served, til he hadde him ete;
> That he ne wiste hou that it stod,
> Bot thus his oughne fleissh and blod
> Himself devoureth ayein kinde,
> As he that was tofore unkinde.   (V.5901–6)

The pun of the last two lines indicates that the cannibalistic feast of Tereus is a punishment in kind for his infidelity, ingratitude, and cruelty, or "un-kindness" in the modern sense of the term. The taunting blame with which the women accompany the presentation of the boy's head to the unfaithful husband promises to occasion more bloodshed, but as Tereus takes up his sword,

> The goddes, that the meschief syhe,
> Here formes changen alle thre.
> Echon of him in his degre
> Was torned into briddes kinde;
> Diverseliche, as men mai finde,
> After thastat that thei were inne,
> Here formes were set atwinne.   (V.5936–42)

By means of divine aid, Nature finally triumphs after many defeats, and transformation mirrors condition with Tereus becoming the faithless lapwing, Procne the admonishing swallow, and, most important, Philomene the gently complaining nightingale. The sense of loss in the story is of such horrible proportions that any sense of excessive desire for anything, or avarice, is completely frustrated in the characters themselves and, presumably, in the reader. Philomene loses her honor and her tongue. Procne and Tereus lose their son in a banquet which is a final terrifying witness to "unkindeschipe" in the infidelity of the husband and the derangement of the wife.

But the mood of the narration changes significantly at this point. When

Philomene becomes the nightingale, there is a distancing of the treachery, mutilation, and cannibalism which induces in the reader a response analogous to that of Troilus in the Eighth Sphere. Just as that victim of infidelity no longer feels the pain of his early frustrations and laughs at the vanity of human pursuits, the reader of the *Confessio Amantis* is made to see Tereus, Procne, and Philomene in a significantly different perspective. It is as if Gower's basic response to evil in the *Confessio Amantis* can be best represented by complaint not in the sense of anxious, vehement, even presumptuous adjudication, but complaint tempered with trust in "Nature" controlled by Providence and viewed as passing in the primal movement of comedy from winter to spring—the complaint of Philomene, the nightingale:

> Bot whan the wynter goth away,
> And that Nature the goddesse
> Wole of hir oughne *fre largesse*
> With herbes and with floures bothe
> The feldes and the medwes clothe,
> And ek the wodes and the greves
> Ben heled al with grene leves,
> So that a brid hire hyde mai,
> Betwen Averil and March and Maii,
> Sche that the wynter hield hir clos,
> For pure schame and noght aros,
> Whan that sche seth the bowes thikke,
> And that there is no bare sticke,
> Bot al is hid with leves grene,
> To wode comth this Philomene
> And makth hir ferste yeres flyht;
> Wher as sche singeth day and nyht,
> And in hir song al openly
> Sche makth hir pleignte. . . .   (V.5960–78; my italics)

When Philomene is absorbed into Nature, "Unkindeschipe" is most fully rectified in a transformation which points to the final triumph of justice and transcends the histories of individuals. She becomes not an artifice of eternity but a sign of the enduring beneficence of Nature as an adjutant to the world of grace. The treatment of "unkindeschipe," which in Gower's immediate context in Book V means the ungratefulness of avaricious complaint, embodies, as I have attempted to show, the rejection of a certain kind of blame—that too earnest rhetoric of condemnation represented by the *Vox Clamantis* and the *Mirour de l'omme*. Providentially guided Nature, as a most appropriate object of praise, finally overcomes those instances of the additional meaning of "unkindeschipe"—unnaturalness.

If without further elaboration we may suggest that this sequence of themes and images represents the tone of the whole poem, we can confirm from a new perspective that Gower found his true voice in the *Confessio Amantis*. The conversion at the end of the poem shows us not a fiery, transformed Saul, but a man saying a prayer that has unmistakable but gentle homiletic overtones. From the Latin and Anglo-Norman poems, he has moved not to satire, but to an effectively poetic variation of complaint, still intently didactic, but with a mixture of earnest and game unique in medieval literature.

Epilogue

Gower's regular and inevitable reference to sins of speech countered by the word of God in some form, his resolution of the tension between amorous persuasion and prayer, his framework of the confessional dialogue clearly define an explicit pattern of emphasis on the faculty of speech. The three literary principles that I defined at the beginning of the book—inexpressibility, reversibility, and synecdoche—illuminate the various forms this emphasis has taken. The experience of semantically or morally imperfect speech—that all things to some extent are ontologically or willfully inexpressible—generates the logical necessity of an allusion to the Word, which becomes actual through the presence of four significantly placed appearances of the god Mercury; Annunciation allusions; mysterious, divinely authoritative voices; and the identification of the image of God in man with his faculty of speech. The mythography of Mercury, as we have reviewed it, itself demonstrates this movement from words to Word, because the incidents of his history are interpreted as vices or virtues of speech, which point finally to perfect speech, or Mercury as the Word. Mercury pleasantly varies the Augustinian model quoted in Chapter 1, extending the theology of the Word into classical literature and mythology, astronomy, and even physiology in the commentary of Boccaccio. We have seen that as an agent, he is sometimes interpreted as the Word, sometimes as eloquence, sometimes as the devil, diabolically persuasive. Mercury can be indirectly involved in physical combat, as when Perseus uses his sword to decapitate Medusa, or kill the monster who imprisons Andromeda. He can be a lover, as when he marries Philologia with all the Seven Liberal Arts in attendance. He can be an adviser or lawgiver, as when Gower substitutes Mercury for Apollo in the story of Lycurgus in Book VII of the *Confessio Amantis.* He can be a savior, as when he liberates Io from the wardship of Argus. The usefulness of Mercury in a poetic narrative lies in the fact that he can be an emblem of individual or communal history conceived as all the thoughts and deeds which are true or false in regard to their verbal expression and hence conducive to union with, or final separation

159

from, the Word Himself. Or he can be a minute part of that history, but a part
with a sufficient microcosmic dynamism to invoke synecdochally the presence
of the Whole. The critical principle of Kenneth Burke seems especially true
for the *Confessio Amantis* and other medieval literary works as well:
awareness of the imperfect use of words leads to the Word, Who in turn is the
final cause of all the verbal causes.

In medieval verbal art, the ontological omnipresence of the Word is most
relevant as a critical model especially in those poems where the tradition is
explicit. The famous line from the *Adoro Te* of Thomas Aquinas—"Nil hoc
verbo veritatis verius"—displays a pun on *verbum* which asserts that every
word of the Word is the Word, who in turn is the source of all truth. In
Chaucer's *Merchant's Tale*, there is an ironic inversion of this pattern in the
reference to the marriage of Philology to Mercury, who of course, as
Alexander Neckam reminds the readers of Martianus Capella, is the Word.
The many references to counsel, the self-consciously verbal roles of Placebo
and Justinus, January's "eloquence," and the final endowment of May with
the ability always to have the last word enrich the pattern with comedy and
pungently ironic morality.

Even where there is no literal or allegorical allusion to the Word as such,
many other conventions occur which fall clearly within a dialectic between
impotent and powerful, or imperfect and perfect speech. When Sir Launfal,
in a Middle English romance, is provoked by Guinevere into boasting of his
otherworld mistress, Triamour, she disappears, his purse is emptied, his
winnings melt like snow, and his armor turns black. A misuse of speech
dramatizes the relationship of speech to the whole hierarchical structure of
man's place in nature. When Beowulf encounters the dragon, his shout, in a
memorable instance of heroic synecdoche, epitomizes his own dignity as a
man and sacral warrior in a challenge to the forces of evil in a final
apocalyptic combat:

> Lēt ðā of brēostum,   ðā hē gebolgen waes,
> Weder-Gēata lēod   word ūt faran,
> stearcheort styrmde;   stefn in becōm
> heaðotorht hlynnan   under hārne stān.
> Hete waes onhrēred,   hordweard oncnīow
> mannes reorde. . .   (2550–55)

> Then the man of the Weather-Geats, enraged as he was,
> let a word break from his breast.
> Stout-hearted he shouted; his voice went roaring,
> clear in battle, in under the gray stone.
> Hate was stirred up, the hoard's guard knew
> the voice of a man.[1]

Speaking out, the result of a process of understanding, defining, and judging, can have the effect of a structurally climactic action, as when, at the end of the *Paradiso,* Dante formally defines Faith for St. Peter, Hope for St. James, and Love for St. John—a series of declarations that all the timid questionings of the Inferno and Purgatorio have been a prologue to. John Gower's prayer for all of society at the end of the *Confessio Amantis* emerges from and climaxes his experience of amorous persuasion and confession. And, of course, failure to speak can be a climactic omission, as when Parzifal fails to ask the healing question of the Fisher King. The way in which the theology of the Word affected and was in turn affected by, not only such morally and ontologically conspicuous examples of human speech in medieval literature, but also the whole tradition of rhetoric in the Middle Ages and the Renaissance, deserves further investigation.

Furthermore, the literary criticism of the twentieth century has had much to say about the poetic word, or how words in a poem differ from their use in prose. Most obviously, the poetic word is less restricted in meaning and effects a greater internal unity. Northrop Frye, attempting to sum up the formalist critical practice, uses the notion of a "connector" which handily describes what he calls the centripetal movement of words in a poem—the tendency to link or "connect" to all the other words and to a symbolic center which contains and climaxes them.[2] Elsewhere in the *Anatomy of Criticism,* Frye actually uses the word *Logos* to describe literature as a total form, that hypothetical sum total which is made up of all the works of literature, themselves acting as connectors.[3] The historical debt that such criticism owes to the literary implications of the medieval theology of the Word, which remains One throughout an infinity of verbal instances and which is the final cause of all the verbal causes, is apparent, I hope, from what I have written about John Gower's *Confessio Amantis.*

Notes

Introduction

1. Erik H. Erikson, *Young Man Luther* (New York: W. W. Norton & Co., 1958), p. 47.
2. Maria Wickert, *Studien zu John Gower*, p. 66.
3. Donald G. Schueler, "Some Comments on the Structure of John Gower's *Confessio Amantis*."
4. James J. Murphy, "John Gower's *Confessio Amantis* and the First Discussion of Rhetoric in the English Language," p. 404n.11.
5. J. A. W. Bennett, "Gower's 'Honeste Love.'"
6. Derek Pearsall, "Gower's Narrative Art."
7. C. S. Lewis, *The Allegory of Love*, pp. 198–222.
8. Russell A. Peck, ed., *Confessio Amantis*, by John Gower (New York: Holt, Rinehart and Winston, 1968).
9. J. A. Burrow, *Ricardian Poetry: Chaucer, Gower, Langland and the Gawain Poet* (New Haven: Yale University Press, 1971).

Chapter 1

1. John H. Fisher, *John Gower: Moral Philosopher and Friend of Chaucer*, p. 138.
2. John Barry Dwyer, S.J., "The Tradition of Medieval Manuals of Religious Instruction in the Poems of John Gower, with Special Reference to the Development of the Book of Virtues," p. 37.
3. I discovered, after becoming acquainted with the medieval Aristotelian virtue of truth, that Northrop Frye, in his *Anatomy of Criticism*, p. 40, cites the *eiron* and the *alazon*, the self-deprecator and the boaster respectively, as poles which constitute the basis of all literary characterization. The terms are from Aristotle's *Ethics*. See below, n.24.
4. In formulating these principles, I have been influenced by the discussion of "Inexpressibility Topoi," in Ernst Robert Curtius, *European Literature and the Latin Middle Ages*, trans. Willard R. Trask (New York: Pantheon Books, 1953), pp. 159–62; Kenneth Burke, *The Rhetoric of Religion* (1961; rpt. Berkeley and Los Angeles: University of California Press, 1970), pp. 7–42; and Marcia L. Colish, *The Mirror of Language*, pp. 8–82. Although I believe that the validity of my approach is corroborated by Professor Colish's study, I came to it independently; the sources of my documentation are substantially different; and I am more concerned with practical literary analysis than she.
5. Colish, *Mirror*, pp. 34–35.

6. Burke, *Rhetoric*, pp. 17–23.

7. Boethius, *The Consolation of Philosophy*, trans. Richard Green (New York: Bobbs-Merrill Co., Library of Liberal Arts, 1962), Book Three, Prose Ten, p. 61: "It follows that if something is found to be imperfect in its kind, there must necessarily be something of that same kind which is perfect. For without a standard of perfection we cannot judge anything to be imperfect."

8. Burke, *Rhetoric*, pp. 7–8.

9. Augustine, *Confessions*, Book Eleven, 28–31, 6–8.

10. Henri de Lubac, S.J., *Exégèse Médiévale*, 2:1:181–97.

11. Quintilian, *The Institutes of Oratory*, trans. H. E. Butler (London and Cambridge, Mass.: Loeb Classics, 1953), VIII, vi, sec. 21.

12. Guillaume de Lorris and Jean de Meun, *Le Roman de la Rose*, ed. Felix Lecoy; see ll. 2347–2490 passim, especially ll. 2349–57:

> et quant partir t'en covendra,
> trestot le jor te sovendra
> de ce que tu avras veü,
> si te tendras a deceü
> d'une chose mout laidement,
> car onques cuer ne hardement
> n'eüs de li aressoner,
> ainz as esté sanz mot soner
> lez li, con fox et entrepris.

And ll. 2379–98:

> S'il avient chose que tu troves
> la bele ou point que tu la doives
> araisoner ne saluer,
> lors t'estovra color muer,
> si te fremira tot li sans,
> parole te faudra et sens
> quant tu cuideras comancier;
> et se tant te puez avancier
> que ta resson comencier oses,
> quant tu devras dire .III. choses
> tu n'en diras mie les .II.,
> tant seras vers li vergondeus.
> Il n'ert ja nus si apensez
> qui en ce point n'oblit asez,
> si tex n'est que de guille serve.
> Mes faus amanz content lor verve
> si come il veulent, sanz peor;
> icil sont fort losengeor;
> il dient un et pensent el,
> li traïtres felon mortel.

13. Dante Alighieri, *La Vita Nuova*, ed. T. Casini, p. 13:

> . . . e, passando per una via, volse gli occhi verso quella parte ov' io era molto pauroso; e per la sua ineffabile cortesia, la quale è oggi meritata nel grande secolo, mi salutò molto virtuosamente, tanto che mi parve allora vedere tutti li termini de la beatitudine.
>
> L'ora, che 'l su' dolcissimo salutare mi giunse, era fermamente nona di quel giorno; e però che quella fu la prima volta che le sue parole si mossero per venire a' miei orecchi, presi tanta dolcezza, che come inebriato mi partio da le genti, e ricorsi al solingo luogo d'una mia camera, e puosimi a pensare di questa cortesissima.

14. *Njal's Saga*, trans. Magnus Magnusson and Hermann Palsson, p. 91. In the edition of Einar Ól. Sveinsson, *Brennu-Njáls Saga*, p. 83, the passage is as follows:

> At jólum gaf jarl honum gullhring. Gunnarr lagði hug a Bergljótu, fraendkonu jarls, ok fannsk at opt á, at jarl mundi hana hafa gipta Gunnari, ef hann hef i nokkut ess leitat.

15. *Troilus and Criseyde*, III.50–56:

> Lay al this mene while Troilus,
> Recordyng his lesson in this manere:
> "Mafay," thoughte he, "thus wol I sey and thus;
> Thus wol I pleyne unto my lady dere;
> That word is good, and this shal be my cheere;
> This nyl I nought foryeten is no wise."
> God leve hym werken as he kan devyse!

And again when actually confronted by Criseyde, III.78–84:

> This Troilus, that herde his lady preye
> Of lordshipe hym, wax neither quyk ne ded,
> Ne myghte o word for shame to it seye,
> Although men sholde smyten of his hed.
> But, Lord, so he wex sodeynliche red,
> And sire, his lessoun, that he wende konne
> To preyen hire, is thorugh his wit ironne.

All quotations from Chaucer will be from *The Works of Geoffrey Chaucer*, ed. F. N. Robinson, 2d ed.

16. Mes celi, don plus li remanbre,
> N'ose aparler ne aresnier.
> S'ele osast vers lui desresnier
> Le droit, que ele i cuide avoir,
> Volantiers li feïst savior;
> Mes ele n'ose ne ne doit.
> Et ce que li uns l'autre voit,
> Ne plus n'osent dire ne feire. . . .

Chrétien de Troyes, *Cligés*, ed. Wendelin Foerster, ll. 582–89. All quotations from this poem are from this edition.

17. Ibid., ll. 992–1001:

> Cui chaut, quant il ne le savra,
> Se je meïsme ne li di?
> Que ferai je, se ne le pri?
> Qui de la chose a desirrier,
> Bien la doit requerre et proiier.
> Comant? Proierai le je donques?
> Nenil. Por quoi? Ce n'avint onques,
> Que fame tel forsan feïst,
> Que d'amor home requeïst,
> Se plus d'autre ne fu desvee.

18. Ibid., ll. 1018–29:

> Bien le savra, ce cuit, devoir,
> S'il onques d'amors s'antremist
> Ou se *par parole an aprist.*

Aprist? Or ai je dit oiseuse.
Amors n'est pas si gracïeuse,
Que *par parole* an soit nus sages,
S'avuec n'i est li buens usages.
Par moi meisme le sai bien;
Car onques n'an poi savoir rien
Par losange ne par parole,
S'an ai mout esté a escole
Et par maintes foiz *losangiee.* . . . (My italics.)

19. Ibid., ll. 3835–38:

Des iauz parolent par esgart;
Mes des langues sont si coart,
Que de l'amor qui les justise
N'osent parler an nule guise.

20. Ibid, ll. 4410–28:

Cligés par quel antancion,
'Je sui toz vostre' me deïst,
S'amors dire ne li feist?
De quoi le puis je justisier,
Por quoi tant me doie prisier,
Que dame me face de lui?
N'est il plus biaus que je ne sui
Et mout plus jantis hon de moi?
Nule rien fors amor n'i voi,
Qui cest don me poïst franchir.
Par moi, qui ne li puis ganchir,
Proverai que, s'il ne m'amast,
Ja por miens toz ne se clamast:
Ne plus que je soe ne fusse
Tote, ne dire nel deüsse,
S'amors ne m'eüst a lui mise,
Ne redeüst an nule guise
Cligés dir qu'il fust toz miens,
S'amors ne l'a an ses liiens.

ll. 4432–38:

Mes ce me resmaie de bot,
Que c'est une parole usee,
Si repuis tost estre amusee;
Car tes i a, qui par losange
Dïent nes a la jant estrange:
'Je sui toz vostre et quanque j'ai,'
Si sont plus jeingleor que jai.

Translation in text from Chrétien de Troyes, *Arthurian Romances*, trans. W. W. Comfort, p. 148.

21. *The Romance of Flamenca*, trans. Merton Jerome Hubert, revised Provencal text by Marion E. Porter, ll. 3949–54.

22. Ibid., ll. 4303–15.

23. Robinson, I(A)1806–10.

24. Saint Thomas Aquinas, *In Aristotelis Stagiritae Nonnullos Libros Commentaria*, "In X. Libros Ethicorum ad Nicomachum," *Opera Omnia*, 21:147. All translations in this study, unless

otherwise indicated, are my own. The availability to Gower of the Aristotelian teaching on the virtue of truth is verified by its presence in one of his recognized sources, *Li Livres dou Tresor* of Brunetto Latini. I quote the relevant passage from page 196 of Francis J. Carmody's edition:

> Home verais est cil ki tient le mi entre celui ki se vante et moustre k'il face grans choses et s'enhauce plus k'il ne doit, et entre celui ki se desprise et humelie et ki wet celer et abaissier le bien ki est en lui; mais li verais reconoist et conferme de lui tant de bien come il a en lui, et non plus ne mains.

For Gower's use of this work, see Macaulay's notes to Book VII of the *Confessio Amantis*, *The Complete Works of John Gower*, 3:522.

25. Aquinas, *In Aristotelis*, p. 147. The virtue of truth extends also to action: "Est enim verax inquantum de se confitetur ea quae sunt; et hoc non solum sermone, sed etiam vita; inquantum scilicet exterior sua conversatio conformis est suae conditioni, sicut et sua locutio" (Ibid). Thomas's discussion of truth as a moral virtue in the *Summa* repeats in the main what Aristotle says. Truth is a mean between excess and defect in that a person says neither more nor less about himself than what is so. Truth, from the point of view of what is fitting, is also a mean. One should speak the truth at the proper time and in the proper circumstances "quando oportet, et secundum quod oportet" (*Summa Theologiae*, II-II, 109). He who manifests something about himself importunately errs by excess. He who conceals when he should reveal errs by defect.

26.   Or te lo et veil que tu quieres
    un compaig sege et celant
    a cui tu dies ton talant
    et descuevres tot ton corage.
    Cil te fera grant avantage;
    quant ti mal t'angoisseront fort,
    tu iras a li par confort
    et paraleroiz endui ensemble
    de la bele qui ton cuer emble
    Tot ton estre li conteras
    et conseil li demanderas
    coment tu poras chose fere
    qui a t'amie puise pleire.
    Se cil qui tant ert tes amis
    en bien amer son cuer a mis,
    lors vaudra mieuz sa compaignie.
    Si est reson qu'il te redie
    se s'amie est pucele ou non,
    qui ele est et coment a non;
    si n'avras pas peor qu'il muse
    a t'amie ne qu'il t'en ruse,
    ainz vos entreporteroiz foi
    et tu a li, et il a toi.
    Saches que c'est mout plesant chose
    quant l'en a home a qui l'en ose
    son conseil dire et son secre.   (ll. 2672–97).

Cf. also ll. 3083 ff.

27. *Le Roman de la Rose*, ll. 12511–14688; *Troilus and Criseyde*, Book I, passim.

28. The point is also made at length by John V. Fleming, The Roman de la Rose: *A Study in Allegory and Iconography*, pp. 121 ff.

29. In Book IV of the *Nicomachean Ethics*, Aristotle discusses the virtues pertaining to life in society; and Lectio XIV of Aquinas's commentary concerns chapter 6 of Book IV, where the two

extremes to be avoided are obsequiousness and quarrelsomeness. Although life in society consists of both speech and action, Thomas, following Aristotle, emphasizes speech, which has an essential relationship to man's nature:

> Et dicit, quod circa *colloquia humana, per quas maxime homines ad invicem convivunt secundum proprietatem suae naturae,* et universaliter circa totum convictum humanum, qui fit per hoc, quod homines sibi invicem communicantur in sermonibus et in rebus, quidam videntur esse placidi, quasi hominibus placere intendentes. (*In Aristotelis,* p. 145; my italics)

Those who represent the extreme opposite to obsequiousness are called quarrelsome ("dyscoli vel litigiosi"). Though the mean has no name, it is most like friendship. It differs from friendship in that it is "sine amore, qui est passio appetitus sensitivi, et sine dilectione ad eos *quibus colloquitur,* quae pertinet ad appetitum intellectivum." (My italics; ibid.) Here again Thomas deals specifically with speech, and the emphasis is maintained throughout the discussion. The first property of this virtue, for example, "sumitur *ex modo colloquendi.* Et dicit, quod sicut dictum est, universaliter omnibus colloquitur, sicut opportet." This virtue enables a man to live pleasantly with others and pertains "ad bonum honestum, et ad conferens, id est utile, quia est circa delectationes et tristitias quae fiunt in *colloquiis, in quibus principaliter et proprie consistit* convictus humanus." Furthermore, the man who possesses this virtue is aware of the rules of decorum in speaking to persons of different quality:

> Et dicit, quod virtuosus diversimode colloquitur et versatur cum his qui sunt in dignitatibus constituti, et quibuscumque privatis personis. Et similiter diversimode cum magis vel minus notis, et secundum alias diversitates personarum. Singulis enim attribuit quod est conveniens.

Although Aristotle concludes that the virtue has no name, Thomas gives it the designation of *affability.* All the quotations from Thomas's commentary on the *Ethics* are from *In Aristotelis,* p. 145.

In his treatment of the same problem in the *Summa Theologiae,* Thomas considers *affabilitas* a synonym of friendship: ". . . Eccli. vi. dicitur: 'Congregationi pauperum affabilem te facio.' Ergo affabilitas, quae hic amicitia dicitur, est quaedam specialis virtus." *Summa Theologiae,* II-II, 114, 1, c. The extremes, between which the virtue of friendship constitutes a mean, are the same as those named in the commentary on Aristotle. Again, although the virtue regulates both speech and action, the emphasis falls on speech. The first extreme discussed has two manifestations, obsequiousness and flattery:

> Si ergo aliquis in omnibus velit ad delectationem alteri loqui, excedit modum in delectando, et ideo peccat per excessum. Et si quidem hoc faciat, sola intentione delectandi, vocatur placidus, secundum Philosophum; si autem faciat hoc intentione alicuius lucri consequendi, vocatur blanditor sive adulator. (Ibid., 115, 1, c)

The focus on speech in the opposite extreme is even more emphatic:

> Dicendum quod proprie litigium in verbis consistit, cum scilicet unus verbis alterius contradicit. (Ibid., 116, 1, c)

The availability of these ideas to Gower can again be verified by reference to Brunetto Latini:

> Apres ce deviserons des choses ki afierent a compaignie des gens et en la conversation des homes et en lor parleure, pour ce que tenir le mi en ces choses fet a loer, et tenir les estremites fet a blasmer. Et en tenir le mi doit on estre plaisant en parler, et en demorer avec les gens et en converser entrer les homes, et k'il soit de bele compaignie. . . . (*Li Livres,* p. 196)

30. My analysis of the *De arte honeste amandi* is greatly influenced by D. W. Robertson, *A Preface to Chaucer,* pp. 402 ff. The Aristotelian elements together with the emphasis which I

put on speech as such and the allusions to prayer constitute an important difference from Robertson's analysis, however.

31. Andreas Capellanus, *The Art of Courtly Love*, trans., John Jay Parry, p. 33.

32. Ibid., p. 35. Robert Bossuat, in *Drouart la Vache, traducteur d'André le Chapelain*, p. 76, also asserts the centrality of speech in medieval love theory:

> Drouart devine également que le Chapelain ne fait que s'insourer d'Ovide, quand il considère le charme du beau langage comme le plus utile auxiliaire de l'amant; c'est pourquoi il ajoute:
>> Biau parler a amour aide,
>> Selonc la parole d'Ovide
> faisant allusion d'une facon générale à tout un développement du livre II de l'Ars Amatoria, et plus spécialement à ce vers:
>> Dulcibus est verbis mollis alendus amor.
> (Ars. Amat II.152)

Bossuat goes on to refer especially to Ovid's *Ars Amatoria*, II.145–60.

An interesting reference in the *Etymologiae* of Isidore of Seville, Lib. X, *PL* 82:483, lists the wisdom expressed in speech as the principal cause of love:

> In eligendo marito quatuor spectari solent: virtus, genus, pulchritudo, sapientia. Ex his sapientia potentior est ad amoris affectum. Refert haec quatuor Virgilius de Aenea, quod his Dido impulsa est in amorem ejus. Pulchritudine: *Quem sese ore ferens*. Virtute: *Quam forti pectore, et armis. Oratione:*
>> . . . . Heu! quibus ille
> Jactatus fatis, quae bella exhausta canebat! (My italics.)

33. Andreas, *Art of Courtly Love*, pp. 36–37.
34. Ibid., p. 37.
35. Ibid., p. 57.
36. Ibid., p. 52.
37. Ibid., p. 64.
38. Ibid., p. 129.
39. Ibid., pp. 129–30.
40. Ibid., p. 130. See also in the *Mirour*, ll. 14893–97, on the requirement of completeness in confession.
41. Exhortations to oral confession are full of intense and vivid imagery. Guilielmus Peraldus, in a work erroneously attributed to William of Auvergne, *Opera Omnia*, 2(supplement):229, indicates the requirement of oral declaration through his interpretation of a mute demon:

> Primum in hoc quod daemonium mutum dicitur. In hoc enim innuitur quod diaboli machinatione efficitur ut a confessione peccatorum suorum aliquis obmutescat.

Such a culpable silence occasions laughter among the demons who mockingly contrast the response of an injured animal: "Videte de fatuo isto qui permittit se furari, et nescit clamare, quod brutum animal sciret facere" (Ibid.). Peraldus further relates the failure to confess sins with the refusal of the learned to teach:

> *Confundentur confusione vehementi, quia non intellexerunt opprobrium quod nulla oblivione delebitur. Et illud erat mutum.* Notandum quod cum daemon sciens interpretatur daemonium mutum, esse videtur literatus, qui alios aedificare neglexit. Proverbiorum 11, *maledicetur in populis*. Ecclesiastici 30. *Bona abscondita in ore clauso quasi appositiones epularum circumpositae sepulchro.* Item daemonium mutum esse videntur, qui sic volunt loqui ut non intelligantur, 1 Corinth. 14. *Si venero ad vos linguis loquens, quid prodest?*

It is necessary to state the condition of one's soul according to the rules of effective speech, that is, with clarity and thoroughness, and in this context it is significant to note that the confessional manual itself, in its formal structure, fits into the larger genre of the *ars dicendi:* see D. W. Robertson, Jr., "A Note on the Classical Origin of 'Circumstances' in the Medieval Confessional," pp. 6–14. In Gower's *Mirour de l'omme,* the questions that must be answered to ensure the thorough treatment of a topic in an oration come to make up "La fourme de confessioun" (14834):

> C'est qui, quoy, u, qant et comment,
> Ove qui, pour quoy darreinement. . . . (14839–40)

See also in the *Mirour,* ll. 14893–97, on the requirement of completeness in confession.

42. *Dictionnaire de théologie Catholique (DTC),* 12:1, cols. 723–24, contains a discussion of sin as an offense against the order of the Creator. Reference is also made, col. 736, to the *Summa Theologiae* of Aquinas, IIIa, 85, where penance is defined as a special virtue related to justice. Cf. also *Summa Theologiae,* Suppl., 7, "De Quidditate Confessionis." A quotation from Aulus Gellius *Noct. att.* XVII, 1, cited in *DTC,* ibid., col. 723, concerning the use of the word *paenitentia* is also illuminating: "Paenitere tunc dicere solemus cum quae ipsi fecimus aut quae de nostra voluntate nostroque consilio facta sunt ea nobis post incipiunt displicere, *sententiam-que in iis nostram demutamus."* (My italics.) Peraldus, in William of Auvergne, 2:482, lists as part of the act of confession, "divini juris recognitio."

43. "Sicut autem poenitens celare non debet peccatum, quia superbia est; ita nec humilitatis causa fateri se reum illius quod non commisisse noscit, quia incauta est talis humilitas et peccatorem constituit." Peter Lombard, *Sententiae,* Lib. IV, Dist. XXI, Pars II, Cap. VIII, *PL,* 192:897.

Robert de Sorbon, *De Confessione, Maxima Bibliotheca veterum patrum,* 25:354; quoted in D. W. Robertson, "A Study of Certain Aspects of the Cultural Tradition of *Handlyng Synne,"* p. 182:

"Dicebat autem Cardinalis Odo, quod mentiens in confessione, tria peccata mortalia committit de novo; scilicet mendacium perniciosum, hypocrisim; et tertium, quia pollutus scienter, recipit sacramentum confessionis."

According to John H. Fisher, *John Gower, Moral Philosopher,* p. 354, Robertson's dissertation is still the best treatment of the development of the penitential tradition.

Alan of Lille emphasizes the wrong of accepting guilt falsely: "Confiteri nemo debet quae non fecit, Sed caveat ne ex falsa humilitate se dicat esse reum hujus peccati quod non est. . ." (*Liber Poenitentialis, PL* 210:300).

44. Nota, ista observando in confessione: primo ut simplex sit iuxta illud: "Non declinet cor meum in verba malitiae ad excusandas excusationes in peccatis." [Ps. 140:4] Simplex est confessio, ubi totum imputo mihi peccatum, non refundens culpam in alium ut Adam; simplex, sine plica fraudis. . . . . . . nuda, quia sine omni palliatione peccata revelare debemus. . . .

Quoted in Robertson, "Cultural Tradition," p. 182. Robertson's source here is "Le 'Liber Poenitentialis' de Pierre de Poitiers," *Beitrage zur Geschichte der Philosophie und Theologie des Mittelalters,* Supplementband III (1935), p. 317.

45. Robert Mannyng of Brunne, *Handlyng Synne,* ed. Frederick J. Furnival. See also *The Book of Virtues and Vices,* ed. W. Nelson Francis, p. 176.

For more extended research into the sources of the nature and requirements of confession, see Herm. Jos. Schmitz, *Die Bussbücher und die Bussdisciplin der Kirche,* and Oscar D. Watkins, *A History of Penance.*

46. This passage has an extraordinary resemblance to the Augustinian description of the generation of the interior word from knowledge: "It is begotten from the knowledge which remains in the soul, when that knowledge is said as it is." The truth of this word, or *parole,* depends on this knowledge, in Augustine as in Gower: "But the word is true, when it is begotten

from the knowledge of doing well, that even there may be preserved the yes, yes, no, no, that if it is, it is in that by which we must live, that it may also be in that word by which it is brought about." See p. 22.

47. Aquinas, *Summa Theologiae*, II-II, 83, c; repeated in Vincent of Beauvais, *Speculum Quadruplex*, vol. 3 (Morale), Lib. III, Pars X, Dist. XXXI, 1511. All references to Vincent of Beauvais will be to this edition. Cf. 3:III:X:XXXII, 1522, where prayer is described as an address before the whole heavenly court:

> Item honorabile est officium; quia qui orat cum Deo loquitur. Magnus honor est loqui frequenter cum aliquo magno Principe, maior cum Rege, multo fortius cum Rege Regum. Isidor. *Cum oramus, cum Deo loquimur, cum autem legimus, ipse nobiscum loquitur.* Magna igitur est orationis dignitas, quia ipse Deus, et tota curia coelestis, attenta est audire orationes nostras, laudes; et delectantur in eis: et ipsi Angeli orationes et laudes Deo referunt et offerunt. Psalmus 67. *Astiterunt principes coniuncti psallentibus,* scilicet hominibus, et c. Item 137. *in conspectu Angelorum psallam tibi,* et. c. id est conspicientibus Angelis, vel conspiciendo Angelos, qui orationibus nostris attendunt, et eas deferunt. Canticor. 8. *Quae habitas in hortis, amici auscultant: fac me audire vocem tuam,* I. Corinth. 4 *Spectaculum facti sumus Angelis hominibus.*

Cf. also Augustine, *Enarrationes in Psalmos*, LXXXV, PL 37:1086: "Oratio tua locutio est ad Deum: quando legis, Deus tibi loquitur; quando oras, Deo loqueris." The relation of the reading of scripture or the word of God to prayer is developed further by Vincent of Beauvais, 3:III:X:XXXIII, 1522–23.

48. See also Augustine, *Epistulae*, 130, 10, 20, PL 33:501.

> Absit enim ab oratione multa locutio, sed non desit multa precatio, si fervens perseverat intentio. Nam multum loqui est in orando rem necessariam superfluis agere verbis; multum autem precari est ad eum, quem precamur, diuturna et pia cordia excitatione pulsare. Nam plerumque hoc negotium plus gemitibus quam sermonibus agitur, plus fletu quam affatu. Ponit autem lacrimas nostras in conspectu suo et gemitus noster non est absconditur ab eo, qui omni per Verbum condidit et humana verba non quaerit.

The final reference to the Verbum as an ultimate criterion of the speech of prayer is important to our general thesis about the *Confessio Amantis*. For the unimportance of words in prayer, see also Clement of Alexandria, *Stromata*, 7, 7, 43, 4, PG 9:460 C; and Gregory, *Moralia*, 22, 17, 23, PL 76:238C. A positive analogy between the art of rhetoric and prayer is extensively developed by William of Auvergne (1:336 ff.) in an interesting treatise entitled *Rhetorica Divina sive Ars Oratoria eloquentiae divinae.* I quote from a summary of intention, p. 338:

> Scito igitur, quod oratio, de qua hic intendo, septem habet perfectiones, seu differentias, et quia prima est velut oratio rhetorica, et intentio, habens similitudinem orationis rhetoricae saecularis, et ad similitudinem et proportionem illius, partes, videlicet exordium, narrationem, petitionem, confirmationem, et infirmationem, novissime vero conclusionem.

In this context, Colish, p. 61n.140, refers to Augustine's "tendency to play on the word *oratio,* using it to mean 'speech' and 'prayer' at the same time." Her source is C. S. Baldwin, *Medieval Rhetoric and Poetic,* p. 67.

49. *DTC*, 13:175.

50. "Dicendum quod non est necessarium nos Deo preces porrigere ut ei nostras indigentias vel desideria manifestemus," (Aquinas, *Summa Theologiae*, II-II, 83, 2, ad 1). This whole article is reproduced almost verbatim in Vincent of Beauvais, XXXI, 1512. On the idea of God's foreknowledge of the content of man's prayer, cf. also Clement of Alexandria, *Stromata*, 7, 7, 43, 4, PG 9:460 C.:

> Unde loquaces Deus linguas non exspectat, ut hominum interpretes, sed cognoscit omnium, ut semel dicam, mentes; et quod nobis vox significat, hoc Deo nostra loquitur cogitatio, *quam etiam ante creationem sciebat esse venturam in mentem.* 5. Licet ergo etiam absque voce emittere orationem, modo quid quidquid est intrinsecus spiritale, intendat in vocem quae mente percipitur, per indiculsam ad Deum conversionem. (My italics.)

Cf. also St. Basil, *PG* 31:244 A.:

> Precatio est boni petitio, a piis Deo exhibita. Petitionem autem non omnino in verbis circumscribimus, *Neque enim Deum arbitramur monitorum voce prolatorum indigere, immo eum nosse, ne petentibus quidem nobis, quae conducibilia sint.* Quid igitur est, quod dicimus? Nimirum precationem in syllabis constitui non oportere, sed vim precum in proposito animi et in iis virtutis operibus, quae ad omnem vitam esse extendant, collocandum esse. (My italics.)

Both writers obviously stress the superiority of the intention over the spoken word in prayer. The objection that prayer is useless because of God's foreknowledge is answered by Origen, *De Oratione,* 5–8, *PG* 2:429–42.

51. Aquinas, *Summa,* II-II, 83, 2, ad 1, c. Cf. also Vincent of Beauvais, 3:III:X:XXXI, 1512.

52. The relationship of prayer to the character or nature of the person praying is illustrated by a question in the *Sentences* of Peter Lombard, Dist. XVII, "Si omnis Christi oratio vel voluntas impleta sit" which becomes a discussion of what may legitimately be prayed for and the two natures in Christ:

> Post praedicta considerari oportet, utrum Christus aliquid voluerit vel oraverit quod factum non sit. Hoc enim existimari potest per hoc quod ipse ait (Math. 26,39): "Pater, si possibile est, transfer a me calicem istum; verumtamen non sicut ego volo, sed sicut tu vis." Hic namque voluntatem suam a Patris voluntate discernere vicetur. Quocirca ambigendum non est, diversas in Christo fuisse voluntates, juxta duas naturas; divinam scilicet voluntatem, et humanam. Et humana voluntas est affectus rationis, vel affectus sensualitatis: et alius est affectus animae secundam rationem, alius secundum sensualitatem; uterque tamen dicitur humana voluntas. Affectu autem rationis id volebat quod voluntate divina, scilicet pati et mori; sed affectu sensualitatis non volebat, immo refugiebat.

See Aquinas's commentary, *Opera Omnia,* 7:180–87.

53. It would be out of place here, as well as impossible, to attempt a complete description of the role of the Verbum in medieval theology. See the lengthy article by A. Michel in *DTC,* vol. 25, pt. 2, 2639–72; Etienne Gilson, *History of Christian Philosophy in the Middle Ages,* p. 6. Cf. also Karl Rahner et al., *The Word: Readings in Theology.*

54. John L. McKenzie, S.J., *Myths and Realities,* pp. 41–44.

55. *De Trinitate,* 15:11.

56. See Bernard J. Lonergan, S.J., *Verbum,* p. x:

> The context of his [Augustine's] thought on verbum was trinitarian, and its underlying preoccupation was anti-Arian. It followed that the prologue to the Fourth Gospel had to be freed from any Arian implication. To achieve this end Augustine did not employ our contemporary techniques of linguistic and literary history. He did not attempt a fresh translation of the Greek word "λογος," but retained the traditional verbum. Church tradition, perhaps, precluded any appeal to the Stoic distinction between *verbum prolatum* and *verbum insitum.* In any case he cut between these Stoic terms to discover a third *verbum* that was neither the *verbum prolatum* of human speech nor the *verbum insitum* of man's native rationality but an intermediate *verbum intus prolatum.* Naturally enough, as Augustine's discovery was part and parcel of his own mind's knowledge of itself, so he begged his readers to look within

themselves and there to discover the speech of spirit within spirit, an inner *verbum* prior to any use of language, yet distinct both from the mind itself and from its memory or its present apprehension of objects.

For further discussion, Lonergan cites M. Schmaus, *Die psychologische Trinitätslehre des hl. Augustinus.*

57. Translation by Rev. Arthur West Haddan, in *A Select Library of the Nicene and Post-Nicene Fathers of the Christian Church,* ed. Philip Schaff, 3:210.

58. Ibid.

59. Ibid.

60. Ibid. The whole Latin text from Augustine, quoted from Vincent of Beauvais, *Speculum Quadruplex,* vol. 1 (Naturale), lib. XXVII, col. 1921, is as follows:

Nam illud quod carnis ore profertur, vox verbi est, verbum est ipsum dicitur, propter id a quo ut foris appareret assumptum est. Ita enim verbum vox quodammodo corporis fit, assumendo eam in qua manifestetur sensibus hominum sicut Verbum Dei caro factum est, assumendo eam in qua et ipsum manifestetur sensibus hominum. Quisquis itaque cupit ad qualemcunque verbi similitudinem pervenire, non intueatur verbum nostrum quod sonat in auribus, nec quando voce profertur, nec quando silentio cogitatur, sed transeunda sunt haec, ut ad id perveniatur hominis verbum quod in corde dicimus, et tandem per id ad verbum non de Deo natae, sed a Deo factae imaginis Dei, quod neque prolativum est in sono neque cogitativum in similitudine soni, quod alicuius linguae esse necesse sit, sed quod omnia quibus signatur signa praecedit. Et gignitur de scientia quae manet in animo, quando eadem scientia dicitur sicuti est.

Simillima est enim visio cogitationis visioni scientiae. Nam quando per sonum dicitur vel aliquod corporale signum, non dicitur sicuti est, sed sicuti videri audirive per corpus potest: quando ergo quod est in notitia, hoc est in verbo, tunc est verum verbum et veritas, qualis ab homine expectatur, ut quod est in ista, hoc sit et in isto, quod non est in ista, non sit et in isto, hic agnoscitur est, est, non, non. Sic accedit quantum potest illa similitudo imaginis factae ad illam similitudinem imaginis natae, qua Deus filius per omnia substantialiter similis patri praedicatur, sicut etiam de ipso dictum est. Omnia per ipsum facta sunt, ubi Deus per unigenitum suum praedicatur universa fecisse se, ita hominis opera hominis nulla sunt, quae non prius dicantur in corde, sed etiam hoc cum verum verbum est, tunc est initium boni operis. Verum autem verbum est, cum de scientia bene operandi gignitur, ut etiam ibi servetur est, est, non, non, ut si est, est in ea scientia qua vivendum est, sit et in verbo per quod operandum est. Si non, non. Alioquin mendacium erit verbum tale nec veritas, et inde peccatum erit, nec opus rectum.

Et haec similitudo verbi nostri cum Verbo Dei, quia potest esse verbum nostrum quod non sequatur opus, opus autem esse non potest, nisi praecedat verbum, sicut Verbum Dei potuit esse nulla existente creatura, creatura vero nulla esse potest, nisi per ipsum per quod omnia facta sunt omnia. Ideoque non Deus pater, non Deus spiritus, non ipsa Trinitas, sed solus Deus filius qui est Verbum Dei caro factum est, quamvis Trinitate faciente, ut sequente atque imitante verbo nostro eius exemplo recte viveremus, id est, nullum habentes in verbi nostri vel contemplatione vel operatione mendacium. Verum haec huiusmodi imaginis quandoque futura est perfectio. Ad hanc consequendam nos erudit magister bonus fide Christiana et pietate doctrinae ut revelata facie a legis velamine quod est umbra futurorum, gloriam domini speculantes, per speculum scilicet intuentes in imaginem eandem transformemur.

The text can also be found in *PL* 42:1072 ff.

61. Augustine, *Sermones,* 12, 4, 4, *PL* 38:102:

Multi autem modi sunt, quibus nobiscum loquitur Deus. Loquitur aliquando per aliquod instrumentum, sicut per codicem divinarum Scripturarum; loquitur per aliquod elementum mundi, sicut per stellam Magis locutus est [cf. Mt 2,2]. Quid est enim locutio, nisi significatio voluntatis? Loquitur per sortem, sicut de Matthia in locum Iudae ordinando locutus est; loquitur per animam humanam, sicut per prophetam; loquitur per angelum, sicut patriarcharum et prophetarum et apostolorum quibusdam locutum esse accipimus; loquitur per aliquam vocalem sonantemque creaturam, sicut de caelo voces factas, cum oculis nullus videretur, legimus et tenemus. Ipsi denique homini, non extrinsecus per aures eius aut oculos, sed intus in animo non uno modo Deus loquitur, sed aut in somnis, sicut Laban Syro, ne Iacob servum eius in aliquo laederet, et Pharaoni de septem annis opulentis totidemque sterilibus demonstratum est; aut spiritu hominis assumpto, quam Graeci ecstasin vocant, sicut oranti Petro vas plenum similitudinibus crediturarum gentium visum est submissum esse de caelo; aut in ipsa mente, cum quisque maiestatem vel voluntatem intellegit, sicut ipse Petrus ex illa ipsa visione, quid se agere vellet Dominus, apud seipsum cogitando cognovit. Non enim hoc quisquam potest nisi apud se intus sonante quodam tacito clamore veritatis agnoscere.

62. Vincent of Beauvais, *Speculum Quadruplex*, vol. 3 (Morale) Lib. III, Dist. X, Pars I, col. 905–11.

63. A more theologically oriented tradition of friendship than the one we have discussed, contributed to by Ambrose, Augustine, Aelred of Rievaulx, and Peter of Blois, has as its preeminent model for the friendly exchange of secrets the series of conversations that Christ had with his disciples precisely in his role as an expression of the Father. The analogy seems to originate in Ambrose:

> Dedit formam [Christus] amicitiae quam sequamur, ut faciamus amici voluntatem, ut aperiamus secreta nostra amico quaecunque in pectore habemus, et illius arcana non ignoremus. Ostendamus illi nos pectus nostrum, et ille nobis aperiat suum. *Ideo, inquit, vos dixi amicos quia omnia quaecunque audivi a Patre meo, nota feci vobis* (Joan. XV, 15). Nihil vero occultat amicus, si verus est; effundit animum suum, sicut effundebat mysteria Patris Dominus Jesus. (*De Officiis*, III, 22, *PL* 16:193)

The wording in the other two authors is sufficiently different to make direct quotation valuable. Aelred, *De Spirituali Amicitia*, *PL* 195:671:

> . . . et quod his omnibus excelsius, quidam gradus est amicitia vicinus perfectioni, quae in Dei dilectione et cognitione consistit; ut homo ex amico hominis Dei efficiatur amicus, secundum illud Salvatoris in Evangelio: Jam non dicam vos servos, sed amicos meos (Joan. XV, 15).

Peter of Blois in *Un traité de l'amour de xiie siècle: Pierre de Blois*, ed. M. M. Davy, pp. 195–96:

> Veritas in Evangelio loquens ait: *Jam non dicam* vos servos, vos autem dixi amicos, quia omnia quaecumque audivi a Patre meo, nota feci vobis quae ego principio vobis [Joan. XV, 14, 15]. In his verbis, sicut ait beatus Ambrosius, dedit nobis formam amicitiae quam amicorum voluntatem alterutrum faciamus.

64. Gregory the Great, in Garner of St. Victor's *Gregorianum*, *PL*, 193, 174:

> Bene ergo dicitur: si separaveris pretiosum a vili, quasi os meus eris. [Jerem. 15:19]. Vilis quippe Deo est mundus presens, pretiosa est ei anima humana. Quia ergo pretiosum a vili separatur, quasi os Domini vocatur, quia per eum Dominus sua verba, qui ab amore saeculi, loquendo quae potest humanam animam evellit.

65. Rabanus Maurus, *De Vitiis et Virtutibus*, *PL* 112:1395:

> Egregius praedicator Paulus generaliter cunctos ab omnibus malis et pestiferis

refrenare cupiens sermonibus ait: omnis sermo malus de ore vestro non procedat, sed si quis bonus ad aedificationem fidei, ut det gratiam audientibus (Ephes. IV, 29); et super haec adjicit: Nolite contristare Spiritum Sanctum Dei, in quo signati estis in die redemptionis, quo utique gravius malum nullum esse poterit (*Ibid.*, v. 30). Patet igitur quia omnis sermo prolatus qui non proficit ad aedificationem fidei audientium contristat Spiritum Sanctum Dei. Et si sermo prolatus non aedificat, is ab Apostolo Christi est prohibitus, ne Spiritum sanctum contristet, quanto magis ille sermo qui destruit et polluit os dicentis et aures audientis, sicuti est falsitas, detractio, maledictio, et similia?

66. Lubac, *Exégèse médiévale*, 2:I:187–88.
67. Ibid., p. 188*n*.1: "Quoniam (homo) divisus est, et alius factus, ut non sit unus totus."
68. Bernard of Clairvaux, *Sermones de Diversis*, PL 183:735–36:

Quanta est miseria nostra, et indigentia nostra quam multiplex. Etiam verbis opus habemus. Et cum utrumque sit miserum, non jam mirum quod inter nos; mirum magis, quod etiam ad nos ipsos. Nemo scit quae sunt in homine, nisi spiritus hominis qui est in ipso (I Cor. II, 11). Chaos magnum inter nos firmatum est, nisi interveniente quasi instrumento verborum fiat ad invicem transitus quidam cordium in communicatione cogitationum. Hac necessitate inventa sunt verba: quis nesciat? Verumtamen et nos ipsos verbis jam alloqui necesse est. *Nonne Deo subjecta eris, anima mea?* Propheta ait, *ab ipso enim salutare meum* (Psal. LXI, 1). Et cui non frequenter necesse est animam revocare suam, advocare rationem suam, suos convocare affectus? Cui non opus est crebro se ipsum convenire verbis, increpare minis, sollicitare monitis, urgere accusationibus? Quin etiam ratiociniis suadere expedit; quale est, *Ab ipso enim salutare meum;* et consolari aliquando, juxta illud, *Quare tristis es, anima mea, et quare conturbas me.* (Psal. CXLV, 1): et nonnunquam diligentius commonere de quibus oportet, ut est, *Benedic, anima mea, Domino, et noli oblivisci omnes retributiones ejus* (Psal. CII, 2). Nempe cor meum dereliquit me, et necesse habeo ad me ipsum, imo ad me alterum loqui. Atque id interim tanto amplius, quanto minus sum adhuc reversus ad cor, reversus in me, unitus denique mihi ipsi: Nam ne invicem quidem erit jam verbis uti, ubi in unum utique virum perfectum occurremus omnes. Opportune igitur linguae cessabunt; nec medius requiretur interpres, ubi usque adeo medium omne charitate constraverit ille unicus Mediator, ut et nos in unum facti simus in ipsis, qui vere sempiterneque unum sunt, Deo Patre, et ipso Domino Jesu Christo.

Chapter 2

1. J. S. P. Tatlock, "Notes on Chaucer," pp. 141–42.
2. Seán O'Súilleabháin, *A Handbook of Irish Folklore*, p. 403.
3. Robert Adger Law, "In Principio," p. 212.
4. Another revealing passage in Chaucer is a detail about the performing repertoire of "hende Nicholas":

And al above ther lay a gay sautrie,
On which he made a-nyghtes melodie
So swetely that all the chambre rong;
And Angelus ad virginem he song. . . . (I[A]3213–16)

5. Stith Thompson, *Motif-Index of Folk-Literature.*
6. Ambrose, *Expositio Evangelii Secundam Lucam*, PL 15:1636; Bede, *In Lucae Evangelium Expositio*, PL 92:517:

Disce virginem moribus, disce virginem verecundia, disce virginem oraculo, disce mysterio. Trepidare virginum est, et ad omnes ingressus viri ingressus pavere, omnes viri affatus vereri. Discant mulieres propositum pudoris imitari. Sola in penetralibus quam nemo virorum videret, solus angelus reperit, sola sine comite, sola sine teste, ne quo degeneri depravaretur affectu, ab angelo salutatur. Disce, virgo, verborum vitare lasciviam.

7. Lucy Toulmin Smith, ed., *York Plays*.
8. Justinus, *Dialogus cum Tryphone Iudaeo*. In *Enchiridion Patristicum*, ed. M. J. Rouet de Journel, and J. Dutilleul, S.J., p. 56; *PG* 6:709:

Eva enim cum virgo esset et incorrupta, sermone serpentis concepto, inobedientiam et mortem peperit. Maria autem virgo, cum fidem et gaudium percepisset, nuntianti angelo Gabrieli laetum nuntium, nempe Spiritum Domini in eam superventurum et virtutem altissimi ei obumbraturam, ideoque et quod nasceretur ex ea sanctum esse Filium Dei, respondit: *Fiat mihi secundum verbum tuum.*

9. St. Ephraem, *Hymni de instauratione ecclesiae*, 4,1. Rouet and Dutilleul, *Enchir. Pat.*, p. 251:

Adam, suadente serpente, iustitiae debitorem se constituit, et delicti poena in omnes generationes transmissa est. Angelus et puella sese ordinaverunt, locuti sunt et audierunt et debitum solverunt . . . Deus constituit mediatores angelum et puellam, ut suis verbis rem converterent et reconciliatio fieret atque inter supernos et infimos chirographum debitorum dilaceraretur.

10. Jacobus de Voragine, *Sermones de Sanctis*, pp. 142–43:

Missus est Gabriel Angelus a Deo in ciuitatem Galileae &c. Olim missus fuit diabolus ad Euam inferens prauam suggestionem, mendacem assertionem, fallacem promissionem. Sed hodie mittitur Angelus ad Virginem offerens reverendam salutationem cum dixit. Aue gratia plena, ueram assertionem cum dixit. Inuenisti enim gratiam apud dominum. Vtilem promissionem cum dixit. Ecce concipies.

11. Mabel Day, ed., *The English Text of the Ancrene Riwle*, p. 28.
12. Hugh of St. Victor, Sermo XVIII, *In Annuntiatione Dominica*, PL 177:933–34:

Debemus, fratres, nosmetipsi mater esse Christi. . . . Debemus Christum concipere, Christum parturire, Christum parere, Christum natum possidere. . . . Sic in spirituali generatione, in qua Deus masculus est, anima femina. Quando ipse Deus animae conjungitur, concipit anima Christum per fidem.

13. Hildebert, *Sermones de Sanctis, LV, In Festo Annuntiationis*, PL 171:609:

Virgo enim Maria facta est Ecclesia, vel quaelibet anima fidelis, quae incorruptione voluntatis casta et sinceritate fidei virgo est. Unde Apostolus "Despondi enim vos uni viro virginem castam exhibere Christo (II Cor. XI, 2)." Angelo quoque nuntiante quod Maria concepit, predicator est veritatis, quo evangelizante, mens fidelis concipit Verbum Dei, deinde parit.

14. Guérric d'Igny, *De Annuntiatione Sermo II*, PL 185:123–23:

Et ut plenius noveris conceptum Virginis non solum esse mysticum, sed et moralem; quod sacramentum est ad redemptionem, exemplum quoque tibi est ad imitationem; ut manifeste evacues in te gratiam sacramenti, si non imiteris virtutem exempli. Quae enim Deum fide concepit, si fidem habeas, idem tibi promittit, quod videlicet si verbum ex ore nuntii coelestis fideliter velis suscipere, Deum quem totus orbis non potest capere, possis et ipse concipere. Concipere autem corde, imo et corpore, licet non corporali opere aut specie, tamen plane corpore tuo; quandoquidem jubemur ab Apostolo glorificare et portare Deum in corpore nostro (I. Cor. vi 20).

15. Ibid.:

Attende itaque, ut scriptum est, diligenter auditui tuo, nam fides ex auditu, auditus autem per Verbum Dei (Rom. X, 17); quod tibi absque dubio evangelizat angelus Dei, cum de timore aut amore ejus tecum agit predicator fidelis, quem angelum Domini exercituum dici et esse non est tibi fas ambigire (Malach. II, 16, 17). Quam beati qui dicere possunt: *A timore Tuo, Domine, concepimus et parturivimus spiritum salutis* (Isa. XXVI, 17, 18)! qui nimirum non est alius quam spiritus salvatoris, quam veritas Jesu Christi. Vide ineffabilem dignationem Dei, simulque virtutem incomprehensibilis mysterii: qui creavit te, creatur in te; et, quasi parum esset te ipsum habere patrem, vult etiam te sibi fieri matrem. *Quicumque*, inquit, *fecerit voluntatem patris mei, ipse meus et frater, et mater est* (Matth. XII, 50). O fidelis anima, expande sinus, dilata affectus; ne angustieris in visceribus tuis, concipe quem creatura non capit. Aperi Verbo Dei aurem audiendi, haec est, ad uterum cordis via spiritus concipiendi, hac ratione compiguntur ossa Christi, id est, virtutes in ventre praegnantis.

16. Angus Fletcher, *Allegory*, pp. 181–219.

17. Peter Chrysologus, Sermo CXLII, *De Annuntiatione Beatae Mariae Virginis*, PL 52:582:

Fiat nihi secundum verbum tuum. Quae credit verbo, merito concipit Verbum: *In principio erat Verbum, et Verbum erat apud Deum* (Kn. I); et ad totam rem pervenit, quae secretum fidei consentit auditu. Quantum peccat haereticus, qui post causam non credit, cum tantum hanc credisse conspicit ante causam.

18. Peter Abelard, *Sermo I, In Annuntiatione Beatae Virginis Mariae*, PL 178–388: "Fiat mihi secundum verbum tuum. Hoc est, ut ipsum Dei Verbum juxta tuae promissionis verbum concipiam integra, et pariam incorrupta."

19. Ibid., 387:

Quia non erit impossibile apud Deum omne verbum. Verbum Dei hoc loco ipsa est divina locutio, quae a beato describitur Augustino, divina dispositio non habens sonum strepentem et transeuntem, sed vim in perpetuo manentem. Nullum igitur verbum Dei impossibile est ipsi, quum quidquid ipse disponit ut faciat, nullo impediri casu queat.

20. Guérric d' Igny, *De Annuntiatione Sermo I*, PL 185:115:

Sic quippe scriptum habes: Moeror in corde viri humiliabit eum; et sermone bono laetificabitur. (Prov. XII, 25). Prorsus sermo bonus, sermo fidelis et omni acceptione dignus, Evangelium nostrae salutis; quod angelus missus a Deo, hodierna die Mariae evangelizavit, ac laetum de Incarnatione Verbi, dies diei, Angelus Virgini verbum eructavit. Sermo ille, dum Filium promittit Virgini, veniam pollicetur reis, redemptionem captivis, adapertionem clausis, vitamque sepultis. Sermo ille, dum Filii regnum, praedicat, justorum quoque gloriam annuntiat; terret inferos, laetificat coelos; et sicut cognitione mysteriorum, sic etiam novitate gaudiorum perfectionem auxisse videtur angelorum. Quem ergo non laetificet ille sermo bonus in afflictione sua, quem non consoletur verbum illud in humilitate sua.

21. The similarity between the rhetoric of the commentaries and the technique of Gower can be further illuminated by Angus Fletcher, who has shown that in allegorical literature, the inexplicit meaning is suggested by what he calls "rhythmic encoding," a process that readers of medieval literature have long been aware of (*Allegory*, pp. 172–74). A quotation will illustrate the direction of our own reading of Gower. It is a process by which

the author communicates an allegorical intent, not by the content, but by the rhythm. How is this so? Very simply, we can understand the process in terms of an encoding technique. If one wanted to establish a code using a series of unfamiliar signals, let us say bell sounds of different pitches instead of dots and dashes, one would have to repeat certain key combinations in a sort of ritual. The listener who picked up the repeated sounds would at first see no message in them, but gradually would perceive the repetitive pattern, an imposed "code," and would try deciphering what he heard. (Fletcher, *Allegory*, p. 172)

The repeated functions of speech in the stories I have selected from the *Confessio Amantis* display this patterning, and the commentaries unlock the code.

22. For an important analogue of this story in which a woman is seduced by a priest who pretends to be the angel Gabriel, see Giovanni Boccaccio, *Decameron*, ed. Vittore Branca, (1:477–93. Also, Paul A. Olson, *"Le Roman de Flamenca,"* p. 16, finds an Annunciation allusion in an epistle Guillaume sends to Flamenca:

> Its illuminations picture an angel kneeling before a woman who is called 'la bella de Belmont.' From the angel's mouth issue two flowers wreathed together, one of which touches the edge of the verses, and the other leads to the lady. The angel is counseling the lady to listen to the words of the flower, to hear the verses written on the manuscript.

See *Flamenca*, ll. 7100 ff.

23. Giovanni Boccaccio, *Genealogie Deorum Gentilium Libri*, ed. Vincenzo Romano, p. 358. See p. 73.

24. C. S. Lewis, *The Allegory of Love*, p. 212. Although the Nectanabus story is mentioned also, there is no development of the insight; and, in fact, it is accompanied by a curiously disparaging observation:

> The heathen theogamies which form the pivot of *Mundus and Paulina* and Nectanabus are conceived in the light of the Christian sentiment of the Annunciation. . . . This is not art, for doubtless Gower never dreamed of envisaging the story otherwise; but it makes the story better.

My interpretation proves, I hope, that considerable art is involved.

25. For a discussion of the continuation of Roman syncretism in medieval mythography, see Jean Seznec, *The Survival of the Pagan Gods*, trans. Barbara F. Sessions, p. 238.

26. Servius the Grammarian, *In Vergilii Carmina Commentarii*, ed. George Thilo and Hermann Hagen, 2:302: "*Latrator Anubis* quia capite canino pingitur, hunc volunt esse Mercurium, ideo quia nihil est cane sagacius."

27. Robert Holcot, *In librum Sapientiae praelectiones*, lect. cxli, p. 473: "Colebant Iovem sub specie Arietis et Mercurium sub specie canis."

28. Mythographus Primus, *Scriptores rerum mythicarum latini tres Romae nuper repertae*, ed. G. H. Bode: "Canino autem capite pingitur (unde et Anubis dicitur), quia nihil cane sagacius esse dinoscitur."

29. Petrus Berchorius (Pierre Bersuire), *De Formis Figurisque Deorum*, typescript, fol. viii[a]: "Aliqui etiam ut dicit ibidem Rabanus depingebant eum cum capite canino: unde Ovidius: et tu latrator anubis."

30. Ibid.: ". . . quapropter etiam caninum caput habebat quod latratum eloquentiae significat." The elaboration of the image of the dog's head in terms of the effects of preaching is as follows:

> Dicamus igitur quod mystice Mercurius potest designare quem libet bonum praelatum: qui in primis debet habere caput canis inquantum scilicet custos gregis dominici et subditorum speculator et pugil debet esse qui lupos id est daemones et

tyrannos latratu praedicationis et redargutionis deterreat et dente punitionis mordeat inquantum fidelis debet esse domino suo I. Corinth. IIII. Hic iam quaeritur inter dispensatores vt fidelis quis inueniatur.

See also Seznec, *Survival,* p. 238*n.*70.
   31. See Chapter 4, pp. 77–80.

Chapter 3

   1. See chap. 1, pp. 7–8.
   2. See chap. 1, *n.*21.
   3. See chap. 1, p. 20.
   4. Gower, *Works,* 3:512; note to ll. 399 ff.
   5. "L' 'Ovidius Moralizatus' di Pierre Bersuire," ed. F. Ghisalberti, pp. 111–12.
   6. Ibid., p. 112:

> Vel quod Liber pater cum exercitu suo signat beatum Petrum cum exercitu suo *scilicet* cum collegio apostolorum et aliorum sanctorum patrum. Istis enim sicientibus et aquam gratie appetentibus apparuit Jupiter in specie arietis id est Dei filius in humana natura qui fontem baptismatis, Spiritus Sancti et gratie omnibus aperuit et eos donis et virtutibus adaquavit. . . .

   7. See chap. 1, pp. 18–19.
   8. There seems to be an analogy here to virtuous action as prayer. See chap. 1, *n.*44.
   9. Alexander Neckam, *De Naturis Rerum,* p. 91:

> Sed dum quis secularis scientiae totum se dedit exercitatio, eloquentia quae sine sapientia multum nocet, intellectum, per caput designatum cum usu discretionis ei aufert et adimit, ita quod oculi ejus inani gloriae dediti sunt. Per oculos intellige intentionem.

  10. Boccaccio, *Genealogie,* p. 358:

> Demum hic [homo] iam natus Argo servandus committitur, id est rationi, cui profecto multa sunt lumina semper, et in salutem nostram vigilantia. Sane Mercurius, id est blande carnis astutia, caduceo, id est suasionibus pessimis, in somnum rationem deducit atque interimit, eaque superata atque deiecta, Juno, id est regnorum preminentiorum atque divitiarum concupiscentia, vacce, id est humano appetitui, summittit oestrum, id est solicitudinis acquirendi stimulum; hinc miseri cursum rapimus, vagamur, et circum agimur fluctuantes, quietem eis in rebus querentes, in quibus ne dum sit quies, sed continuus labor inest talis, ut anxios nos ad ultimum deducat in Egyptum, id est in tenebras exteriores, ubi fletus et stridor dentium; et ni nobis divino munere suffragium prestetur, Ysis effici efficimur, id est terra, sic enim Ysis interpretatur, et a cunctis, tamquam res vilis atque deiecta calcamur.

Boccaccio's interpretation of the Mercury and Argus story is so close to the explicit intention of Genius that it may be a direct source. In the present context Mercury represents a force that must be resisted if the fault of somnolence is to be overcome. In Boccaccio, Io, as is evident from the above quotation, is human nature. "Et ideo in vaccam transformatus dicitur homo, qui uti vacca laboriosum et fructuosum sit animal, sic et homo . . ." (ibid.; IV.2363–2700, in Gower). The uses of labor form the subject of a fairly lengthy digression immediately after which come Somnolence and the present Mercury story. When introducing the section on labor, Gower quotes Solomon as saying,

> As the briddes to the flihte
> Ben made, so the man is bore
> To labour. . . .

Boccaccio uses the same comparison in describing Io as human nature: "Uti ad volatum avis, sic et ipse nascitur ad laborem. . . ."

11. John of Garland, *Integumenta Ovidii*, ed. Fausto Ghisalberti, p. 43:

> Mercurius mentes curans deus eloquiorum
> Verbi mobilitas dicitur ala duplex.
> Sermonis virga vis est sopire tyrannos,
> Fertur, et egrotis mentibus addit opem.

12. *Arnolfo d'Orleans, Un cultore di Ovidio nel secolo XII*, ed. Fausto Ghisalberti, p. 203: "Quemlibet facundum qui sua persuasione mundanas concupiscencias in ea mortificavit. . . ."

13. Bersuire, *Ovidius*, fol. XXI b:

> Vel dic quod Argus est diabolus oculatissimus et subtilis qui Yo mutatam in vacam i. animas peccatrices in suo dominio detinet. Sed Mercurius i. Christus qui de masculo est factus femina, de deo factus est homo quando *Verbum caro factum est*, assumpta humanitatis nostre fistula, ipsum Argum i. diabolum consopivit. . . . (My italics.)

Chapter 4

1. *Dante's Convivio*, trans. William W. Jackson, p. 149.
2. Ibid., pp. 149–50.
3. Ibid., p. 150.
4. Hugo Rahner, *Greek Myths and Christian Mystery*, trans. Brian Battershaw, pp. 354–55, and passim.
5. *Symposium*, 216 A; quoted by Rahner, *Greek Myths*, p. 355.
6. Proclus, *Comment. in Platonis Cratylum*, 157; *In Rempubl.*, 34, 10; quoted by Rahner, *Greek Myths*, p. 356.
7. Ibid.
8. Vincent of Beauvais, *Speculum Quadruplex*, vol. 3 (Morale), Lib III, Dist. iv, Pars I, col. 879:

> Sexto a verbis ociosis; et hoc audiendo aedificatoria verba, vel stupendo in eis, Prouerb. 2. Audiat sapientiam auris tua. Hoc signatur, 2. Reg. 22. Bananias qui Aedificatio Domini, vel responsio, vel secretarius interpretatur, erat auricularius Dauid, et significat verbum Dei quod debet esse custos aurium nostrarum.

Preceding this passage in the section "De Auditu" is a reference to Ulysses and the Sirens which concludes with a quotation from St. Jerome:

> Dicitur de Ulysse, quod cum iret per mare per loca ubi consueuerant audiri cantus Syrenarum (que finguntur et describuntur a Poetis pisces ex parte inferiori, et mulieres ex parte superiori) canentes cum cytharis et tibijs, ille sapiens dicitur obturasse aures suas pice, ne attractus cantus earum dulcedine, praecipitaret se in mare. Quod multi faciunt allecti suauitate musicorum, et muliebrium cantuum, se praecipitantes in periculum luxuriae, et amaritudinem inferni. Aures pice sibi obturat, qui cogitans quam turpe, tenax, faetidum, et combustile in inferno sit peccatum, aures euertit ab huiusmodi. Hieronym. in prologo super Iosue: *Nos ad patriam festinantes*, Syrenarum mortiferos cantus debemus surda aure transire. . . .

9. Boccaccio, *Genealogie*, p. 355:

> Hec de his legisse memini, in quibus quid figentes senserint advertendum est. . . . Et Leontius asserit vetustissima haberi fama apud Etholos prima Grecorum fuisse meretricia, *et tantum lenocinio facundie valuisse*, ut fere omnem Achayam in suam

vertissent predam; et ex hoc arbitrari fabule originis Syrenarum locum fuisse concessum. (My italics.)

10. Ibid.: "Quibus ob blandam fere omnium facundiam Caliopes, id est bona sonoritas, mater ascribitur."

11. For the word of God as food, see chap. 1, p. 23.

12. Gregory the Great, *Homiliarum in Evangelia Libri Duo*, XL, *PL* 76:1302; Bede, *Homiliae*, Lib. III, *PL* 94:271, repeats what Gregory says; so does Smaragdus, *Collectiones in Epistolas et Evangelia*, *PL* 102:353–3:

> Sed Lazarus vulneratus cupiebat saturari de micis quae cadebant de mensa divitis et nemo illi dabat, quia gentilem quemque ad cognitionem legis admittere superbus ille populus despiciebat. Qui dum doctrinam legis non ad charitatem habuit, sed ad elationem, quasi de acceptis opibus tumuit. Et quia ei verba defluebant de scientia quasi micae cadebant de mensa.

13. Ibid.:

> At contra jacentis pauperis vulnera lingebant canes. Nonnunquam solent in sacro eloquio per canes praedicatores intelligi. Canum etenim lingua vulnus dum lingit, curat, quia et doctores sancti dum in confessione peccati nostri nos instruunt, quasi vulnus mentis per linguam tangunt; et quia nos loquendo a peccatis eripiunt, quasi tangendo vulnera ad salutem reducunt.

14. Peter Riga, *Aurora . . . Biblia Versificata*, ed. Paul E. Beichner, C. S. C., 2:505:

> Gentes quas curat confessio signat egenus
> Cuius curabat uulnera lingua canum. (2061–62)

For Gower's knowledge of this poem, see Beichner's remarks in *Speculum* 30 (1955):582; also Fisher, *John Gower*, pp. 147, 150.

15. Gregory, *Homiliarum*, *PL* 76:1302:

> In lingua autem amplius ardere ostenditur, cum dicit: Mitte Lazarum, ut intingat extremum digiti sui in aquam, ut refrigeret linguam meam, quia crucior in hac flamma (Luc. XVI, 24). Infidelis populus verba legis in ore tenuit, quae opere servare contempsit. Ibi ergo amplius ardebit, ubi se ostendit scire quod facere noluit. Quapropter bene de doctis et neglegentibus per Salamonem dicitur: omnis labor hominis in ore ejus, sed anima illius non implebitur (Eccle. VI, 7), quia quisquis hoc solummodo laborat, ut sciat quid loqui debeat, ab ipsa refectione suae scientiae mente vacua jejunat.

16. For the motif of falling in love through hearsay, see Olin H. Moore, "Jaufre Rudel and the Lady of Dreams," pp. 527 ff.; also D. W. Robertson, Jr., "Love Conventions in Marie's *Equitan*," p. 243. The whole tradition of Christian reflection upon the nature of fame is significant in this context: see B. G. Koonce, *Chaucer and the Tradition of Fame*.

17. Edward A. Block, "Originality, Controlling Purpose, and Craftsmanship in Chaucer's *Man of Law's Tale*," pp. 587–88.

18. W. F. Bryan and Germaine Dempster, eds. *Sources and Analogues of Chaucer's Canterbury Tales*, p. 176: "Et taunt com fu plus curious, Constaunce, pur sa chastete sawer, priueement luy vient rere au dos e le tresbucha en la mer."

19. Ibid., p. 175, where Constance is entertained by the lord of the castle, an episode absent from Chaucer and Gower.

20. 3 Esdras, 3, 55:

> Vinum iniquum, iniquus rex, iniquae mulieres, iniqui omnes filii hominum, et iniqua illorum omnium opera, et non est in ipsis veritas, et in sua iniquitate peribunt, et veritas manet et invalescit in aeternum et vivit et obtinet in saecula saeculorum.

St. Jerome considered the third and fourth books of Esdras apocryphal, but they are commonly included in Latin biblical manuscripts. In 1546, the Council of Trent excluded these books from the Roman Catholic Canon; and in subsequent editions of the Vulgate, they often appear in an appendix after the New Testament. See *The Oxford Dictionary of the Christian Church*, ed. F. L. Cross (London: Oxford University Press, 1957), pp. 462–63. The story told here by Gower seems to have been cited frequently in the Middle Ages: see *A Dictionary of the Bible*, ed. James Hastings and John A. Selbie (New York: Charles Scribner's Sons, 1898), 1:758. In fact, Augustine's allegorical interpretation of Christ as the Truth in this very story may have influenced Gower to apply an analogous interpretation to woman:

> . . . perhaps, Esdras is to be understood as prophesying of Christ in that passage where, on a question having arisen among certain young men as to what is the strongest thing, when one had said kings, another wine, the third women, who for the most part rule kings, yet that same third youth demonstrated that the truth is victorious over all. For by consulting the Gospel we learn that Christ is the Truth.

Saint Augustine, *The City of God*, trans. Marcus Dods (New York: Modern Library, 1950), Bk. 18, 36, p. 645.

Chapter 5

1. *Aristotle's Poetics, A Translation and Commentary for Students of Literature*, trans. Leon Golden, p. 19:

> Recognition, as the name indicates, is a change from ignorance to knowledge, bringing about either a state of friendship or one of hostility on the part of those who have been marked out for good fortune or bad. The most effective recognition is one that occurs together with reversal, for example, as in the *Oedipus*. There are also other kinds of recognition for, indeed, what we have said happens, in a way, in regard to inanimate things, even things of a very casual kind; and it is possible, further, to "recognize" whether someone has or has not done something. But the type of recognition that is especially a part of the plot and the action is the one that has been mentioned. For such a recognition and reversal will evoke pity or fear, and we have defined tragedy as an imitation of actions of this type; and furthermore, happiness and misery will appear in circumstances of this type. Since this kind of recognition is of persons, some recognitions that belong to this class will merely involve the identification of one person by another when the identity of the second person is clear; on other occasions it will be necessary for there to be a recognition on the part of both parties; for example, Iphigenia is recognized by Orestes from her sending of the letter; but it is necessary that there be another recognition of him on her part.

2. The convergence of the dramatic recognition scene and Christian repentance is discussed by Edmund H. Creeth, "Moral and Tragic Recognition: the Uniqueness of Othello, Macbeth, and King Lear," p. 382: "The uniqueness of Othello, Macbeth, and King Lear lies not simply in their employment of tragic recognition, however, but in its employment within traditional dramatic structure. . . . A recognition scene, leading to contrition and spiritual restoration, had formed a regular part of Tudor moral interludes. . . ." I am indebted for this reference to Professor Nancy Harvey of the University of Cincinnati.

The important role played by the doctrine of repentance in the whole vernacular drama is the subject of Eleanor Prosser's *Drama and Religion in the English Mystery Plays* (Stanford: Stanford University Press, 1961). See also chap. 1, *n.*34.

3. See Richard Hamilton Green, "Alan of Lille's *De Planctu Naturae*," pp. 660 ff.

4. Ovid *Metamorphoses*, IV.792–801, trans. Mary M. Innes (Baltimore: Penguin Books, 1955), p. 125.

> Clarissima forma
> multorum fuit spes invidiosa procorum
> illa, nec in tota conspectior ulla capillis
> pars fuit: inveni, qui se vidisse referret.
> hanc pelagi rector templo vitiasse Minervae
> dicitur: aversa est et castos aegide vultus
> nata Iovis texit, neve hoc inpune fuisset,
> Gorgoneum crinem turpes mutavit in hydros.
> nunc quoque, ut attonitos formidine terreat hostes,
> pectore in adverso, quos fecit, sustinet angues.

5. Boccaccio, *Genealogie,* p. 496:

> Quod autem prospectantes in saxa converterent, ob id fictum existimo, quia tam grandis esset earum pulchritudo, quod eis visis obstupescerent intuentes, et muti atque immobiles non aliter quam essent saxei devenirent.

6. Petrus Berchorius, *Ovidius Moralizatus,* fol. XLI a and b:

> Ista serpentina monstra possunt signare malas et pulchras mulieres quae serpentinae id est maliciosae sunt naturae. . . . Ipse enim videntes in lapides convertunt: quia ex visu et aspectu mulierum homines in lapides: id est insensibiles efficiuntur et prae stupore et temptatione quam concipiunt sensu debite discretionis priuantur. . . .

7. Gower, *Works,* 2:35–36.
8. Giovanni del Virgilio, *Allegorie Librorum Ovidii Metamorphoseos,* ed. Fausto Ghisalberti, p. 60: "Homo igitur virtuosus vult hanc occidere et accipere scutum sapientie et gladium virtutis scilicet *eloquium* et eam superat." (My italics.)
9. *Mirour de l'omme,* 14593–15096.
10. Bersuire, *Ovidius Moralizatus,* fol. XLI b.: "gladium fulcatum id est verbum dei et orationem."
11. John of Garland, *Integumenta Ovidii,* p. 56: "Est Perseus virtus, harpe facundia fertur."
12. Ibid., p. 55, note to ll. 225–32: ". . . arpe Mercurij, id est consilio facundo eloquentissimorum hominum. . . ."
13. Giovanni del Virgilio, *Allegorie,* p. 61: "Sed per Perseum intellige virtutem, que accipit mentem rationalem in suam uxorem, et liberat eam a diabolo cum pulchris verbis."
14. See chap. 1, nn.16–20.
15. Giovanni del Virgilio, *Allegorie,* 61: "faminis ense sacri."
16. Ibid.: "Hec secat eloquio virtus."
17. Arnulph of Orleans, ed. Fausto Ghisalberti, p. 212: "Arpis enim ensis est recurvus et signat facundiam virtuosi que ad modum gladii curvi in se ipsam recurvans in supercilium iactantie numquam attingit."
18. See chap. 1, pp. 5–6.
19. Boccaccio, *Genealogie,* pp. 615–16:

> Credo tantum quemcunque Mercurium eloquentie deum veteres voluisse, eo quod ad Mercurium planetam mathematici asserant spectare omne sonans organum, seu fistulam in corporibus nostris disponere, et hinc credant nonnulli eum deorum dictum nuntium et interpretem, quia per organa ab eo disposita cordis nostri pandantur intrinseca, que deorum secreta dici possunt, in quantum nisi exprimantur nutu vel verbis, nemo preter deum cognoscit, et in hoc interpres secretorum talium est quia verba, que organizata sunt per organa, ab eodem disposita interpretantur et aperiunt, que ex nutu solo satis percipi non poterant.

For further information on the tradition of Mercury and speech, especially in love, see Norman O. Brown, *Hermes the Thief,* p. 15 and passim.

20. Rémi of Auxerre, *Commentum in Martianum Capellam*, ed. Cora E. Lutz, p. 81:

> Puer depingitur quia turpis amor puerilis est et sic in amantibus sermo deficit sicut in pueris. Hinc Virgilius: "Incipit effari, mediaque in voce resistit" [Aen. IV, 76].

21. Servius the Grammarian, *In Vergilii Carmina Commentarii*, ed. Georg Thilo and Hermann Hagen, 1:478.

22. Trans. James Michie, *The Odes of Horace*, p. 209.

> Sed cur heu, Ligurine, cur
> > Manat rara meas lacrima per genas?
>
> Cur facunda parum decoro
> > Inter verba cadit lingua silentio?

23. Justin, *Apologia*, I, 22, quoted by Rahner, *Greek Myths*, pp. 196–97.

24. *Recognitiones*, X, 41, *PG*, X, 1441B; quoted by Rahner, *Greek Myths*, p. 197: "Mercurius Verbum esse traditur."

25. Ibid.

26. Augustine, *Ennarationes in Psalmos*, 38, *PL* 36, pp. 115–16:

> *Obsurdui, et humiliatus sum, et silui a bonis*, Ps. 38:3. Unde enim dicebam bona, nisi quia audiebam? *Auditui enim meo dabis exultationem et laetitiam.* Et amicus sponsi stat, et audit eum, et gaudio gaudet propter uocem, non suam sed sponsi. Ut uera dicat, audit quae dicat. Nam qui loquitur mendacium, de suo loquitur.

27. Alexander Neckam, *De Naturis Rerum*, pp. 65–66:

> Etsi enim vocem non credam esse aerem, tamen sine aeris beneficio nec proferri potest nec audiri. Vox itaque a multis sine sui dispendio auditur, adeo ut quadam naturae munificentia usum sui multorum quilibet sine invidia aut diminutione concedat. Unde et verbum Patris toti mundo sufficit, totum se ecclesiae toti concessit, commune solatium, communis salus. Verbum Patris sapientia est. Sapientia autem thesaurus nobilis est, quia sine sui detrimento omnibus se offert, omnibus sufficit. Vox item affectus animi exponit, adeo ut littera. Vox viva efficacius imprimit mentibus auditorum sententiarum characterem quam mortui apices. Nescio quid latentis energiae, id est interioris operationis, habet in se viva vox. Vox etiam, cum jam proferri desiit, interius tamen in anima auditoris adhuc loqui videtur. Verba item sunt sagittae acutae, ex intimis cordis sanguinem quendam devotionis elicientes. Verba namque penetrant usque ad penitiores partes animi, adeo ut nunc aculeo doloris animus pungatur, nunc imagines laetitiae letus sibi depingat. *Numquid enim frustra in virga Mercurii quaedam pars esse vivificans, quaedam esse mortifera, fingitur?* Nonne in manibus linguae mors et vita?

28. MS Bod. Digby 221, fol. 81; quoted by E. Faye Wilson, "Pastoral and Epithalamium in Latin Literature," p. 45. See also Henri de Lubac, *Exégèse Médiévale*, p. 216:

> Et quod ubicumque dignitas Mercurii Philologie dignitati proponitur in hoc loco. Mercurius Verbum, id est filius Dei intelligitur. Aliter enim non procederet cum rationem mentis sermone oris liqueat esse digniorem. Ei autem, id est filio Dei Philologia coniungitur, id est homo qui duce ratione tendit ad suum principium. Quid ergo per Mercurium et Philologiam nisi sponsum et sponsam, id est, Christum et Ecclesiam intelligimus?

29. *Gesta Romanorum*, ed. Hermann Oesterley, p. 557:

> Narrat Trogus Pompejus de Ligurio nobili milite, qui civitatem quandam cum populo jurare indixerat, ad servandum leges quasdam justas et utiles licet principio graves,

donec ipse ab *Appolline* deifico, quem ipse finxit esse auctorem dictarum legum, responsum reportaret. (My italics.)

30. Aquinas, *Summa Theologiae*, I-II, 91, 1, ad 2:

. . . promulgatio fit et verbo et scripto, et utroque modo lex aeterna habet promulgationem ex parte Dei promulgantis, quia et Verbum divinum est aeternum, et scriptura libri vitae est aeterna.

For a discussion of law and the Word in medieval thought, see Etienne Gilson, *The Spirit of Medieval Philosophy*, trans. A. H. C. Downes, pp. 334 ff.

31. Brunetto Latini, *Li Livres dou Tresor*, ed. Francis J. Carmody, p. 31: "La divine loi est par nature; et neporquant ele fut mise en escrit et fut confermee premierement par les prophetes et c'est le viel testament. Puis fu li noviaus testament, et fu conferme par Jhesukrist et par ses disciples."

32. Boccaccio, *Genealogie*, p. 245:

. . . Orpheus movet silvas radices habentes firmissimas et infixas solo, id est obstinate opinionis homines, qui, nisi per eloquentie vires queunt a sua pertinacia removeri, Sistit flumina, id est fluxos et lascivos homines, qui, nisi validis eloquentie demonstrationibus in virile robur firmentur, in mare usque defluunt, id est in perpetuam amaritudinem. Feras mites facit, id est homines sanguinum rapacesque, quod sepissime eloquentia sapientis revocat in mansuetudinem et humanitatem.

Bersuire's interpretation, *Ovidius Moralizatus*, fol. LXXIII a, makes Orpheus a preacher:

Orpheus significat praedicatorem et diuini verbi carminum dictatorem: qui . . . saxa et arbores id est insensibiles et induratos peccatores trahere et ex eis verbi diuini dulcedine populum aggregare.

33. Boccaccio, *Genealogie*, p. 274:

Eum [Amphyonem] autem cythara movisse saxa in muros Thebanos construendos dicit Albericus, nil aliud fuisse, quam melliflua oratione suasisse ignaris, atque rudibus et duris hominibus, et sparsim degentibus, ut in unum convenirent, et civiliter viverent, et in defensionem publicam, civitatem mentibus circumdarent, quod et factum est. *Quod autem a Mercurio cytharam susceperit, est quod eloquentiam ab influentia Mercurii* habuerit, ut mathematici asserunt. (My italics.)

34. Ma come Constantin chiese Silvestro
    d'entro Siratti a guerir della lebbre;
      cosi mi chiese questi per maestro
    a guerir della sua superba febbre. . . .   (ll.94–97)

The Divine Comedy of Dante Alighieri, trans. John D. Sinclair, 1:339.

35. For an extensive discussion of the real and spurious history of Constantine, see Christopher Bush Coleman, *Constantine the Great and Christianity*.

36. Brunetto Latini, *Li Livres*, p. 31.

37. Künc Constantîn der gap sô vil,
    Als ich ez iu bescheiden wil:
      dem stuol ze Rôme sper kriuz unde krône.
    Zehant der engel lûte schrê:
    'owê, owê, zem dritten wê.'
      ê stuont diu kristenheit mit zühten schône:
    Der ist ein gift nû . . gevallen,
    ir honec ist worden zeiner gallen.
      daz wirt der werlt her nâch vil leit.'

alle fürsten lebent nû mit êren,
wan der hoe heste ist geswachet:
    daz hât der pfaffen wal gemachet.
    daz sî dir, süezer got, gekleit.
die pfaffen wellent leien reht verkêren.
    der engel hât uns wâr geseit.

Walther von der Vogelweide, pp. 128–29. The poem is translated by Frank C. Nicholson, *Old German Love Songs*, pp. 74–75:

> King Constantine, he gave of yore
> Spear, Cross, and Crown, no less, no more,
> Unto the See of Rome: I tell you truly.
> Aloud thereat the Angel cried:—
> "Woe, woe, and once more woe betide!
> Once Christendom was governed well and duly.
> Some poison now hath fallen in it:
> The honey turns to gall within it.
> This soon will fill the world with ruth!
> All princes now live honoured and renowned:
> Only the highest is brought to shame.
> The priests' election is to blame.
> Sweet God, to Thee we cry, in sooth!
> The priests would fain the layman's rights confound.—
> The Angel told us nought but truth.

38. Sinclair translation, p. 243. *Inferno* XIX. 115–17:

> Ahi, Constantin, di quanto mal fu matre,
>   non la tua conversion, ma quella dote
>   che da te prese il primo ricco patre!

39. A concise account of this whole sequence of events can be found in Maurice Keen, *The Pelican History of Medieval Europe*, pp. 207–21, 159–61. For a more extended discussion of the spiritual Franciscans, see D. L. Douie, *The Nature and the Effect of the Heresy of the Fraticelli*.

40. Larry D. Benson, *Art and Tradition in Sir Gawain and the Green Knight*, pp. 23–24, 231–40.

41. Gerald Bordman, *Motif-Index of the English Metrical Romances*, H 13.5 ff.

42. Stith Thompson, *Motif-Index*, H.11.1.: "Recognition by telling life history."

43. See Elimar Klebs, *Die Erzählung von Apollonius aus Tyrus*.

Chapter 6

1. Robert Scholes and Robert Kellogg, *The Nature of Narrative*, pp. 236 ff.

2. Fletcher, *Allegory*, pp. 214 ff.

3. See chap. 5, pp. 139–40.

4. John Peter, *Complaint and Satire in Early English Literature*, pp. 9–10.

5. Fisher, *Gower*, pp. 206 ff.

6. Frye, *Anatomy of Criticism*, pp. 223–39; Robert C. Elliott, *The Power of Satire*.

7. Frye, *Anatomy*, p. 224.

8. Fisher, *Gower*, pp. 105, 109.

9. In the *Summa Praedicantium* of John Bromyard, the following association between infidelity to a spoken promise, ingratitude, and unnaturalness occurs:

Istorum vero sive quorumcunque aliorum temerarie et consuetudinarie iurantium: voventium/ vel peierantium [*sic*] ingratitudo: et peccati magnitudo multis ostenditur evidentiis.

Primo quia deum inhonorant in membro in quo deus plus pro eis fecit: quod pro quacunque alia creatura id est in lingua et ore homini namque soli dedit os et linguam ad loquendum. Ex quo sequitur quod in illa parte in qua deus illum specialius et excellentius honoravit ex lege gratitudinis et mutue vicissitudinis obtentu specialius deum laudare deberet: dicens cum psal. XXXIII semper laus eius in ore meo. Sed heu a contrario iurantes: et voventes contra omnem mundi curialitatem: plus deum in illa parte inhonorant contra omnem mundi curialitatem. . . .

Later in the article, J, XII, ix, a metamorphosis is described which, along with the whole section, may well have influenced Gower in his composition of Book V of the *Confessio Amantis:*

Tales vero bestiis assimilantur. . . Vel quibuscumque rebus peioris sunt conditionis: et maioris ingratitudinis. Primum patet: quia sicut cornicule super aquilam vel falconem garrunt. Ita isti cornicule inferni super deum et sanctos. Sed sicut avis illa nobilis: si illos garrientes attingere posset; illis redderet quod meruerunt. Ita deus et sancti qui illis attingere possunt illis reddunt tam hic diversis eos infirmitatibus percutientes. . . .

Epilogue

1. The text is that of Fr. Klaeber, *Beowulf and the Fight at Finnsburg,* 3d ed. (Boston: D. C. Heath and Co., 1950); the translation is that of E. Talbot Donaldson, *Beowulf: A New Prose Translation* (New York: W. W. Norton and Co., 1966), p. 45.

2. Frye, *Anatomy,* p. 73.

3. Ibid., pp. 120–21, 126.

Bibliography

The following abbreviations are used for J. P. Migne, *Patrologiae cursus completus:*
PG:Series graeca, Paris, 1857–1903; *PL:Series latina,* Paris, 1844–1903.

Abelard, Peter. *Sermones. PL* 178:379–610.

Aelred of Rievaulx. *De Spirituali Amicitia. PL* 195:659–702.

Alan of Lille. *Liber Poenitentialis. PL* 210:281–304.

Ambrose. *De Officiis. PL* 16:25–194.

————. *Expositio Evangelii Secundam Lucam. PL* 15:1603–1944.

Andreas Capellanus. *The Art of Courtly Love.* Translated by John Jay Parry. New York: Frederick Ungar Publishing Co., 1964.

————. *De Amore Libri Tres.* Edited by Amadeo Pages. Castellón de la Plana, Spain: Sociedad Castellonense de Cultura, 1929.

Aquinas, Saint Thomas. *Opera Omnia.* New York: Musurgia Publishers, 1949.

Aristotle. *Aristotle's Poetics, A Translation and Commentary for Students of Literature.* Translated by Leon Golden. Commentary by O. B. Hardison. Englewood Cliffs, N.J.: Prentice-Hall, 1968.

Arnulph of Orleans. *Arnolfo D'Orleans, Un Cultore di Ovido nel Secolo XII.* Edited by Fausto Ghisalberti. Memorie del Reale Instituto Lombardo di Scienze e Lettere, vol. 24. Milan, 1932.

Augustine. *The City of God.* Trans. Marcus Dods. New York: Modern Library, 1950.

————. *De Trinitate Libri XV. PL* 42:815–1098.

————. *Enarrationes in Psalmos. PL* 36–37.

————. *Sermones. PL* 38:16–39:1638.

Baldwin, C. S. *Medieval Rhetoric and Poetic.* New York: Macmillan Co., 1928.

Bede. *Homiliae. PL* 94:9–516.

————. *In Lucae Evangelium Expositio. PL* 92:301–634.

Beichner, Paul E., C.S.C. "Gower's Use of Aurora in *Vox Clamantis.*" *Speculum* 30 (1955):582–95.

Bennett, J. A. W. "Gower's 'Honeste Love.'" In *Patterns of Love and Courtesy: Essays in Memory of C. S. Lewis,* edited by John Lawlor. London: Edward Arnold Publishers, 1966.

Benson, Larry D. *Art and Tradition in Sir Gawain and the Green Knight.* New Brunswick, N.J.: Rutgers University Press, 1965.

Berchorius, Petrus. *See* Bersuire.

Bersuire, Pierre (Petrus Berchorius). *De Formis Figurisque Deorum.* Utrecht: Instituut voor Laat Latijn der Rijksuniversiteit, 1962.

————. *L' "Ovidius Moralizatus" di Pierre Bersuire.* Edited by Fausto Ghisalberti. Studi Romanzi, vol. 23. Rome: V. Rossi and C. Salvioni, 1933.

———. *Opera Omnia.* 4 vols. Cologne, 1731.

———. *Ovidius Moralizatus.* Utrecht: Instituut voor Laat Latijn der Rijksuniversiteit, 1962. A typescript edition of the Paris, Aedibus Ascensianis, 1509 edition, wrongly attributed to Thomas Waleys, entitled *Metamorphosis Ouidiana Moraliter a Magistro Thoma Walleys Anglico de professione praedicatorum sub sanctissimo patre Dominico explanata.*

Block, Edward A. "Originality, Controlling Purpose, and Craftsmanship in Chaucer's *Man of Law's Tale.*" *PMLA* 68 (1953):572–616.

Boccaccio, Giovanni. *Decameron.* Edited by Vittore Branca. 2 vols. Florence: F. LeMonnier, 1960.

———. *Genealogie Deorum Gentilium Libri.* Edited by Vincenzo Romano. Scrittori d'Italia, no. 201. Bari: G. Laterza, 1951.

The Book of Virtues and Vices. Edited by W. Nelson Francis. Early English Text Society, no. 217. London, 1942.

Bordman, Gerald. *Motif-Index of the English Metrical Romances.* Helsinki: Suomalainen Tiedeakatemia, 1963.

Bossuat, Robert. *Drouart la Vache, traducteur d'André le Chapelain.* Paris: Champion, 1926.

Brennu-Njáls Saga. Edited by Einar Ól. Sveinsson. Reykjavik, 1954.

Bromyard, John. *Summa Praedicantium.* Basel: Johann Amerbach, about 1484. Hanes Collection, University of North Carolina, no. 499.

Brown, Norman O. *Hermes the Thief.* New York: Random House, 1969.

Bryan, W. F., and Dempster, Germaine, eds. *Sources and Analogues of Chaucer's Canterbury Tales.* New York: Humanities Press, 1958.

Burrow, J. A. *Ricardian Poetry: Chaucer, Gower, Langland and the Gawain Poet.* New Haven: Yale University Press, 1971.

di Capua, Francesco. *Scritti Minori.* Rome: Desclée, 1959.

Chaucer, Geoffrey. *The Works of Geoffrey Chaucer.* Edited by F. N. Robinson. 2d ed. Cambridge, Mass.: Houghton Mifflin Co., 1957.

Chrétien de Troyes. *Arthurian Romances.* Translated by W. W. Comfort. New York: E. P. Dutton and Co., 1963.

———. *Cligès.* Edited by Wendelin Foerster. Halle, Germany: M. Niemayer, 1910.

Coleman, Christopher Bush. *Constantine the Great and Christianity.* Columbia University Studies in History, Economics, and Public Law, no. 60. New York: Columbia University Press, 1914.

Colish, Marcia L. *The Mirror of Language.* New Haven: Yale University Press, 1968.

Creeth, Edmund H. "Moral and Tragic Recognition: The Uniqueness of Othello, Macbeth, and King Lear." *Papers of the Michigan Academy of Science, Arts, and Letters* 45 (1960):381–94.

Dante Alighieri. *Dante's Convivio.* Translated by William W. Jackson. Oxford: Clarendon Press, 1909.

———. *The Divine Comedy of Dante Alighieri.* Translated by John D. Sinclair. 3 vols. New York: Oxford University Press, 1958.

———. *La Vita Nuova.* Edited by T. Casini. Florence: Sansoni, 1962.

Day, Mabel, ed. *The English Text of the Ancrene Riwle.* Early English Text Society, no. 227. London, 1952.

A Dictionary of the Bible. Ed. James Hastings and John A. Selbie. 5 vols. New York: Charles Scribner's Sons, 1898.

Dictionnaire de théologie Catholique. Paris: Letouzey et Ané, 1903–50.

Douie, D. L. *The Nature and the Effect of the Heresy of the Fraticelli.* Manchester, Eng.: University Press, 1932.

Dwyer, John Barry, S.J. "The Tradition of Medieval Manuals of Religious Instruction in the Poems of John Gower, with Special Reference to the Development of the Book of Virtues." Ph.D. dissertation, University of North Carolina, 1950.

Elliott, Robert C. *The Power of Satire.* Princeton: Princeton University Press, 1960.

Fisher, John H. *John Gower: Moral Philosopher and Friend of Chaucer.* New York: New York University Press, 1964.

Fleming, John V. *The Roman de la Rose: A Study in Allegory and Iconography.* Princeton: Princeton University Press, 1969.

Fletcher, Angus. *Allegory: The Theory of a Symbolic Mode.* Ithaca, N.Y.: Cornell University Press, 1964.

Frye, Northrop. *Anatomy of Criticism: Four Essays.* Princeton: Princeton University Press, 1957.

Gesta Romanorum. Edited by Hermann Oesterley. Berlin: Weidmann, 1872. Reprinted by Georg Olms Verlagsbuchandlung, Hildesheim, W. Germany, 1963.

Gilson, Étienne. *History of Christian Philosophy in the Middle Ages.* New York: Random House, 1955.

———. *The Spirit of Medieval Philosophy.* Translated by A. H. C. Downes. New York: Charles Scribner's Sons, 1936.

Gower, John. *The Complete Works of John Gower.* Edited by G. C. Macaulay. 4 vols. Oxford: Clarendon Press, 1899–1902.

Green, Richard Hamilton. "Alan of Lille's *De Planctu Naturae.*" *Speculum* 31 (1956):649–74.

Gregory the Great. *Gregorianum.* Edited by Garner of St. Victor. *PL* 193:9–462.

———. *Homiliarum in Evangelia Libri Duo. PL* 76:1075–1312.

———. *Moralia in Job. PL* 75:509–76:782.

Guérric d'Igny. *Sermones per Annum. PL* 185:11–214.

Haddan, Rev. Arthur West. *A Select Library of the Nicene and Post-Nicene Fathers of the Christian Church.* Edited by Philip Schaff. New York: Christian Literature Co., 1905.

Hildebert of Lavardin. *Sermones de Sanctis. PL* 171:606–752.

Holcot, Robert. *In librum Sapientiae praelectiones.* Basel, 1586.

Horace. *The Odes of Horace.* Translated by James Michie. New York: Washington Square Press, 1965.

Hugh of St. Victor. *Sermones Centum. PL* 177:899–1222.

Isidore of Seville. *Etymologiae. PL* 82:73–728.

Jerome. *Epistolae. PL* 22:325–1224.

John of Garland. *Integumenta Ovidii.* Edited by Fausto Ghisalberti. Testi e Documenti Inediti o Rari, no. 2. Messina and Milan: Guiseppe Principato, 1933.

John of Salisbury. *The Metalogicon of John of Salisbury.* Translated by Daniel D. McGarry. Berkeley and Los Angeles: University of California Press, 1955.

Justinus. *Dialogus cum Tryphone Iudaeo. PG* 6:471–800.

Keen, Maurice. *The Pelican History of Medieval Europe.* Baltimore: Penguin Books, 1969.

Klebs, Elimar. *Die Erzählung von Apollonius aus Tyrus.* Berlin: G. Reimer, 1899.

Koonce, B. G. *Chaucer and the Tradition of Fame.* Princeton: Princeton University Press, 1966.

Latini, Brunetto. *Li Livres dou Tresor.* Edited by Francis J. Carmody. University of California Publications in Modern Philology, no. 22. Berkeley: University of California Press, 1948.

Law, Robert Adger. "In Principio." *PMLA* 37 (1922):208–15.

Lewis, C. S. *The Allegory of Love.* London: Oxford University Press, 1936.

Lonergan, Bernard, S.J. *Verbum: Word and Idea in Aquinas.* Notre Dame, Ind.: University of Notre Dame Press, 1967.

de Lorris, Guillaume, and de Meun, Jean. *Le Roman de la Rose.* Edited by Felix Lecoy. 2 vols. Paris: H. Champion, 1965.

de Lubac, Henri, S.J. *Exégèe Médiévale: les quatre sens de l'écriture.* 4 vols. Paris: Aubier, 1961.

McKenzie, John L., S.J. *Myths and Realities: Studies in Biblical Theology.* Milwaukee: Bruce Publishing Co., 1963.

McNally, John J. "The Penitential and Courtly Traditions in Gower's *Confessio Amantis.*" In *Studies in Medieval Culture,* edited by John R. Sommerfeldt. Kalamazoo: Western Michigan University, 1964.

Mannyng, Robert. *Handlyng Synne.* Edited by Frederick J. Furnival. Early English Text Society, no. 123 London, 1862.

Moore, Olin H. "Jaufre Rudel and the Lady of Dreams." *PMLA* 24 (1914):517–36.

Murphy, James J. "John Gower's *Confessio Amantis* and the First Discussion of Rhetoric in the English Language." *Philological Quarterly* 41 (1962:401–11.

Neckam, Alexander. *De Naturis Rerum.* Edited by T. Wright. Rerum Britannicarum Medii Aevi Scriptores, no. 34. London, 1863.

Nicholson, Frank C. *Old German Love Songs.* Chicago: University of Chicago Press, 1907.

Njal's Saga. Translated by Magnus Magnusson and Hermann Palsson. Harmondsworth, Eng.: Penguin Books, 1960.

Olson, Paul A. *"Le Roman de Flamenca:* History and Literary Convention." *Studies in Philology* 55 (1958):7–23.

Origen. *De Oratione. PG* 2:429–42.

O'Súlleabháin, Sean. *A Handbook of Irish Folklore.* London: Jenkins, 1963.

Ovid. *The Metamorphoses of Ovid.* Translated by Mary M. Innes. Baltimore: Penguin Books, 1955.

The Oxford Dictionary of the Christian Church. Edited by F. L. Cross. London: Oxford University Press, 1957.

Pearsall, Derek. "Gower's Narrative Art." *PMLA* 81 (1966):475–84.

Peck, Russell A., ed. *Confessio Amantis,* by John Gower. New York: Holt, Rinehart and Winston, 1968.

Peraldus, Guilielmus. *Summa de Vitiis.* Basel.: Berthold Ruppel, ca. 1469.

Peter, John. *Complaint and Satire in Early English Literature.* Oxford: Clarendon Press, 1956.

Peter Chrysologus. *Sermones. PL* 52:183–680.

Peter Lombard. *Sententiae. PL* 192:519–962.

Peter of Blois. *Un traité de l'amour du xiie siècle: Pierre de Blois.* Edited by M. M. Davy. Paris: E. de Boccard, 1932.

Prosser, Eleanor. *Drama and Religion in the English Mystery Plays.* Stanford: Stanford University Press, 1961.

Rabanus Maurus. *De Vitiis et Virtutibus. PL* 112:1335–98.

Rahner, Hugo. *Greek Myths and Christian Mystery.* Translated by Brian Battershaw. London: Burns and Oates, 1963.

Rahner, Karl, et al. *The Word: Readings in Theology.* New York: P. J. Kennedy, 1964.

Rémi of Auxerre. *Commentum in Martianum Capellam.* Edited by Cora E. Lutz. Leiden: E. J. Brill, 1962.

Riga, Peter. *Aurora . . . Biblia Versificata.* Edited by Paul E. Beichner, C.S.C. 2 vols. Notre Dame, Ind.: University of Notre Dame Press, 1965.

Robert de Sorbon. *De Confessione, Maxima bibliotheca veterum patrum.* 25 vols. Lyons, 1677.

Robertson, D. W., Jr. "Love Conventions in Marie's *Equitan." Romanic Review* 44 (1953): 241–45.

———. "A Note on the Classical Origin of 'Circumstances' in the Medieval Confessional." *Studies in Philology* 43 (1946):6–14.

———. *A Preface to Chaucer.* Princeton: Princeton University Press, 1962.

———. "A Study of Certain Aspects of the Cultural Tradition of *Handlyng Synne.* " Ph.D. dissertation, University of North Carolina, 1944.

The Romance of Flamenca. Translated by Merton Jerome Hubert. Edited by Marion E. Porter. Princeton: Princeton University Press, 1962.

Rouet de Journel, M. J., S.J., and Dutilleul, J., S.J. *Enchiridion Patristicum: Loci S. Patrum et Scriptorum Ecclesiasticorum ad Ascesim Spectantes.* 4th ed. Barcelona: Editorial Herder, 1947.

Schmaus, M. *Die psychologische Trinitätslehre des hl. Augustinus.* Münster, 1927.

Schmitz, Herm Jos. *Die Bussbücher and die Bussdisciplin der Kirche.* Mainz, 1883.

Scholes, Robert, and Kellogg, Robert. *The Nature of Narrative.* New York: Oxford University Press, 1966.

Schueler, Donald G. "The Age of the Lover in Gower's *Confessio Amantis*." *Medium Aevum* 36, no. 2 (1967):152–58.

————. "Some Comments on the Structure of John Gower's *Confessio Amantis*." In *Explorations of Literature,* edited by Rima Drell Reck. LSU Studies, no. 18. Baton Rouge, 1966.

Scriptores rerum mythicarum latini tres Romae nuper repertae. Edited by G. H. Bode. Celle, Germany: E. H. C. Schulze, 1834.

Servius the Grammarian. *In Vergilii Carmina Commentarii.* Edited by George Thilo and Hermann Hagen. 3 vols. Leipzig, Germany 1881–87. Reprinted by Georg Olms Verlagsbuchhandlung, Hildesheim, W. Germany, 1961.

Seznec, Jean. *The Survival of the Pagan Gods.* Translated by Barbara F. Sessions. Bollingen Series, no. 38. New York: Pantheon Books, 1953.

Smaragdus. *Collectiones in Epistolas et Evangelia. PL* 102:9–552.

Smith, Lucy Toulmin, ed. *York Plays,* Oxford, 1885.

Tatlock, J. S. P. "Notes on Chaucer: the Canterbury Tales." *Modern Language Notes* 29 (1914):140–44.

Thompson, Stith. *Motif-Index of Folk Literature.* 6 vols. Bloomington: Indiana University Press, 1955–58.

Vincent of Beauvais. *Speculum Quadruplex.* 4 vols. Douai: Ex Officina Typographica B. Belleri, 1624. Reprinted by Akademische Druck-u. Verlagsanstalt, Graz, 1964–65.

del Virgilio, Giovanni. *Allegorie Librorum Ovidii Metamorphoseos.* Edited by Fausto Ghisalberti. *Giornale Dantesco* 34 (1931).

de Voragine, Jacobus. *Sermones de Sanctis.* Venice, 1573.

Walther von der Vogelweide. Edited by W. Wilmanns. Halle: Buchhandlung des Waisenhauses, 1924.

Watkins, Oscar D. *A History of Penance.* London: Longmans, Green and Co., 1920. Reprinted by Burt Franklin, New York, 1961.

Wickert, Maria. *Studien zu John Gower.* Cologne: Kölner Universitäts-Verlag, 1953.

William of Auvergne. *Opera Omnia.* 2 vols. Paris: Edmundus Couterot, 1674.

Wilson, E. Faye. "Pastoral and Epithalamium in Latin Literature." *Speculum* 23 (1948):42–50.

Index